UNDERSTANDING CENTRAL AMERICA

About the Book and Authors

Since the 1960s political violence has taken 300,000 lives, displaced millions, and reversed decades of economic gains in Nicaragua, El Salvador, and Guatemala. Despite the turmoil in these countries, however, neighboring Costa Rica and Honduras have remained relatively stable. And in a region long dominated by the United States, political events have increasingly eluded U.S. control. In this book, two of the most respected writers on politics in Latin America examine these paradoxes.

The authors trace the roots of underdevelopment and crisis in the region by examining the shared and individual histories of the Central American nations. They offer an original theory about rebellion and political stability to account for the region's peculiar mixture of violence and relative placidity. Drs. Booth and Walker look in particular at the forces driving popular mobilization—including economic change, liberation theology, and Marxism—and evaluate the origins, successes, and failures of U.S. efforts to affect the course of political events and to contain the perceived Soviet influences. Finally, they assess the prospects for peace in Central America and the future role of U.S. policy.

John A. Booth is professor and chair of the Department of Political Science at the University of North Texas. He is the author of *The End and the Beginning: The Nicaraguan Revolution* (Westview, revised edition, 1985) and has written widely on politics and democracy in Latin America. He chairs the Latin American Studies Association's Task Force on Scholarly Relations with Nicaragua and Central America and is a member of the editorial board of the *Latin American Research Review.* **Thomas W. Walker** is professor of political science and director of the Latin American Studies Program at Ohio University. He is the author of *Nicaragua: The Land of Sandino* (Westview, second edition, 1986) and the editor/coauthor of *Reagan Versus the Sandinistas: The Undeclared War on Nicaragua* (Westview, 1987) and *Revolution and Counterrevolution in Nicaragua: The First Decade* (forthcoming from Westview Press). He has participated in the United Presbyterian Church's National Task Force on Central America and in 1983–1984 served as founding chair of the Latin American Studies Association's Task Force on Scholarly Relations with Nicaragua.

UNDERSTANDING CENTRAL AMERICA

John A. Booth
UNIVERSITY OF NORTH TEXAS

Thomas W. Walker
OHIO UNIVERSITY

Westview Press
BOULDER, SAN FRANCISCO, & LONDON

The drawing on the paperback cover was created especially for this book by Leoncio Sáenz of Managua, Nicaragua. Sáenz, whose works hang in the outer office of Nicaraguan President Daniel Ortega and have been featured in exhibitions in New York and throughout the world, is a frequent artistic contributor to *Nicaráuac*, *Pensamiento Propio*, and other Nicaraguan publications.

Published in 1989 in the United States of America by Westview Press, Inc., 5500 Central Avenue, Boulder, Colorado 80301, and in the United Kingdom by Westview Press, Inc., 13 Brunswick Centre, London WC1N 1AF, England

Library of Congress Cataloging-in-Publication Data
Booth, John A.
Understanding Central America / John A. Booth and Thomas W. Walker.
p. cm.
Includes bibliographical references.
ISBN 0-8133-0002-9.—ISBN 0-8133-0003-7 (pbk.)
1. Central America—Politics and government—1979- 2. Central America—History. 3. Central America—Economic conditions. 4. Central America—Social conditions. 5. Central America—Foreign relations—United States. 6. United States—Foreign relations—Central America. 7. Revolutions—Central America—History—20th century. I. Walker, Thomas W. II. Title.
F1439.5.B66 1989 89-37517
CIP

Printed and bound in the United States of America

∞ The paper used in this publication meets the requirements of the American National Standard for Permanence of Paper for Printed Library Materials Z39.48-1984.

10 9 8 7 6 5 4 3 2 1

To Julie
and
to Anne

CONTENTS

TABLES AND ILLUSTRATIONS

Tables

Figures

Photographs

Map

ACKNOWLEDGMENTS

We owe many people and institutions in the United States and Central America our sincerest thanks for their time, support, encouragement, and patience. For support that has gotten us into the field during the years this manuscript has been in preparation we wish to thank the Latin American Studies Association; the Advisory Council on Church and Society of the United Presbyterian Church, USA; the Inter-American Dialogue; the International Human Rights Law Group; the Washington Office on Latin America; the University of North Texas; and Ohio University. For collaboration in Central America we gratefully acknowledge the assistance of the Facultad Latinoamericana de Ciencias Sociales (FLACSO) and the Centro Superior Universitaria Centroamericana (CSUCA) in Costa Rica, the Asociación de Investigación y Estudios Sociales (ASIES) in Guatemala, and the Confederación Nacional de Profesionales (CONAPRO) Héroes y Mártires in Nicaragua. For generously granting Thomas Walker the right to reuse some material he had originally written for a Presbyterian Church publication (incorporated into Chapters 1 through 4 and Chapter 9), we are indebted to the United Presbyterian Church, USA. Several dozen kind folks in Central America have granted us interviews and helped us collect data on their countries, without which this book would have been completely impossible to write. E. Bradford Burns, Sung Ho Kim, Harold Molineu, and Mitch Seligson read portions of the manuscript at different stages in its evolution and made valuable suggestions. Our thanks to Cece Hannah for her excellent typing of the manuscript. Most of all, we thank Miriam Gilbert and Westview Press for their encouragement and great patience with this long-delayed project.

John A. Booth
Thomas W. Walker

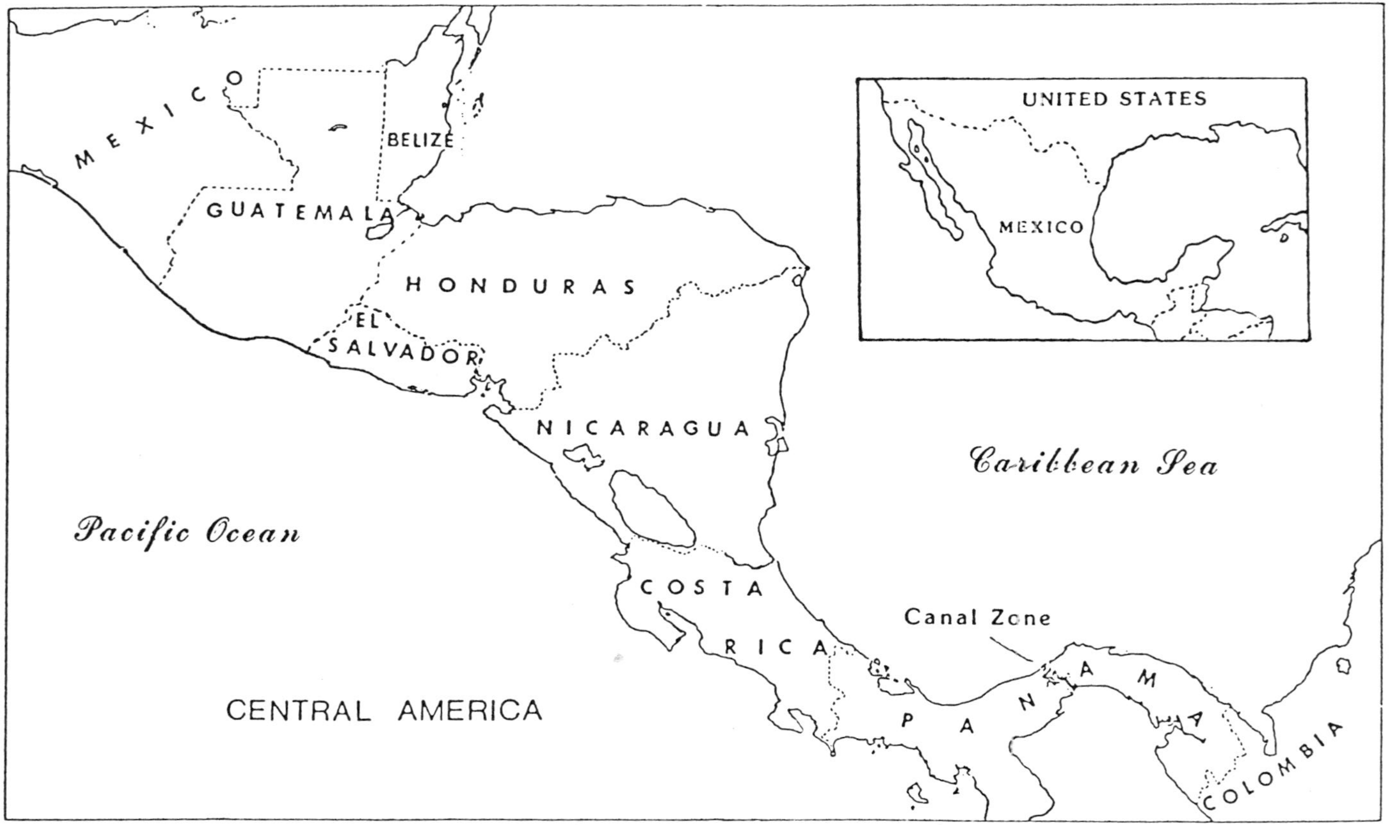

Reprinted from *U.S. Policy Toward Latin America*, by Harold Molineu (Boulder, Colo.: Westview Press, 1986, p. 4). Copyright Westview Press, Inc., 1986.

1

THE CENTRAL AMERICAN CRISIS

In its 1984 report, President Reagan's National Bipartisan Commission on Central America (the Kissinger Commission) explained the turmoil in Central America and dramatized its gravity:

> Central America is gripped by a profound crisis. That crisis has deep roots in the region's history. . . . The crisis is the product of *both* indigenous and foreign factors. Poverty, repression, inequity all were there breeding fear and hate; stirring in a world recession created a potent witch's brew, while outside forces have intervened to exacerbate the area's troubles and to exploit its anguish.[1]

No one familiar with Central America and its problems could disagree that both internal and external factors have shaped the region. However, there is indeed much to question about the commission's conclusions as to the nature and relative importance of such factors.

The commission looked at Central American reality in a very particular way. It sought written advice from only about one-fourth of the fifty most active U.S. scholars specializing on Central America at the time and heard oral testimony from still fewer. The commission consulted almost no scholars from Central America itself. The groups the commission visited during its one-week Central American visit were predominantly from the political center and right and generally represented dominant elites and powerful vested interests. Commission staff and expert advice were drawn from conservative think tanks, large U.S. business firms and pressure groups with Central American interests, and from the U.S. military and foreign service. At least eight of the commission's twelve members were conservatives.[2]

Given its composition and operation, it is no great surprise that the Kissinger Commission's report was a highly ideological, partisan, and analytically biased document that presented an unclear picture of Central America and stimulated a barrage of criticism.[3] The commission apparently was not intended to conduct an impartial and open enquiry about Central America and its problems. Rather, its purpose seems to have been to give the imprimatur of bipartisanship and its members' collective stature—and thus to ratify and legitimate—the Reagan administration's policy preferences for Central America. We do not pretend to rebut or correct the Kissinger Commission's report. We do, however, seek to supply the reader with keys to understanding Central America by briefly and systematically describing the region and its major problems, its historical evolution, and the major social and political forces that have taken at least 200,000 Central American lives and displaced nearly 2 million refugees since 1978.

The dramatic passage cited above suggests that mysterious forces have conspired to disturb Central America. We disagree that the causes of this turmoil are mysterious or obscure—even though solutions to the problems will likely prove elusive. In fact, much of what is wrong in Central America today stems from fairly simple, direct, and man-made causes. We believe that regional traditions of economic and political exploitation and the external reinforcement of those patterns of repression of the many by the few laid the groundwork for turmoil. Rapid but unbalanced economic growth, the product of deliberate public policy decisions by Central American elites, backed financially and militarily by the United States, created the conditions for popular rebellion and turmoil in the late 1970s.

The "Central America" upon which we focus in this report consists of five countries: Guatemala, El Salvador, Honduras, Nicaragua, and Costa Rica.[4] Belize and Panama will not receive individual attention. Though Belize is technically Central American, that English-speaking microstate has a history that is fairly distinct from that of the other states in the region. At present this tiny republic, which only became formally independent from Great Britain in 1981, does not figure significantly in the "Central American" problem. Panama, though often lumped with the other countries of the region, is not technically Central American. Its pre-Columbian indigenous cultures were South American, and from the beginning of the national period until 1903, Panama was an integral (though poor) part of the South American republic of Colombia. "The five," however, share a common political heritage from the colonial period—in which they were administered as a unit by Spain—to the early national period, when for fifteen years (1823–1838) they formed a single state called the United Provinces of Central America. In the late nineteenth century, several ill-fated attempts at reunification once again took place, and in the 1960s the five joined to form a common market. Out of this history comes a sense of Central American national identity and, among a surprisingly large segment of the region's educated elite, an almost utopian belief that someday the larger homeland will once again be united.

Central America, as defined above, is not a big region. Indeed, its combined land mass of 431,812 square kilometers is barely larger than that of the state of California (404,975 square kilometers). Moreover, its total 1988 population of around 25.9 million is just slightly more than California's (25 million). The country with the smallest surface area, El Salvador, is smaller even than the state of

Maryland, whereas the largest, Nicaragua, is only slightly larger than Iowa. In population, the five vary between a low of 2.82 million in Costa Rica (Arkansas, in comparison, has 2.28 million) and a high of 8.61 million in Guatemala (New Jersey has 7.36 million).[5]

Central America's natural resources are not particularly remarkable. However, under a different sort of political system than currently rules most of Central America, there would certainly be enough arable land to provide adequate sustenance for the present population, while at the same time producing some primary products for export. Yet the unregulated response to international market demands by the region's agrarian elite has led to land concentration, an overemphasis on export, and inadequate production of consumer food staples. Instead of growing beans, corn, rice, plantain, and cassava for local consumption, big landholders normally concentrate on lucrative exports such as coffee, cotton, sugar, and beef. Central America also has a variety of mineral resources, though apparently not in remarkable abundance. One possible exception is Guatemala, with its nickel and its newly discovered oil reserves. Historically, Central America, or more precisely, Nicaragua, was (for a while) viewed as the logical site for a future transisthmian waterway. However, the building of the Panama Canal and the development of modern air and surface communication have made it unlikely that this potential will ever be developed.

Central America's main resource is clearly its people. Contrary to the ethnocentric stereotype often held by North Americans, Central Americans are as hardworking as most other humans on this planet. To verify that statement, one need only observe the hustle and bustle of most Central American cities at daybreak, or follow the activity of a typical Central American through the long hours of his or her daily routine. Central Americans are also remarkably resilient. The strength with which they have faced more than their share of hardship—including endemic repression, occasional civil war, foreign occupation, and frequent natural disasters, such as volcanic eruptions, earthquakes, hurricanes, and floods—is impressive to outside observers, especially those used to fairly safe natural and human environments.

This is not to say that there are not characteristics of the population of some Central American countries that pose problems. Guatemala, for instance, no matter which type of political system it adopts, will long have to struggle with the question of how to integrate the approximately half of the population that is Indian, and that, by and large, does not speak Spanish. Similarly, any government in El Salvador is going to face an enormous social headache posed by the country's high density of population. Moreover, all of the countries face severe problems of poverty that affect the vast majority of their people. But such poverty is not inevitable, and, overall, the human resources of the region are a very positive factor. The dignity, determination, and remarkable humor of the Central American people must be taken as a cause for hope.

In sum, Central America is small in size and population, poor in resources, and holds a wealth of problems and troubles—for its own people as well for its neighbors and for the United States. Its small nation-states are riven by severe internal strains. They are pushed and pulled by international pressures, both economic and political, pressures that often intensify domestic strains rather than reduce them. The deepening U.S. involvement there and the efforts that numerous Latin American and European nations have made to promote negotiated settlements to the various open and latent conflicts in the region have made these strains and conflicts worthy of serious study.

U.S. interests and involvement in Central America have fluctuated widely over the past century and a half. A period of protracted U.S. inattention to Central America after the mid-1950s changed suddenly into intense U.S. concern in the late 1970s when Nicaraguans rebelled against the Somoza regime. Though they lavished attention on Central America, the Carter and Reagan administrations treated and described the region so differently as to bewilder many observers—including academic and policy experts, and especially Central Americans themselves.

There is also evidence that Soviet and Eastern bloc interest and involvement in Central America have changed. The presidential commission on Central America expressed grave reservations about the Soviet role in the region.[6] Although there is ample reason to question the validity of what might well be described as the commission's "devil theory" of Cuban/Nicaraguan influence in Central America, the issue of external involvement must be examined. There are also crises of poverty, development, and political order. In our effort to help the reader understand Central America, we will examine these crises and consider the relative importance of domestic and foreign influence over the region.

CENTRAL AMERICANS (photo of baby in hammock by John Booth; other photos by Steve Cagan).

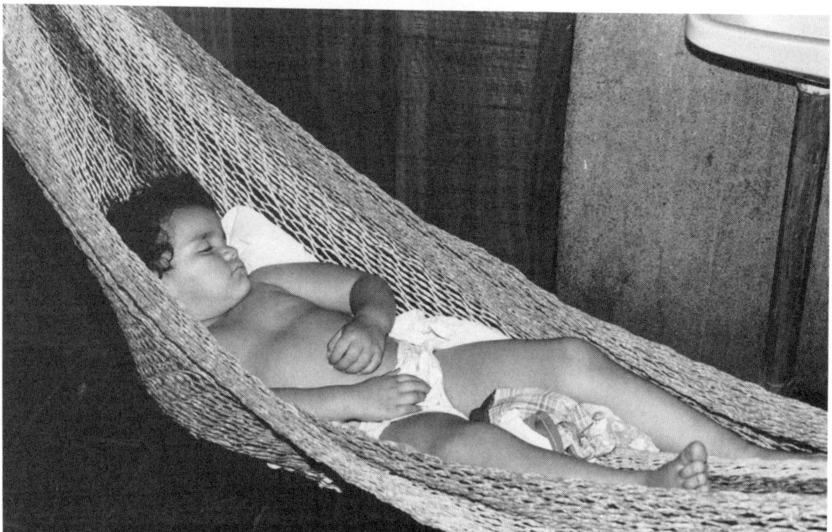

2

THE CRISIS OF POVERTY AND ITS CAUSES

Commonsense interpretations of the causes of the Central American turmoil often stress poverty. Poverty is, indeed, a serious problem in the region. Even the most prosperous nation, Costa Rica, has severe economic difficulties that afflict much of its populace. In Honduras, until recently the poorest of the Central American nations, the living standard of most citizens is abysmal. Most experts and even passing observers of the region recognize that poverty constitutes a crisis of great human cost that cries out for dramatic reform in social and economic systems.

Common sense betrays us, however, if we attempt to explain Central America's rebellions as simply the product of poverty. Most of the world's population live in poverty, yet rebellion against constituted authority by the most disadvantaged is rare. Poverty alone cannot account for the revolts in Nicaragua, El Salvador, or Guatemala. Indeed, if poverty alone were sufficient to cause rebellions, Honduras should have exploded with popular fury long before Nicaragua or El Salvador. We thus encounter the paradox that among Central America's five nations, the poorest historically (Honduras) and the richest (Costa Rica) are the most stable, while those that had the most rapid industrialization and economic growth in the 1960s and 1970s have been the most unsettled.

To affirm that poverty itself is not a direct or sufficient cause of Central America's rebellions, however, is not to say that poverty is unrelated to the turmoil. In fact, there is an important link between *becoming* impoverished and popular unrest. Large segments of Central America's poor and middle classes were becoming much worse off during the 1970s and early 1980s. It is not, then, the grinding, long-term deprivation of poverty, but this change—impoverishment, declining living conditions—that has motivated much of the region's unrest. In this chapter we will focus on the nature of Central American poverty—the long-term, grinding deprivation that affects large segments of the population. We will describe in rather technical and abstract ways what this far-too-real poverty means for the lives of

Central Americans. In Chapters 4 and 5 we will examine how impoverishment has contributed to recent popular unrest and rebellion.

POVERTY

The human condition in Latin America generally lies somewhere between the extreme deprivation and despair of large areas of Africa and Asia and the relative prosperity of North America, Europe, and Japan. Within Latin America, the economic indicators of Central America as a whole fall slightly below the median for the entire region. Latin America in 1986 had a gross domestic product (GDP) per capita of $2,151, but not even relatively wealthy Costa Rica, with a GDP of $1,926, approached that figure. The other four ranged from Guatemala, with a GDP of $1,282 per capita, down to Honduras with $780.[1]

Of course, such GDP per capita figures should be explained and put into context. First, for comparison, it should be noted that the United States in 1981 had a gross national product per capita of $12,820. Second, we should consider the fact that whereas "average" Guatemalans were attempting to make do on less than one-tenth of that amount, they and other Central Americans were facing prices for many consumer products—food, clothing, health care—that were as high as, or higher than, those in the United States. And, finally, we should remember that the "average" indicated GDP in per capita figures is simply a statistical artifact that distorts reality. GDP per capita figures are obtained by dividing the annual total value of goods and services produced in a given country by the total population. In regions such as Central America where a small minority controls most of the resources and earns most of the income, averaging the income of the wealthy with that of the rest of the population results in per capita values that grossly overstate the real condition of most people. Indeed, the real monetary income per capita of the poorer half of the population in most of Central America probably runs between $200 and $400 per year.

The extremely low annual expendable income of the majority of Central Americans manifests itself in deplorable social conditions. Although Costa Rica from 1950 until 1980 and Nicaragua (at least for a few years after the victory of the Sandinista revolution in 1979) made strides in dealing with their most acute social problems, much remains to be done even in those countries. And if we consider the region as a whole, it is certainly fair to say that the typical Central American is poorly fed, poorly housed, and has little or no access to medical care, education, and cultural, or recreational opportunities.

Nutrition is a case in point. Land in the region is very inequitably distributed. Typically, the rich and the powerful, who control the best land, use it to grow export products rather than to produce staples. In a profit-driven, "free enterprise" system, this makes good sense: Export products bring greater profits than staples grown for sale internally. What this means for most Central Americans, however, is that as landownership becomes more and more concentrated in fewer hands and as fewer and fewer staples (in relation to population) are grown, the price of staples, though not as high as that of export products, rises inexorably, thus forcing the common citizen to make do on less and cheaper food. At present, Central Americans generally eat very little animal protein, deriving their essential amino acids, instead, from corn and beans. But even these foods are highly priced since domestic production is normally insufficient and has to be supplemented by costly imports.

The absolute poverty of the region is also reflected in the area of education. A substantial segment of the people has virtually no education. Official illiteracy rates for 1986 ran from a fairly respectable low of 10.2 percent in Costa Rica to a high of 43.3 percent in Guatemala. Honduras, El Salvador, and Nicaragua registered 40.3 percent, 33.1 percent, and 27.7 percent, respectively. (Nicaragua's 1980-1981 Literacy Crusade dropped the illiteracy rate from the 1978 level of 47.4 percent).[2] In addition, even the bulk of those people who are literate have only the most basic education. In elite-dominated systems geared to the export of primary products, there is little or no premium placed on educating the general citizenry. Indeed, efforts made to improve mass education are frequently viewed by local elites as dangerous. Accordingly, it is not surprising that illiteracy is so high and that even most Central Americans described as literate have only a few years of primary education.

In the area of public health, conditions are somewhat, though not much, better. Especially since World War II, with the discovery of a variety of techniques for the prevention of several communicable diseases, international health organizations have had some success in cajoling and assisting Central American regimes to reduce the frequency of certain killer diseases. This has occasioned a gradual lowering of death rates and a raising of life expectancies, which in 1986 ranged from lows of 59.8 years in Nicaragua, 62.0 years in Honduras and in Guatemala, 63.3 years in El Salvador, to a very respectable high of 73.1 years in Costa Rica.[3]

Nevertheless, though "easy" and externally imposed advances in preventive medicine have allowed Central Americans to live longer, most still face serious health problems. Local hygiene is normally poor. Most houses lack interior plumbing. Many do not even have backyard latrines. The curative medical system is grossly inadequate. Private medical care—nearly as expensive in Central America as in the United States—is simply out of the reach of the common citizen. Public facilities in most countries are so scarce as to be available only to a minority of the middle class and wealthy in the larger cities and towns. As a result, good health is largely a matter of privilege or luck.

Exacerbating the problems of poverty are strikingly high annual rates of natural increase in population. In 1986, population growth rates ranged from a "low" of 2.1 percent in El Salvador, to 2.6 percent in Costa Rica, 2.8 percent in Guatemala, and to highs of 3.2 percent in Honduras and 3.4 percent in Nicaragua.[4] The population is growing so rapidly for several reasons. First, the easy advances in medicine brought to Central America in the past four decades have significantly reduced death rates, especially among infants. Second, with the median age of the population falling into the midteens (as opposed to around thirty in the United States), a far greater share of the female population is of childbearing age. Finally, high fertility is normally related to poverty and low levels of urbanization. Unlike most of the rest of Latin America, Central America in the 1980s was still predominantly rural (Honduras and Guatemala, 64 percent; El Salvador, 59 percent; Costa Rica, 57 percent; and Nicaragua, 47 percent).[5] And of course, the overwhelming majority of the area's inhabitants are very poor. If the current rates of population growth remain constant, the countries of the region will double in population every twenty (Honduras) to twenty-five years (Costa Rica).[6] However, high growth rates of a decade ago in other parts of Latin America have actually begun to tail off, and they are now slowing in Central America. This seems to relate to the widespread use of birth control devices, to a rapid process of urbanization, and especially in El Salvador, to the impact of the war. As long as rapid increases in population persist, they will make meaningful efforts to reduce social inequities and uplift the human condition not only more difficult but also more urgent.

THE CAUSES OF POVERTY

Poverty in Central America is neither natural nor inevitable. It used to be argued by foreigners that Central Americans were poor because they were racially inferior. For instance, in the words of one geography text used widely in U.S. primary schools a half century ago, "except where white men have established plantations, the resources [of Central America] are poorly developed. Most of the Indians, mestizos, and negroes are poor and ignorant . . . few care to work hard. More white men are needed to start plantations and to fight tropical diseases."[7]

Of course, today we recognize that statements of that sort, which can also be found in prominent encyclopedias of the era, are racist nonsense. Likewise, it cannot be maintained that the region is lacking in sufficient resources to support its human population. El Salvador *is* overpopulated. But Central America as a whole has sufficient good land, not only to engage in some export of primary products for foreign exchange but also to grow sufficient staples to feed its people. And though not exceptional, the region also has significant energy and mineral resources.

In fact, Central America's poverty is a human artifact—produced by exploitation of the many by the few. The latter, who have traditionally ruled the region for their own selfish ends, were often joined and supported in this exploitative behavior by powerful foreign interests.

What developed over time was a system that many scholars—Latin and North American alike—came to label as "dependency."[8] Though there is some disagreement on specifics, most people who write about this subject agree that dependency is a complex political, economic, and social phenomenon that serves to block the human development of the majority in certain privilege-dominated Third World countries where the economies are heavily externally oriented. In such countries, one finds that even during periods of rapid economic growth the benefit of such growth normally fails to "trickle down" in any but the most trivial way to the majority of the people. The *dependentistas* (as those who write about this subject are called) argue that the social stagnation of dependent countries is due to the combination of an income-concentrating, externally oriented, and externally conditioned form of capitalism with political systems controlled by those privileged minorities who benefit from such poorly distributed growth.

It is very important to note that in order for the dependency syndrome—with all of its negative human consequences—to exist, it is necessary for a country to have *both* an externally oriented economy *and* a socially irresponsible political elite. External economic orientation, though essential, is not enough in and of itself to cause the socially regressive dependency syndrome. The economies of Korea and Japan are both heavily externally oriented. However, the elites of those two more tightly knit societies seem to have a greater sense of social responsibility than the elites of Latin America, and, hence, externally stimulated growth has led to a general rise in standard of living. Another example of dependence without the poverty-generating dependency syndrome has been provided by Cuba in the three decades since 1959. Critics of the Cuban revolution are quick to point out that island republic under its revolutionary government has simply substituted dependence on the United States for dependence on the Socialist bloc. Quite so. However, what is now crucially different about post-1959 Cuba is that its revolutionary elite has had the will to distribute the income from its externally dependent economy in such a way as to significantly improve general levels of health, education, housing, and nutrition. Thus it would be incorrect to argue that Cuba, whatever other problems it may have, suffers from the dependency syndrome per se.

Capitalist development in dependent countries such as those of Central America is very different from that which took place in the industrialized countries. In the Western industrial nations the common citizen became crucially important to the economy as a consumer. In the United States, for instance, over 80 percent of industrial production is absorbed by domestic consumers. Therefore, even if we were to accept the argument that there is a "ruling class" in the United States, we would say that it would not be in that group's interest to exploit common citizens to the extent that they could no longer consume. For these reasons, in an internally oriented economic system like that of the United States, income redistribution devices such as the graduated income tax, social welfare programs, and a free labor movement actually serve the interest of the moneyed elite as well as that of the common citizen. However, in dependent Third World countries the tiny middle and upper classes that control the political system derive most of their income directly or indirectly from export or from the local multinational corporation–manufacture of products that the members of those classes, not the masses, consume. Accordingly, the common citizen in such a system is important, not as a consumer, but rather as a cheap and vulnerable source of labor.

Under this type of system, average citizens have virtually no opportunity to lift themselves up by the bootstraps because there is almost no access either to the means of production or to the riches that flow therefrom. By its very nature, the elite-run dependency system produces an inexorable concentration of both property and income. In the rural areas, stimulated by the growing lure of high profits through export, the rich and the powerful simply buy out or drive the illiterate peasant from the land. In the cities, incipient industrialization is dominated by the local elites and foreign enterprises. The latter, enjoying huge advances in technology and brand recognition, often make the formation of locally based industry very difficult. Nevertheless, the local elites benefit in the form of contracts, services, and employment for the educated few, as well as occasional payoffs and bribes. At the same time, the advantages that accrue to a host country as a whole from the presence of outside firms are usually very limited. Such enterprises export profit directly and through the purchases of licenses, patents, and materials at inflated prices from parent companies. They tend to use capital-intensive rather than labor-intensive technology, thus causing not only a drain on foreign exchange used for the purchase of costly industrial equipment but also minimal "trickle down" in the form of wages. And finally, over 80 percent of the capital they use is raised locally, thus drying up domestic capital sources that might otherwise be available to native entrepreneurs.

This system, then, is one that favors a privileged local elite and its foreign associates while ignoring the interests of the vast majority. There are powerful economic disincentives for the privileged elites to do anything about the miserable condition of the masses. The switch to a more benign consumer-driven economic model or even a more socially responsible and controlled mixed economic system would involve a period of economic dislocation and personal sacrifice to which many among Central America's dominant elites simply will not subject themselves without a fight.

At this point, one might reasonably ask two questions: (1) Why did the dependency system develop in Central America while a consumer-driven economy arose in North America? and (2) Why has the great bulk of the Central American people not been able to alter a system that is so contrary to their interests? Much of the answer to the first question lies in the distinct ways in which North America and Central America were colonized. North America was settled originally by European nonconformists seeking a new life and greater freedom. These people tamed the land by dint of their own labor and eventually developed into a large class of freeholders. North America did develop an aristocracy of sorts, but one that was never able completely to dominate the common citizen.

In Central America, as will be detailed later, the conquistadores sought quick riches. They superimposed their administration over that of the Indians and immediately began exacting tribute in gold and slaves. Within a matter of decades, the region had been plundered of its gold, and much of its Indian population had been decimated by slavery and contagion with Old World diseases. The Spanish system was a mercantile one that, from the very start, drained resources from the region. It was also heavily elitist with most of the physical labor being done by the subjugated masses composed of Indian *peones*, mestizos, and eventually, black slaves and mulattoes. Only in Costa Rica, which had few easily exploitable resources and not many Indians, did even a small number of Spaniards come to till the soil. Small wonder, then, that four and a half centuries later, the four northern countries of Central America were still struggling with problems of mass poverty and huge class disparities, whereas Costa Rica had developed a relatively more democratic, egalitarian, and socially just system.

This also leads us to the answer to the second question: The impoverished majority of Central Americans have not always docilely accepted their imposed lot. In fact, there have been frequent revolts when things got rapidly worse for certain groups: Indians resisted the conquistadores; peasants revolted against land concentration caused by the late-nineteenth-century Liberal reforms and the spread of coffee cultivation; peasants and workers under Nicaraguan nationalist Augusto C. Sandino rebelled against U.S. occupation from 1927 to 1933; workers led by El Salvador's indigenous Communist Augustín Farabundo Martí revolted in 1932; Nicaraguans en masse successfully rebelled against the Somoza regime in 1978–1979, and mass-based insurrections are taking place in El Salvador and Guatemala today.

Such struggles between popular-based movements and those in power, however, have usually been very unequal. The entrenched elite has always enjoyed an overwhelming advantage in military, economic, and propaganda resources. And the privileged elites of the region have normally been able to count on the support of foreign powers, be they the Spaniards in the colonial period or the Americans in the twentieth century. Indeed, since the Russian revolution, Central America's ruling classes have learned that merely by labeling their opposition as "Bolshevik" or "Communist" they can usually win U.S. support ranging from armed intervention to economic and military aid.

All in all, however, it is not the long-term, grinding deprivation of Central Americans that has led to political turmoil and rebellion in three of the region's countries since 1974. It is, in fact, the relative deprivation of becoming rapidly poorer—declining living standards among large segments of the population—that has sparked the recent outbursts, unrest, and rebellion. Indeed, the developmental model (the economic growth plan) adopted by several Central American nations in the 1960s, based on the traditions of dependent capitalism and class exploitation described above, has itself been a major cause of this growing relative deprivation.

3

THE COMMON HISTORY

One great truth about Central America is that whereas there are many similarities among the five countries, there are also a number of striking differences. In large part, these similarities and differences are a product of the early history of the region from the conquest, through the colonial period, to independence, to union with Mexico, to the fifteen-year period in which the five shared a common political identity as part of the United Provinces of Central America.[1]

CONQUEST TO 1838

The conquest itself profoundly affected the nature of Central America's present-day societies. In this period, Costa Rica had an experience that immediately set it apart from the other four countries. The regions that are today Nicaragua, Honduras, El Salvador, and Guatemala were conquered in the two decades following the first Spanish penetration in 1522. As we will detail below, Spanish rule was imposed upon those Indians who were lucky enough to survive the tremendous depopulation of the region that resulted from the effects of slavery and exposure to Old World diseases. Costa Rica, however, was not settled until the 1560s because, unlike the other areas, it offered no easily exploitable resources in either gold or Indian slaves. Indeed, the hostile native inhabitants of the region were a major obstacle to European penetration. In the end, Costa Rica's Indians were neither pacified nor conquered. Instead they were for the most part either exterminated or pushed into remote areas. As a result, the population of the Central Valley of Costa Rica became heavily Iberian, and therefore, a racially distinct and exploited underclass never developed.

In the rest of Central America, however, the Spaniards were able to impose their dominion without destroying the entire population despite both passive and active resistance by the native people. Though this period meant annihilation for most of them, some Indians did survive. When the Spaniards arrived, they encountered millions of Indians in what are today the four northernmost countries of Central America. By co-opting and controlling native caciques (chiefs), the bearded foreigners proved to be very effective in extracting local riches in the form of gold and native slaves. In addition, the conquistadores unwittingly brought with them a variety of diseases to which Old World populations had become essentially immune. The Indians, having no natural immunity, perished in large numbers.

It is estimated that in western Nicaragua alone, a population of over one million natives was reduced to a few tens of thousands by the end of the conquest. It is unlikely that the Spaniards killed very many Indians outright. Careful historical research indicates that as many as half a million native Nicaraguans may have been exported as slaves to Panama and Peru. Most of these died either in passage to their destination or in slavery within a year or two thereafter. The bulk of the rest of the populace appears to have succumbed to disease.[2] Only in Guatemala did large numbers of Indians survive. Perhaps this was due to the greater difficulty the conquistadores had in completely subjugating the relatively more advanced society they encountered in that area. Perhaps, too, the cooler climates of the mountainous parts of Guatemala presented a less congenial environment for the spread of disease.

The drastic reduction in the Indian population was not the only change wrought by the conquest in the region of northern Central America. Prior to the conquest, labor-intensive agriculture typified this area. The common people grew corn, beans, peppers, and squash on land consigned to them by their caciques. Although obliged to turn over to the chief as tribute part of the crop, they were permitted to use the rest either for home consumption or for barter or sale in local markets. By the end of the conquest, however, as a result of depopulation, the bulk of former farmlands had reverted to jungle. The economy had become externally oriented, with the Spaniards controlling the region's human and natural resources to produce articles for trade among the colonies and with the mother country. The labor that produced the gold, silver, timber, and cattle products (hides, tallow, and dried beef) for export was supplied by the surviving Indians (still more numerous than their white masters). However, most of the wealth that this type of economy produced went to the white elite. The culture and process of dependent underdevelopment were now in full swing.

Many aspects of culture were also changed practically overnight as the conquistadores sought to impose their religion, language, and ways on the peoples they had conquered. Of course, nowhere was Indian culture *completely* obliterated. In Guatemala, where hispanization was least effective, the Indians retained their languages and hid many aspects of their old religion under a thin patina of Catholicism. Even in El Salvador, Honduras, Nicaragua, and Costa Rica, where the Indian populations were most decimated, some Indian traits remained. For instance, to this day, everywhere in the region, corn and beans (Indian staples) constitute the heart of local cuisine. Moreover, many place names remain Indian, as do the names of hundreds of common objects, from peppers and turkeys to grindstones. Yet, by and large, Central America was hispanicized. Spanish became the lingua franca except in rural Guatemala and certain remote regions elsewhere.

A mystical, elite-supporting, pre-Reformation version of Catholicism became the nearly universal religion. Even the cities, often built on or next to the sites of pre-Columbian centers of habitation, eventually took on Spanish characteristics, with the typical Iberian arrangement of plazas, cathedrals, and public buildings.

Finally, the conquest established new class patterns. The larger pre-Columbian societies of Central America had been hierarchically ordered, with chiefs and associated elites dominating the masses. Perhaps that is why it was so easy for the Spaniards to superimpose themselves on the system. But what became most different after the conquest was a new racial configuration of class. With the exception of Costa Rica, what emerged was a highly unequal, two-class society, with people of Spanish birth or descent constituting the ruling class and everyone else comprising a downtrodden lower class. Within the lower class, there eventually evolved a subsystem of stratification as the biological union between Spaniards and Indian women produced mestizos, who though never considered equals by the Spaniards, were nonetheless of higher social status than pure Indians.

During the rest of the colonial period, from the late sixteenth century to 1821, the regions that are today the five countries of Central America (plus Chiapas in present-day Mexico) were nominally ruled by the viceroyalty of New Spain (Mexico) as the Kingdom of Guatemala. In fact, however, the viceroyalty had little control over the kingdom, which in practice was administered directly by Spain. In turn, the provinces of Central America were only loosely controlled by Guatemala. Underpopulated, geographically isolated, and economically insignificant, the tiny Costa Rican colony became a neglected backwater, helping to account for its unique evolution.

Elsewhere, resentment grew between the provinces and the central administration in Guatemala as the newly emerging system of dependency inevitably caused the greatest development to take place in that administrative center. Even within individual provinces, such as Nicaragua, regional differences and rivalries developed and festered. Therefore, while Central Americans were sharing a common experience on the one hand, the seeds of division and disintegration were germinating on the other.

Besides these political factors, what is perhaps most important about this period was the continuation of economic and social patterns that had emerged during the conquest. Paradoxically, Costa Rica's relative backwardness and isolation in this period led to a more self-contained economy. A persistent labor shortage, relatively equal land distribution, and the lack of easily exploitable Indians produced a large class of free farmers with generally egalitarian values. Though such factors can easily be given too much importance, they appear to have helped Costa Rica to develop a fairly successful liberal, democratic political system by the mid twentieth century.

In contrast, in the rest of Central America, an externally oriented, elite-controlled, dependent pattern of economic activity was becoming more and more entrenched. At first, the region's human and material resources were exploited to produce cacao, silver, gold, timber, and cattle products for export. Later, this list of exports was expanded to include indigo and cochineal for the blue and red dyes needed by a growing European textile industry. As in present-day Central America, fluctuations in external demand produced periods of boom and bust in the local dependent economies. Though new groups were added to the population—black slaves and, later, the mulatto offspring of white-black unions—the social and economic gap between the white elite and the nonwhite majority remained wide. With the premium placed on export and the maximization of profits for the elites, the masses were generally allowed to consume only at a subsistence level. It is small wonder that the four republics of northern Central America are typified to this day by wide social and economic disparities and by a socially irresponsible economic elite.

Central America passed from colonial rule to formal independence with almost no violence. When Mexico broke from Spain in mid-1821, Central America also declared its independence. In January 1822, it joined the Mexican empire of Agustín de Iturbide. El Salvador resisted union with Mexico but was incorporated by force of arms. However, by mid-1823, soon after the abdication of "Agustín the First," Central America tired of its association with Mexico and declared its independence. Only the former Central American province of Chiapas chose to remain a part of the larger country to the north. From then until 1838, the region was fused—legally, at least—into a federation called the United Provinces of Central America or the Central American Republic.

At first Central Americans were very enthusiastic about the union. The idea made good sense. Clearly, Central America would be stronger politically and economically as a unit than as five tiny independent nations. Yet from the start, several factors undermined the success of the United Provinces. First, there was the long history of resentment of Guatemala by the outlying provinces. This resentment grew as Guatemala, the largest of the five states, received eighteen of the forty-one seats in the congress (according to the principle of proportional representation) and therefore dominated policymaking. Second, although the Constitution of 1824 declared the states to be "free and independent" in their internal affairs, it also contained nationalist and centralist features that tended to block such freedom. Finally, the union was also threatened by the rivalry between two emerging factions of the ruling elite that eventually coalesced into the Liberal and Conservative parties. Liberals and Conservatives clashed both within each province and across provincial boundaries; meddling in their neighbors' affairs became a common practice of Central American leaders.

These factors saddled the union with constant tension and recurrent civil war. The whole experiment finally came unglued in 1838, as first Nicaragua and later the other countries split from the federation. Though there were several attempts to promote reunification later in the nineteenth century, the bitterness and national rivalries that had destroyed the United Provinces in the first place were more than sufficient to block its resurrection.

1838 TO THE PRESENT

The one and a half centuries since the disintegration of the Central American federation have been a time of continuing poverty and hardship for most of the region's people. The patterns of dependency and elite rule, which had taken firm root in each of the republics except Costa Rica during the colonial period, continued through the nineteenth century and into the twentieth century. Costa Rica, too, soon developed debilitating external economic dependencies. Overall, although the region as a whole did experience occasional surges of development, that development seldom benefited the majority of Central Americans.

After independence, Central America's tiny, privileged elites—those who had inherited economic power and social standing—continued to use their control of government to repress popular demands. These elites perpetuated an essentially unregulated, externally oriented economic system for their own benefit. Except in Costa Rica, the continued existence of Liberal-Conservative factionalism, relatively large indigenous communities to supply forced labor, and the emergent hacienda system all helped strengthen the military's political role. Armies (at first belonging to individual caudillos) fought in the civil wars, subdued peasants who had been forceably deprived of their land, and implemented forced labor laws against these new "vagrants." This heavy military involvement in economic and political life retarded the development of civil political institutions and spawned both military rule and considerable political violence. Except for Costa Rica, Central American nations spent most of the period from 1838 until 1945 under either civilian or military dictatorships.

Politics

In the nineteenth century, the basic conflict within the elite was between those people who came to call themselves "Conservatives" and those who described themselves as "Liberals." Before independence and in the first decades afterward, the Conservatives advocated authoritarian, centralized government (sometimes even monarchy), greater economic regulation, and a continuation of special privileges for the Catholic church. Liberals espoused limited representative democracy, decentralized government, free trade and reduced economic regulation, and a separation of church and state. At the same time, Conservatives tended to be more traditional rural landholders who had benefited from Crown licenses and export monopolies. Liberals were more likely to be the disgruntled large landowners who lacked Crown licenses to export their crops or urban elites concerned with commerce.

One important difference between the two groups was that whereas Conservatives generally remained wedded to more traditional economic practices, the Liberals—who by the late nineteenth century had come to dominate all the Central American nations—advocated "modernization" within an externally oriented, laissez-faire economic framework. Specifically, Liberals championed the introduction of new export products—such as coffee and bananas—and the development of government institutions and material infrastructure (highways, railroads, and ports) to facilitate growth in the export economy. Despite such early contrasts and after considerable warfare between the two factions, by the late nineteenth century ideological and policy differences between them had largely vanished. Liberals, when in power, ruled in an authoritarian manner and eventually proved willing to make accommodations with the church. Conservatives eventually came to support laissez-faire economics and the expansion of coffee production.

The Liberal and Conservative parties eventually degenerated into ideologically indistinguishable clan-based political factions. Conservatives generally ruled in the mid nineteenth century but were eventually all replaced by Liberal regimes. Liberal hegemony in Central America then lasted well into the twentieth century, and as it died, spawned an extreme right-wing form of militarism that still plagues Guatemala, El Salvador, and Honduras. One should not confuse the Central American meaning of the term *Liberal* with vernacular meaning of that word in the United States. Central American Liberals were exponents of classical Liberal economic policies (capitalism) and republican government. They were very "conservative" by contemporary U.S. standards. They held elitist attitudes, advocated essentially unregulated free enterprise, and generally believed the proposition: That government is best which governs least. Indeed, in the U.S. political system today, modern conservatives would likely find themselves very much at home with the economic policies of nineteenth-century Central American Liberals. The modernization that liberalism brought simply tended, in most countries, to accelerate the process of concentration of wealth and income in the hands of the elite and to increase the dependency of local economies on the international economic system.

Eventually however, Central American liberalism came under fire from more popularly oriented political movements. In Costa Rica, challenges to Liberal dominance and political reforms began in the late nineteenth century and culminated after 1948 in the abolition of the army and a variety of other changes imposed by local social democratic reformers. In El Salvador, local Liberals responded to labor and peasant discontent in the 1930s by ruling through the military, which massacred thirty thousand peasants in 1932 and occupied the presidency thereafter. By the 1970s, however, the Salvadoran military had become so powerful that it could act independently, often ignoring the wishes of its former Liberal masters.

In Guatemala in 1944, social democrats overthrew a "modernizing" dictator, Jorge Ubico, and began a mild form of democratic revolution. Although a successful CIA-sponsored counterrevolution took place in 1954, the military, not civilian Liberals, took power and ruled the country into the 1980s. In Nicaragua, U.S. armed intervention on behalf of Conservatives between 1909 and 1927 eventually led to the return of the Liberals to power in the form of the Somoza family dictatorship. The Somozas ruled Nicaragua from 1936 until a mass-based insurrection brought the social-revolutionary Sandinista National Liberation Front (Frente

Sandinista de Liberación Nacional—FSLN) to power in 1979. Only in traditional Honduras does a Liberal government currently hold formal power. Even there, however, real political power appears to repose only partly with the civilian president: The armed forces play a determining role in many key political decisions.

External Involvement

International pressures battered Central America after 1850. Great powers (particularly Britain and the United States) pursued economic, political, and security interests in the region. These powers were especially enticed by the possibility of constructing a transisthmian canal. Britain established the colony of British Honduras in the Guatemalan territory of Belize and the Miskito Protectorate in eastern Nicaragua to promote and protect British mining, timber, and geopolitical interests. British influence was greatest during the first half of the nineteenth century but thereafter was increasingly supplanted by that of the United States. Foreign intervention exacerbated the Central American nations' well-established penchant for interfering in each others' internal affairs and led to both international disputes within the region and overt and covert military and political intervention by outside powers.

The most flagrant case of intervention was the filibuster in Nicaragua led by Tennessean William Walker. Contracted by business partners of Cornelius Vanderbilt in an effort to wrest away control of Vanderbilt's transit route across the isthmus, Walker brought a group of mercenaries to Nicaragua in 1855. In league with out-of-power Liberals, he formed an army and toppled the Conservative government. The United States quickly recognized the fledgling Liberal government of Walker, who announced his intention to reinstitute slavery, make English the official language, and seek U.S. statehood.

Conservatives in power in the other four Central American nations agreed to send troops to oust Walker. War ensued in 1856, with Conservative forces partly financed by the British and by Vanderbilt. Walker capitulated in 1857 and fled Nicaragua under U.S. protection. He soon attempted another filibuster but was captured and executed in Honduras in 1860. The 1856–1857 struggle against William Walker's takeover of Nicaragua, known as the National War, briefly rekindled interests in reunification of Central America, reinforced Conservative political hegemony in Nicaragua for many years, and contributed to anti-U.S. nationalism among Central Americans.[3]

By 1900 the dominant outside power in the isthmus, the United States, energetically promoted its economic and security interests. U.S. diplomats served U.S. banks by peddling loans to the region's governments. U.S. customs agents seized Central American customs houses to repay the loans, and U.S. marines intervened in domestic political problems in Honduras, Nicaragua, and Panama. When President Theodore Roosevelt could not win agreement from either Colombia or Nicaragua for a proposed canal lease agreement, he sent U.S. troops in 1903 to ensure that local and foreign insurgents could "liberate" Colombia's province of Panama and thus secured for the United States the right to build a canal through what then became the Republic of Panama.

When Nicaragua's president José Santos Zelaya contemplated making a canal deal with Germany in 1909, the United States helped foment a Conservative rebellion against him and landed U.S. troops to back it up. Zelaya resigned and the new government gave the United States a canal-rights treaty that effectively guaranteed that Nicaragua would never have a canal. U.S. marines returned to Nicaragua in 1912 and remained there most of the period until 1933.

The United States flirted with Rooseveltian good neighborliness toward Central America during the 1930s. During World War II security interests led to heavy U.S. assistance to train and modernize Central America's armies. After 1945 the United States emphasized containment of communism by backing anti-Communist regimes. The United States enlisted other Central American governments to help oust the reformist civilian government of Guatemala in 1954 and to reinforce the Somoza regime after the Managua earthquake in 1972.

Fidel Castro's overthrow of the Batista regime in Cuba in 1959 reinforced the U.S. tendency to concentrate its Central American policy upon the containment of communism. During the Carter administration a novel U.S. emphasis on human rights (1977–1979) led to aid cutoffs for abusive military governments in Guatemala and El Salvador and to the ebbing of U.S. support of Nicaragua's Somoza regime. When the FSLN-led popular rebellion toppled Anastasio Somoza Debayle in 1979, however, U.S. policy in Central America shifted sharply back toward the thirty-year tradition of containment of communism. Washington lifted its military aid ban for El Salvador and involved itself deeply in trying to block the growing rebellion there.

Economic and Social Change

In the economic arena, Central America has specialized in exporting agricultural commodities since 1838. After 1850 coffee gradually became a major export throughout the region (except Honduras). During the twentieth century, other commodity export production developed (bananas, cacao, cotton, sugar, and beef), and, like coffee, each of these products was subject to great world market price swings. Cyclical recessions and depressions in the international economy hit Central America hard. Industrialization was slow, the extreme inequalities in the class systems intensified, and dependency upon imported food and manufactures grew.

Coffee production wrought major socioeconomic changes in the late nineteenth century: It concentrated landownership in the hands of major coffee growers/millers/exporters, who constituted new national economic elites that promoted and protected their interests by controlling (or sharing control of) the state.[+] Other export crops also had regional importance, but their effects on the distribution of wealth and political power were usually similar.

The agro-export elites eventually had to enlist the national armed forces to suppress popular discontent. Together they opposed socioeconomic reform so tenaciously that their rule has been labeled "reactionary despotism."[5] Baloyra described the reactionary coalitions of Central America as

> bent on the preservation of privilege [and their] monopoly of public roles and of the entrepreneurial function. . . . The dominant actors of the reactionary coalitions of Central America do not believe in the suffrage, do not believe in paying taxes, and do not believe in acting through responsible institutions. Their basic ideological premise is that the government exists to protect them from other social groups in order to continue to accumulate capital without the restraints created by labor unions, competition, and government regulation.[6]

During the 1950s and 1960s Central American investors began the extensive cultivation of grains for the regional market and cotton for the international market. Except for Honduras,[7] each Central American nation by the mid-1970s had greatly reduced its smallholding and subsistence agricultural sector (small farmers) and greatly expanded migrant wage-labor forces. A large rural labor surplus developed, cityward migration by unemployable campesinos swelled, domestic food production shrank, and landownership and agricultural production became still more concentrated in fewer hands. National dependency upon imported foodstuffs rose throughout the region, as did the number of citizens directly affected by imported inflation.

Following the 1959 overthrow of Fulgencio Batista in Cuba,[8] Central American governments in 1960 formed the Central American Common Market (CACM) to spur regional economic integration, foreign investment, intraregional trade, and industrialization. One of the stated goals was to diversify and increase production so that wealth might "trickle down" to the poor and undercut the potential appeal of socialism. The CACM's goals converged in 1961 with those of the U.S. Alliance for Progress, which greatly increased public development aid to Central America and thus encouraged private investment there. During the 1960s, to varying degrees in each nation, the surge in domestic and foreign investment concentrated in the capital-intensive production of consumer goods, manufactured mainly with imported raw materials and fuel. Gross domestic products and GDPs per capita grew rapidly well into the 1970s, mainly because of a rapid increase in industrial production and productivity (see Appendix, Tables 1 and 2) and because of stable input prices.

Students of the CACM agree, however, that its industrial boom failed to absorb the rapidly growing labor supply and in some nations shifted wealth and income away from working-class groups. The number of factory and middle-class jobs grew because of industrialization until the early 1970s, but rural and urban unemployment simultaneously rose throughout the region. Moreover, the CACM's development model began to exhaust its potential for growth in the 1970s. Imported industrial raw materials suffered upwardly spiraling prices after 1967—input costs rose 150 percent from 1968 to 1976. These higher costs reduced investment rates, productivity, output growth, and the competitiveness of Central American products.[9] In Nicaragua, El Salvador, and Guatemala, the industrial sector's share of exports declined markedly (averaging roughly 6 percent overall) from the 1970–1974 to the 1975–1979 period. Balance-of-payments pressures afflicted all the Central American economies in the 1970s because of declining terms of trade (the relative costs of imports versus exports), a recession in the world economy, and higher foreign interest rates. According to Weeks, "each government in effect decided to pursue a separate strategy to weather the crisis, rather than a collective one."[10] By the end of the 1970s the CACM accord began to break down, and in the 1980s the breakdown was complete.

After World War II socioeconomic change accelerated in Central America (Appendix, Table 2). Population almost doubled between 1960 and 1980 and high growth rates persisted. The expanding commercial agricultural sector and the increasing concentration of landownership forced peasants off the land and thus swelled both agricultural labor migration and the region's urban populations. Enhanced educational programs increased school attendance, raised literacy rates, and sharply raised participation in higher education everywhere in the isthmus. Ownership of radio and television receivers and of broadcast facilities spread, and roads were improved and means of transportation developed. Such changes made communication easier and faster and brought to more and more people an awareness of their nation and its problems. Economic activity shifted away from agriculture and toward manufacturing and services. Overall economic activity (measured as GDP per capita) more than doubled between 1960 and 1980. However, this growth was unevenly distributed, and, as noted, a sharp recession reduced production regionwide in the late 1970s and the 1980s. By 1987, after productivity had peaked in the late 1970s, four of five isthmian countries (Costa Rica was the exception) saw their per capita GDP levels fall back nearly to 1970 levels (Appendix, Tables 1 and 2).

In summary, each of the five Central American nations entered the 1970s with numerous common economic and social pressures toward ever-greater concentration of wealth, increased rural- and urban-lower-class unemployment, and decreased agricultural self-sufficiency among large segments of the rural poor. The rapid enrichment of the national bourgeoisies and the growth of the middle classes and improvement of their living standards thus held forth to the poor (via ever more sophisticated mass communications) a model of consumption that for larger and larger numbers of people would become unattainable. Clearly such increasing inequality and rapid structural transformation helped to stimulate class conflict and mobilization of protest and pressures to redress growing grievances.

4

INDIVIDUAL HISTORIES OF CENTRAL AMERICAN NATIONS

Although Central America's five nations have had far more in common than most other independent nations, each has had a separate history that has made it unique. Indeed, Central Americans today often dwell upon the differences among their nations. Each country competes with its neighbors in various ways ranging from trade to diplomacy to boundary disputes. Regional governments and elites often interfere in the internal affairs of neighboring countries. Citizens of each country have jokes about and none-too-kind nicknames for their neighbors. This chapter traces the aspects of the national sociopolitical development of each country that have contributed to the distinctive national identity of each nation.

COSTA RICA

Deviant from the patterns set in the rest of Central America during the colonial period, Costa Rica remained an exception to isthmian social, economic, and political norms thereafter. Rather isolated from the rest of Central America because of distance and rugged terrain, Costa Rica retained a much greater degree of racial and economic homogeneity than its neighbors. This is not to say that Costa Rica did not exhibit social disparities, or that it remained forever economically self-contained. Rather, the social inequities in Costa Rica were never great enough to let one class or race completely dominate others to the detriment of the majority of the populace. That is, despite its development of export agriculture, Costa Rica's economic game never became so unequal or so unfair as to allow the development of a full-blown system of dependency, with its tremendous human costs.

In the nineteenth century the roots were planted for Costa Rican democracy, despite a conspicuous absence of democratic rule for much of the era. From 1824 to 1899, one Costa Rican government in five ended by coup d'état and the country was under military rule 44 percent of the time.[1] During most of that epoch, the country was governed by moneyed rural families. Such elections as did occur were indirect, confined to a tiny, literate elite, and often rigged.

However, certain economic trends and political reforms developed that ultimately prevented a total domination of Costa Rican national politics by a landed oligarchy. The first dictator-president, Braulio Carrillo (1835–1842), for instance, increased the already fairly large number of small farmers by distributing municipal lands to the inhabitants. He also promoted the cultivation of coffee, and in contrast to what was to happen elsewhere in Central America, he encouraged the small farmer to produce coffee beans, thus contributing to the emergence of a class of smallholding yeoman farmers.

The incipient landed elite continued to rule the country until its control was broken by Liberal dictator Tomás Guardia (1870–1882). Guardia immediately attacked the wealthy by confiscating some of their properties and exiling a number of their leaders. As a Liberal, Guardia also arranged with foreigners for the construction of roads and railways to move coffee to market. In the late nineteenth century, a labor shortage kept rural wages high as coffee production spread. By that time market forces in the rapidly growing coffee industry had begun to concentrate landownership and thus had pushed many smallholders off the land. But in order to secure the labor supply central to the nation's wealth, large coffee farmers had to pay decent wages and the government had to pass reformist public policies. Costa Rican peasants and workers therefore were not generally exploited or repressed as badly as elsewhere in Central America.

In 1885, Mauro Fernández was named Costa Rican minister of finance, education, and commerce and almost immediately began to carry out a remarkable program of universal public education. Illiteracy, which had stood at around 90 percent at midcentury, was reduced to 69 percent by 1892 and 40 percent by the time Fernández died.[2] Because the ability to read was the key criterion for eligibility to vote in the late nineteenth century, expanding literacy increased the population participating in politics. So, too, did the growth of commerce, government, and urban centers, which swelled the number of people available for and interested in political activity.

In the long run, the presence of a significant number of independent small farmers, the weakening of the socioeconomic elite soon after independence, relative racial homogeneity, the rural labor shortage, and the expansion of popular education combined to create an environment in which democracy could take root. In 1889 "the first really fair election in the country's history" was held.[3] From 1905 to 1914, presidents Cleto González Víquez and Ricardo Jiménez Oreamuno further expanded suffrage, established direct popular election of public officials, and permitted free and open opposition campaigns for office. A brief military regime came to power in 1917 in the hard times associated with World War I. Costa Rica's last military government, it was toppled in 1919 by popular protest and an invasion by exiled elites. Civilian, constitutional rule continued thereafter, and the Costa Rican electorate expanded continuously.

The completion of the Atlantic railroad led to the development of an additional export crop, bananas. The foreign-owned banana industry, concentrated as it was in the sparsely populated Atlantic coastal lowlands, had little effect on Costa Rican politics in the early twentieth century. Later, as hard times developed, labor organizers led by Communists organized the banana plantations, and union influence and political power grew. By the 1940s, the economic slump caused by the Great Depression and World War II had caused great social dislocations. In the early 1940s, President Rafael Calderón Guardia, a popular medical doctor and reformist coffee aristocrat, enacted and began to implement Costa Rica's first labor and social security laws. These policies had the support of the Catholic church and local Communist party and labor unions.

Calderón's alliance with the Communists, however, and his tampering with the results of the 1948 election led to a brief civil war. That year, a broad coalition of groups dominated by social democrats rebelled against the government to protest the electoral fraud. The rebels defeated the government within a few months. From that time to the present, the country's social democrats—the National Liberation party (Partido de Liberación Nacional—PLN), led for three decades by the colorful José "Pepe" Figueres Ferrer—have set the tone of Costa Rican political life. In keeping with a well-established tradition of political accommodation, the victorious National Liberation junta retained Calderón's social reforms for workers. Indeed, the junta went even further by nationalizing the banking and insurance industries. The constitution was rewritten in 1949, abolishing the army, an act that was a key to future political stability. In late 1949, the presidency was turned over to the rightful winner of the 1948 election, Otilio Ulate, who was not a part of the National Liberation movement.

When the PLN and Figueres first won the presidency in 1954, they began to expand the social legislation initiated under Calderón. Increasingly large segments of the populace received health and social security coverage. Even the conservative coalition governments that have periodically replaced the PLN in power have preserved and expanded such social welfare policies. Since 1949, scrupulously honest elections have been held at regular intervals under the auspices of a powerful and independent Supreme Electoral Tribunal. When defeated at the polls, the PLN has willingly given over control of the presidency and Legislative Assembly to an amorphous conservative opposition coalition. The PLN has won the presidency seven times and the opposition has ruled Costa Rica four times between 1949 and 1989. Opinion surveys show that Costa Rican citizens strongly support democratic civil liberties and alternation in power by the competing parties.

Despite its model constitutional democracy, all is not well in contemporary Costa Rica. On the one hand, the cost of its ambitious social welfare programs has outrun the government's ability to collect revenues. Skyrocketing oil costs and plunging export prices caused a foreign debt crisis in the early 1980s. This forced Costa Rica to devalue its currency and to adopt harsh austerity measures that sharply lowered living standards for most citizens. Although the election system remained stable throughout the recession and debt crisis, these problems have had other effects. They have, for example, made recent Costa Rican administrations highly vulnerable to international pressures by the United States, which gave Costa Rica over $1 billion in economic aid during the early and mid-1980s. The administration of Luis Alberto Monge (1982–1986) collaborated with U.S. efforts to isolate and destabilize the Nicaraguan revolution and accepted some military assistance from the United States in an effort to strengthen the Civil Guard. These decisions aroused fears about Costa Rica's civilian democratic institutions and independence.

The administration of Oscar Arias Sánchez somewhat allayed these fears. President Arias resisted U.S. pressure to continue supporting the counterrevolution against Nicaragua. Despite criticism from Washington, Arias took the lead in promoting the Central American Peace Accord, signed in Guatemala in August 1987, for which he received the Nobel Peace Prize. Despite a cutback in U.S. aid during the Arias administration and despite a continuation of Costa Rica's recession in 1986 (Appendix, Table 1), democratic institutions there appeared stable and sound in the late 1980s.

NICARAGUA

Nicaragua is potentially one of the richest countries in Central America, with abundant arable land, considerable hydroelectric, thermal, and (possibly) fossil energy reserves, and significant timber and mineral resources. It also has access to two oceans and a lake and river system that makes it an ideal site for a transisthmian waterway. Ironically, however, Nicaraguans today are among the poorest Central Americans and Latin Americans. The reason for this paradox seems to lie in the extreme degree to which the patterns of dependency, established in the colonial period, were institutionalized and perpetuated into the twentieth century.

Nineteenth-century Nicaragua was plagued by civil wars and foreign interference. During the first several decades, the Liberal and Conservative elites, based in the cities of León and Granada, respectively, struggled with each other to control the national government. At the same time, Britain and the United States—both actively interested in building a transoceanic waterway—maneuvered against each other in an attempt to insert themselves into the power vacuum left by Spain.

At midcentury, foreign interference and the Liberal-Conservative conflict both came to a head in a war. In the late 1840s the British and Americans had almost come to blows over a British attempt to seize the mouth of the San Juan River. In the resulting Clayton-Bulwer Treaty (1850), the United States and Britain mutually renounced the right to embark on any unilateral exploitation of the region. The California gold rush of the 1850s deepened U.S. interest in Central America as a shortcut between the eastern and western coasts of North America.

In 1855 one of two competing transit companies in Nicaragua and Panama became embroiled in Nicaragua's Liberal-Conservative clash. That year the Liberals, in exchange for help in the business dispute, imported a small mercenary army of North Americans commanded by adventurer William Walker to help them defeat the Conservatives. As we noted, the plan backfired when the flamboyant Tennessean seized power for himself. This left Nicaragua's Liberals so discredited by association with the "gringo" interloper that the Conservatives ruled virtually unchallenged until 1893.

In the nineteenth century, Nicaragua experienced profound social and economic changes because of the spreading coffee industry. Before 1870, intraelite turmoil and relatively low foreign economic control had permitted Nicaragua to develop an internal market and a surprisingly large free peasantry. One foreign observer stated: "Peonage such as is seen in Mexico and various parts of Spanish America does not exist in Nicaragua. . . . Any citizen whatever can set himself up on a piece of open land . . . to cultivate plantain and corn."[4] This pattern changed radically when growing international demand for coffee brought widespread cultivation of the bean to Nicaragua. Coffee production required new lands and cheap labor. Accordingly, the elite began in the 1870s to dispossess the peasant and Indian farmers in much of the northern highlands, using chicanery, self-serving legislation, and violence. No longer self-sufficient, former peasants had few options except peonage on coffee plantations. When some of the victims of the process rebelled in the War of the Comuneros of 1881, the elite-run government contained the uprising by killing thousands of the poorly armed insurgents.

The expansion of coffee production at the expense of peasant smallholding accelerated under a modernizing Liberal dictator, José Santos Zelaya (1894–1909). Zelaya also built educational and governmental infrastructure (censuses, archives, a more modern army) and defended the interests of Nicaragua and Central America against a burgeoning imperialist urge in the United States. After the United States decided to build a transisthmian canal in Panama, Zelaya began to seek a canal deal with U.S. rival naval powers Germany and Japan. To protect its canal monopoly, in 1909 the United States encouraged Zelaya's Conservative opposition to rebel against him and then landed marines to protect the rebels. In 1909, Zelaya resigned and in 1910 the Liberals relinquished power to the minority Conservative party. By 1912, however, the Conservatives had made such a mess of public affairs that a combined Liberal-Conservative rebellion occurred. That revolt was put down only after U.S. marines physically occupied Nicaragua.

From 1912 to 1933, with the exception of a short period in the mid-1920s, the United States maintained an occupation force in Nicaragua. U.S.-dominated governments in this era generally followed the dictates of Washington, even when they clearly went contrary to Nicaraguan interests. The Chamorro-Bryan Treaty of 1916, for example, gave the United States rights to build a canal in Nicaragua. The Americans had no intention of constructing such a canal; they simply wanted to block possible competition for the U.S.-built waterway just completed in Panama.

Augusto César Sandino (in checked shirt) (photo courtesy of *Barricada*).

In 1928, another puppet government under U.S. pressure gave Colombia several important Nicaraguan islands, including San Andrés, in order to assuage Colombian resentment of the U.S. role in taking Panama from Colombia in 1903.

And finally, during the latter part of this period, the Nicaraguan government gave in to U.S. pressure to create a modern constabulary—a combined army and police force. A movement to resist U.S. occupation of Nicaragua sprang up in 1927, led by the charismatic local guerrilla-patriot Augusto C. Sandino. U.S. marines could not put down Sandino's resistance, so a Nicaraguan National Guard (Guardia Nacional) was established to assist in the struggle. The war was a standoff, and the United States eventually withdrew its troops at the turn of the year 1932–1933. The National Guard then became the vehicle by which its first Nicaraguan commander, Anastasio Somoza García, created and consolidated the Somoza family dictatorship, which was to brutalize and oppress Nicaragua for over four decades.

As the first Nicaraguan commander of the National Guard, Anastasio Somoza García had Sandino assassinated in 1934 and used the guard to seize political power in 1936. Thereafter, three Somozas held power from 1936 until 1979. Somoza García was either president or the power behind puppets until his assassination in 1956. His son, Luis Somoza Debayle, ruled directly or through puppets until 1967. Luis's younger brother, Anastasio Somoza Debayle, was "elected" to the presidency in 1967 and held power from then until 1979. Throughout this period, there were two primary pillars of support for the Somoza dynasty: the United States and the Nicaraguan National Guard. The guard, always under the command of one of the Somozas, was purposely isolated from the people and allowed to become thoroughly corrupt as means for ensuring its loyalty to the Somozas. It became a sort of Mafia in uniform. The guard ran prostitution, gambling, and protection rackets and took bribes and extorted kickbacks for a variety of activities, both legal and illegal.

U.S. support for the Somozas was secured in two ways: personal ingratiation and political subservience. The Somozas were masters at cultivating Americans. Each was educated in the United States, spoke fluent vernacular English, and knew how to be a "good old boy" among ethnocentric, often homesick North American diplomats and visitors. On the political plane, the Somozas always supported U.S. policy, be it anti-Axis during World War II or anti-Communist thereafter. They allowed Nicaragua to serve as staging grounds for the CIA-organized exile invasions of Guatemala (1954) and Cuba (1961), contributed a small force to participate in the U.S. occupation of the Dominican Republic in 1965, and offered to send Nicaraguan troops to fight in both Korea and Vietnam.

As a result, U.S. support for the Somozas was usually strong and highly visible. Especially after the beginning of the Alliance for Progress in 1961, the United States gave Nicaragua many millions of dollars in aid for social and economic projects (despite ample evidence that the Somozas and their accomplices were stealing much of the aid). U.S. ambassadors were normally unabashedly pro-Somoza. What is more, the dictatorship received U.S. military support far out of proportion to such aid given to other Latin American countries. In fact, by the time the Somozas were finally overthrown, their National Guard was the most heavily U.S.-trained military establishment in Latin America.

The Somoza system accelerated the income-concentrating processes of dependency. In the 1950s, large numbers of peasants were pushed off their Pacific lowlands farms when, in response to increased international demand and prices, the rich and powerful took over these areas to cultivate cotton. Income concentration also took place in cities as the Alliance for Progress and the new Central American Common Market stimulated commercial and industrial growth. Most of the benefit of this growth accrued to Nicaraguan investors in joint ventures with foreign multinational corporations. The bulk of the Nicaraguan economy came to be concentrated in the hands of three huge financial groups, each centered around a local bank with links to corresponding foreign banks. The heart of one of these groups was the Somoza family, which is commonly estimated to have increased its fortune from around $50 million in the 1950s to well over $500 million by 1979. Meanwhile, the situation for the common citizen had become simply intolerable. The Sandinista revolution, which will be discussed separately, was a response to this situation.

EL SALVADOR

To casual visitors in recent decades, El Salvador's most striking characteristic has been its overpopulation. Indeed, foreigners sometimes argue that the tiny country is essentially inviable, lacking the resources to support its teeming population.

That argument, however, is fallacious. Other densely populated countries (Holland, Japan, China) manage to feed their people. In fact, the real problem in El Salvador is an extreme maldistribution of resources brought about, as in the rest of northern Central America, by centuries of external dependence and elite control.[5]

During most of its first century after independence in 1823, El Salvador was controlled by a Liberal elite. Occasionally, Conservative rulers were imposed by Guatemalan intervention, but these were exceptions. Like their counterparts elsewhere in the region, Salvadoran Liberals were staunch advocates of free enterprise and economic modernization through expanding agricultural exports and building up the economic and service infrastructure. The mestizo and Indian masses were regarded somewhat ambivalently as both obstacles to progress and as labor resources to be used as the elite saw fit.

El Salvador entered the national period with most of its economy built around the production, extraction, and export of the dye indigo. However, by the mid nineteenth century, cheaper European chemical dyes sharply cut international demand for the deep blue colorant, forcing El Salvador's privileged elite to turn to coffee production as a substitute. The best land for coffee was the higher, volcanic terrain previously disdained by the large landowners. The mountain slopes, however, were occupied by mestizo and Indian communal farmers whose ancestors had been displaced from the valley floors by the Spanish. The would-be coffee growers thus used their control of the government to gain access to good coffee land by legislating communal landholdings out of existence.

In 1856, the state decreed that individual communes must plant at least two-thirds of their lands in coffee or be confiscated. Lacking the considerable capital necessary to buy and plant coffee trees and wait several years for a crop, many communes were wiped out. Those communes that survived the 1856 legislation received the coup de grace by two laws in the early 1880s. These laws simply declared communal holdings to be illegal and established "vagrancy" rules that effectively forced the now landless peasants to work on the coffee plantations. Salvadoran peasants, of course, were angered by this legalized theft of their land and forced labor schemes. Unsuccessful popular uprisings punctuated the final third of the nineteenth century, but the promoters of coffee prevailed. In the end, the privileged classes brought El Salvador into the twentieth century with one of the most unequal patterns of land distribution in all of Latin America. A coffee elite, henceforth known as the "fourteen families," controlled a lion's share of the country's resources.

Although the seizure of the best lands in the temperate highlands was essentially complete by the end of the nineteenth century, the expansion of coffee continued elsewhere well into the twentieth century. In 1929, for instance, the socially conscious editor of *La Patria* wrote: "The conquest of territory by the coffee industry is alarming. It . . . is now descending into the valleys displacing maize, rice and beans. It is extended like the conquistador, spreading hunger and misery, reducing former proprietors to the worst conditions—woe to those who sell!"[6]

By the 1930s, the situation reached a political breaking point. The Great Depression had lowered the demand and price for Salvadoran exports. Predictably, the coffee elite attempted to cushion itself from the impact of price declines by cutting the already miserable wages of the plantation workers. On top of this, popular hopes for justice were greatly fueled by an aberrant period of democratic reform in 1930–1931 and then dashed by the rise of yet another reactionary dictatorship, led by General Maximiliano Hernández Martínez. The result of all this turmoil and economic travail was an ill-coordinated peasant uprising in January 1932, to which the government security forces and landowners responded with the massacre of over 30,000 peasants (only a small minority of whom were actual insurgents). The original organizer of these uprisings, a charismatic Marxist intellectual, Augustín Farabundo Martí, was captured before the revolt and both shot and beheaded in its wake. His memory, like that of Sandino in Nicaragua, would continue to have an impact on his country decades later.

The half century that has elapsed since the rise of General Hernández Martínez in 1931 and the 1932 massacre (known to this day as the "Slaughter"—*la Matanza*) forms an epoch in Salvadoran history. Whereas previously the Liberal elite had normally ruled through civilian dictators drawn from among themselves, they henceforth entrusted direct control of the government to an uninterrupted series of military regimes. Hernández Martínez ruled dictatorially, both protecting the interests of the coffee elite and initiating modernizing and developmental projects that some of the elite opposed. Post–World War II reformist pressures from labor, middle-class elements, and within the military brought the end of the Hernández Martínez regime in 1944. In 1948 the armed forces restructured its system of rule by establishing a military-dominated political party, the Revolutionary Party of Democratic Unification (Partido Revolucionario de Unificación Democrática—PRUD). Despite its name, the party did not promote revolution, democracy, or unity—it was the military's device for maintaining political control, "an impressive machine of patronage and electoral mobilization."[7] In 1960 the PRUD was replaced by its own clone, the National Conciliation party (Partido de Conciliación Nacional—PCN).

After 1948 the Salvadoran armed forces—with the support of much of the national bourgeoisie, which it defended—ruled essentially in behalf of themselves, becoming increasingly powerful and corrupt. Rule by the military developed a cycle of "change" that kept everything very much the same. First, responding to popular unrest and national problems, a group of progressive young military officers who pledged to break with the past and institute needed reforms overthrew an increasingly repressive regime. Next, the most conservative elements of the army, influenced by members of the oligarchy, reasserted themselves and let the reforms lapse. This produced civil unrest which, in turn, led to increased repression,[8] disaffection by another military faction, and a new reformist coup.

One such cycle produced the PRUD between 1944 and 1948. Another cycle culminated in the PRUD's restructuring itself into the PCN in 1961. On January 25, 1961, just after John F. Kennedy was inaugurated in the United States, a conservative coup that had been encouraged by the Eisenhower administration took place in El Salvador. Although Kennedy quickly recognized the new government, he apparently also pressured the interim junta to begin implementing mild democratic and social reforms. Accordingly, the mid-1960s became a time of reformist rhetoric and growing popular hope for change. During this period the opposition Christian Democratic party (Partido Demócrata Cristiano—PDC) was born. The PDC's very popular leader, José Napoleón Duarte, espoused gradual reformism of the sort supported by the U.S.-created Alliance for Progress and the Central American Common Market. Duarte twice won the mayoralty of San Salvador on the PDC ticket.[9]

This reformism inevitably faded. The moneyed elite was alarmed by the mild reforms proposed under the Alliance for Progress and began to press conservative elements in the military to crack down. Indeed, El Salvador's establishment press had labeled President Kennedy a "Communist" for his insistence on agrarian reform. When the PDC's Duarte apparently won the 1972 election, the regime reacted by throwing out the results and installing rightist Col. Arturo Armando Molina in the presidency. After an unsuccessful barracks revolt on Duarte's behalf, the army arrested and tortured the defrauded candidate, then sent him into exile.

A new reform-repression cycle lasted from 1972 through 1979, spanning the presidencies of two more PCN-imposed military rulers, Molina (1972–1977) and Carlos Humberto Romero (1976–1979). By the late 1960s, the Alliance for Progress and the mild reformism it had espoused had gone the way of the passenger pigeon. Industrial growth had proceeded at a rapid pace, but no "trickling down" of wealth was taking place. Indeed, real wages and living standards for the Salvadoran working classes were deteriorating rapidly and thus spawning unrest. U.S. assistance to El Salvador heavily emphasized military aid. The fact that the Molina and Romero presidencies came to power through vote fraud and became steadily more violently repressive did not alter Nixon and Ford administration policies toward El Salvador. Seeking to contain a feared expansion of Soviet influence, the United States placed paramount importance on maintaining stability and blocking growing pressures for social revolution.

As we shall show in Chapter 6, the accelerating deterioration of economic conditions among the Salvadoran working classes in the 1970s stimulated popular unrest. The period from the 1972 election fraud until 1979 was marked by explosive popular mobilization. Student organizations, labor and peasant unions, and a variety of opposition parties ranging from the Christian Democrats to the small Communist party increased their efforts to politicize the people to defend their interests. Leftist rebel groups appeared for the first time since 1932.

One key element in the political ferment in El Salvador during the 1970s was activist Roman Catholic priests, nuns, and laypersons who had become committed to real social change.[10] This movement, sometimes identified as inspired by "liberation theology," arose as a response to calls by the Second Vatican Council and the Second General Conference of Latin American Bishops of 1968 to make a "preferential option for the poor" and to work for social justice. It organized hundreds of Christian base communities (*comunidades eclesiales de base*—CEBs) to discuss and implement the "social gospel." In addition, between 1970 and 1976, it trained over fifteen thousand catechists and lay "delegates of the Word," who carried a similarly activist message to the rural poor. Logically, these activities heightened grass-roots awareness of the unjust nature of the Salvadoran political and economic system and spurred protests, peasant organization, and other forms of pressure for change.

By mid-1977, the year in which human rights advocate Jimmy Carter became president of the United States, El Salvador had reached an explosive state. The Church was clearly under attack by both the military and the privileged elite. In 1976, presidential candidate Romero had threatened to expel or kill all Jesuits. Soon after Romero assumed the presidency, two priests were killed, ten were exiled, and others were arrested, beaten, or tortured. The Carter administration criticized the Romero regime's human rights record and threatened to cut off military aid. The Salvadoran government, however, astounded Washington by rejecting both the criticism and further military assistance. Unchecked by external or internal brakes and confronted with rising opposition, the Romero government unleashed a wave of terror that was taking over a thousand lives per month by 1979.

El Salvador descended into civil war between 1979 and 1981. A supposedly reformist coup d'état on October 15, 1979, brought to power a junta and cabinet that included the military, business interests, and the Social Democratic and Christian Democratic parties. Fearful of "another Nicaragua" in Central America, the Carter administration reversed field and renewed military assistance to the Salvadoran junta and armed forces. Because the junta did not control human rights abuses, most political moderates withdrew from the government. Several moderate and leftist parties formed the Revolutionary Democratic Front (Frente Democrático Revolucionario–FDR). Five Marxist guerrilla groups united to form the Farabundo Martí National Liberation Front (Frente Farabundo Martí para la Liberación Nacional—FMLN), which received the backing of the FDR. Faced by early 1982 with a burgeoning FMLN-FDR challenge to its sovereignty, the junta—with financial, political, and military aid backing from the United States—embarked upon a dual strategy of building the Salvadoran military and its counterinsurgency capacity while promoting elections to increase the regime's legitimacy at home and abroad. José Napoleón Duarte was elected president in 1984, but his ad-

PRIMERO DE MAYO (MAY DAY) DEMONSTRATION IN EL SALVADOR, 1988. People with signs representing grass-roots organizations; government response (photos by Steve Cagan).

ministration, the military, and the United States were able to achieve no more than a stalemate with the rebel forces.

GUATEMALA

Although its large, unintegrated Indian population sets Guatemala apart from the other countries of modern Central America, it shares many historical legacies with its neighbors, especially with nineteenth-century Nicaragua and El Salvador. An early period of Liberal-Conservative conflict was followed, later in the century, by a consolidation of Liberal control. The Liberals implemented their "reforms," which produced profound socioeconomic realignments and shaped many contemporary social and political problems.

The Liberals, who took control of Guatemala in 1871, dominated the nation, with minor exceptions, until the mid-1940s. They began major reforms under dictator-president Justo Rufino Bárrios (1873–1885). Bárrios pushed hard to modernize his country by building roads, railways, a national army, and a more competent national bureaucracy, by promoting the new crop, coffee, and by encouraging foreign investment. He opened Church and Indian communal lands to "modern" cultivation by large landowners (latifundists). By 1900 coffee accounted for 85 percent of Guatemala's exports, and as landownership concentrated increasingly in their hands, latifundist coffee growers dominated Guatemalan economics and politics. Once they were forced from their land, the Indians were then coerced into being laborers on the coffee plantations through the same sort of debt-peonage systems and "vagrancy" laws seen elsewhere in northern Central America in this period.

In the late nineteenth century, the construction of a rail link to the Atlantic coast gave rise to the banana industry. Soon after the turn of the century, the U.S.-based United Fruit Company (UFCO), at first mainly a shipper/exporter, had squeezed out Guatemalan banana growers and eventually came to own many key public utilities and vast tracts of land. The Liberal development program continued in the twentieth century. In politics, Manuel Estrada Cabrera's brutal dictatorship (1898–1920) inspired Nobel laureate Miguel Angel Asturias's chilling novel of state terror, *El Señor Presidente*. Big coffee plantations, a large number foreign owned, continued to expand inexorably at the expense of many subsistence smallholdings.

When the world economy collapsed in 1929, Guatemala's exports plummeted and worker unrest grew rapidly. The nation's tiny labor movement and incipient Communist party became targets for repression by President Jorge Ubico, who in 1931 assumed dictatorial control of the political system. He violently suppressed the labor movement, Communists, and other political activists, while strongly centralizing power in the national government. Ubico continued to promote the development of government and economic infrastructure (banks, railways, highways, telephones, the telegraph, and electrical utilities). Although originally an admirer of Adolf Hitler, Ubico took the opportunity provided by World War II to confiscate over $150 million in German-owned properties, mainly coffee plantations. He "modernized" vagrancy laws so that the government could oblige Indians to work a certain number of days for the state. This effectively converted the government into Guatemala's major labor contractor.

Labor unrest, middle-class pressures for democratization and reform, and a loss of U.S. support caused Ubico to resign in 1944. Student- and labor-backed military reformers called elections for early 1945. Educator and former exile, Juan José Arévalo Bermejo, who described himself vaguely as a "spiritual socialist," won the presidency. During his five-year term, Arévalo began numerous reforms, instituting social security, a labor code, professionalization of the armed forces, rural education, public health promotion, and the formation of cooperatives. Arévalo vigorously encouraged union and peasant organization and open elections. Arévalo's economic policies, which have been described as an "explicit attempt to create a modern capitalist society,"[11] did not address the root of the country's social problems—the extreme maldistribution of land.

In 1950 Guatemalans elected a young army officer, Jacobo Arbenz Guzmán, to succeed Arévalo. Arbenz sought to deepen the revolution's social reforms despite growing conservative and U.S. opposition. He legalized the Communist party, called the Guatemalan Labor party (Partido Guatemalteco del Trabajo—PGT), in 1951, which became very active in organizing labor and in promoting agrarian reform. A 1952 Agrarian Reform Law began the confiscation and redistribution of farmland to 100,000 peasants. Over 500 peasant unions and 300 peasant leagues formed under the Arbenz government.[12]

Arbenz's reforms and the rapid organization of peasants and workers threatened the rural labor supply system and shifted economic power toward workers and peasants and away from latifundists and employers. The threatened interests took action when Arbenz nationalized land belonging to United Fruit and offered compensation to the company at its previously declared tax value. Several highly placed Eisenhower administration officials had direct ties with UFCO. The nationalization, the presence of a few Communists in the government, and an attempt by Arbenz to purchase light arms from Czechoslovakia caused the United States to label the Arbenz government as Communist.

Beginning about 1953 the United States set out to destabilize Guatemala's Arbenz administration with a program of financial sanctions, diplomatic pressure in the Organization of American States, and Central Intelligence Agency (CIA) disinformation and covert actions. This culminated in a CIA-backed conspiracy with a disloyal rightist army faction. In June 1954 the tiny, CIA-supported National Liberation Army, led by Col. Carlos Castillo Armas, invaded Guatemala. The armed forces refused to defend the government and Arbenz had to resign.[13]

As the head of the National Liberation Movement (Movimiento de Liberación Nacional—MLN), Colonel Castillo Armas assumed the presidency, backed by the United States and the hierarchy of the Catholic church. With ferocious anti-

Communist propaganda, the counterrevolution dismantled the labor and peasant movements, killing and jailing thousands in the process, repressed political parties, revoked the Agrarian Reform Law, and returned confiscated lands to their former owners. As working- and middle-class and prorevolutionary organizations were suppressed, "there began a continuing . . . promotion of upper-sector interests."[14] Military and business sectors made sharp gains in political influence within the government. Foreign policy became closely identified with the United States, and U.S. and multinational aid programs promoted economic growth and financed extensive infrastructure development.

The MLN developed into a substantial political party during the late 1950s, drawing together coffee plantation owners, municipal politicians and bureaucrats, owners of midsized farms, and certain military elements united in anticommunism and in their hostility toward the reforms of the 1944–1954 revolution. Castillo was assassinated in 1957 and confusion followed. Amid accusations of fraud and in an atmosphere of increasingly bitter recriminations between the armed forces and the MLN, the army annulled the 1957 plebiscite, which the MLN had won, and imposed Gen. Miguel Ydígoras Fuentes as president. The Ydígoras government promoted Guatemala's participation in the Central American Common Market, permitted CIA-backed anti-Castro Cuban exile forces to train in Guatemala, and continued police terror against supporters of the revolution and labor and peasant leaders.

Continued violence plus the growing corruption of the Ydígoras government prompted an abortive coup by reformist army officers in 1960. Escaped remnants of the plotters formed the nucleus of the first of several rebel groups. The leaders of the Revolutionary Armed Forces (Fuerzas Armadas Revolucionarias—FAR) and the 13th of November Revolutionary Movement (Movimiento Revolucionario del 13 de Noviembre–MR-13) eventually adopted a Marxist-Leninist ideology and guerrilla war strategy patterned after that of Fidel Castro in Cuba. U.S. military aid to the Guatemalan armed forces increased rapidly, but despite such assistance, early military operations against the guerrillas proved ineffective. Dissatisfaction within military ranks culminated in Col. Enrique Peralta Azurdia's overthrow of Ydígoras in 1963; counterinsurgency operations thereafter expanded rapidly.

In 1965 the military decided to return the government nominally to civilians, and the 1966 election campaign was generally free and open.[15] The Revolutionary party (Partido Revolucionario—PR) candidate, Julio César Méndez Montenegro, who denounced the twelve-year counterrevolution, won the presidency. After Méndez took office, however, military counterinsurgency accelerated while the armed forces' hold on the political system actually deepened—despite the presence of a civilian president in the National Palace. The army's 1968 Zacapa campaign took an estimated ten thousand civilian lives and dealt the guerrillas a severe blow, in the process earning its head, Col. Carlos Arana Osorio, the sobriquet of "the Butcher of Zacapa."

After a decade of reform/revolution and another of counterrevolution, Guatemalan society had become sharply polarized between reformist and conservative segments. For some, the 1966 election signified the breakdown of the counterrevolution and, therefore, a call to radical action. Several right-wing "death squads" formed and commenced acts of terror against persons vaguely associated with the Left and with reformist politics. Regular national security forces (army and police), peasant irregulars armed by the government in areas of insurgency, and right-wing terrorist groups permitted (and encouraged) by the regime conducted the Right's terror campaign. Drastic, often indiscriminate actions by the police and proregime terrorists targeted mainly the government's political opposition, but many victims were completely apolitical. As a result, the reform-oriented opposition was effectively intimidated, demobilized, and disarticulated.

In these circumstances, the presidential elections held in 1970—though the ballots were counted honestly by the Méndez government—resulted in victory for Col. Carlos Arana Osorio, the nominee of both the MLN and the military's own Institutional Democratic party (Partido Institucional Democrático—PID). With U.S. aid at its all-time high during his administration, Arana definitively consolidated the military's political power and deepened its corruption. An aggressive economic modernization program created huge public sector enterprises and projects (some under army control) to increase the financial autonomy of the armed forces and the amounts of graft available to top officers. Terror against unions, political parties, and suspected critics of the regime escalated anew.

Despite the nomination of military officers as presidential candidates by each of the parties, Arana, by a fraudulent count of the 1974 election, imposed Gen. Eugenio Kjell Laugerud García as his successor.[16] Laugerud's government briefly moderated repression, encouraged cooperatives and union resurgence, and pushed a major development project for the potentially oil-rich northeastern Petén, where many high-ranking officers acquired large tracts of land.

The disastrous earthquake of February 4, 1976, took some 25,000 lives, mainly in the western highlands, and sparked new political and economic unrest by unions, university students, and the urban poor. The FAR resurfaced and two new, Indian-based guerrilla organizations, the Guerrilla Army of the Poor (Ejército Guerrillero de los Pobres—EGP) and the Organization of the People in Arms (Organización del Pueblo en Armas—ORPA) also appeared. All grew rapidly and began overt military activity in the late 1970s. When President Laugerud stepped up repression, the Carter administration's State Department criticized Guatemala's human rights record. Guatemala responded in 1977 by refusing to accept further U.S. military assistance. Economic assistance to Guatemala, however, continued during the Carter administration.

In the political turmoil of the 1978 election, all parties again nominated military officers as presidential candidates. Gen. Romeo Lucas García (nominated by the military's PID and the PR) won the election on an apparently fraudulent count.[17] The Lucas García government brutally crushed Guatemala City protests against increased bus fares in late 1978. As opposition parties grew in 1978–1979, security force death squads assassinated dozens of national and local leaders of the Democratic Socialist party (Partido Socialista Demócrata—PSD), Christian Democratic party (Partido Demócrata Cristiano—DC), and the reformist United Front of the Revolution (Frente Unido de la Revolución—FUR). Hundreds of union leaders, university faculty, and student leaders also disappeared or were assassinated during the Lucas government.

In the countryside, peasant organizations led by the Peasant Unity Committee (Comité de Unidad Campesina—CUC) stepped up organizing. The CUC staged a major strike against sugar planters in 1980. In 1978 and 1979 the regrouped FAR and ORPA began military activity in the western highlands; they apparently enjoyed considerable popular support. As a part of its stepped up counterinsurgency efforts, the army implemented draconian measures—including massacres of Indian villagers—to discourage support for the guerrillas. Despite such massive human rights violations, Guatemala continued to receive new economic assistance from the United States that totaled over $60 million from 1979 through 1981.[18]

The relative prosperity of Guatemala had strengthened the military regime in the late 1970s, but the regional recession, with sharp declines in production (Appendix, Table 1), finally arrived in Guatemala in 1981 and 1982. The recession quickly ruined the army's image as an economic manager and alienated the once supportive business community. When President Lucas fraudulently manipulated the results of the 1982 presidential election to benefit his defense minister, Gen. Aníbal Angel Guevara, discontent arose within the army itself. A group of young officers who desired certain reforms (reduced military corruption and withdrawal from direct participation in rule) overthrew Lucas just after the election. They asked a retired general and former DC presidential nominee, Efraín Ríos Montt, to head the government and to take steps to restore the presidency to civilians.

The highly eccentric Ríos—a fundamentalist Protestant—soon proved overly fond of his new job. He took steps to consolidate power fully and gave signs of intending to stay. Ríos had promised a return to civilian rule, but he proposed reforms to the electoral system that would have actually strengthened army control of the elections and weakened the political parties. Although Ríos's rule brought some reduction of urban death squad activity, the army sharply escalated its rural counterinsurgency activities. The unprecedented levels of violence and social dislocation wreaked by the army devastated entire indigenous communities and cultural groups.[19]

Complaints from the parties, external legitimacy problems stemming from the de facto nature and brutality of the regime, and unease about Ríos Montt's increasingly assertive promotion of his sect and religious ideas proliferated. The same reformist element within the army that had put Ríos in power in early 1982 ousted him in an August 1983 coup led by the defense minister, Gen. Oscar Humberto Mejía Víctores. Upon assuming the presidency, Mejía accommodated many of the parties' objections about the election laws, conducted a relatively clean election of delegates to a constituent assembly in 1984—albeit within a climate of extreme political repression. The constituent assembly rewrote the Guatemalan Constitution so as to increase the autonomy of the armed forces and to pave the way for the November 1985 national election. The army's brutal counterinsurgency campaign, political assassinations, disappearances, and overall violence remained largely unchanged under Mejía.

In late 1985 Guatemala conducted a clean national election after a campaign distinguished by the candidates' universal fear of advocating—indeed, even of mentioning publicly—socioeconomic reforms or human rights improvements. Christian Democrat Vinicio Cerezo Arévalo won the presidency in a runoff, and his party captured a majority of the congress.[20]

Guatemala's new civilian regime, with the enthusiastic backing of the United States, then embarked upon what many observers believed was a last chance to avoid a general uprising or bloody civil conflict as in Nicaragua or El Salvador. Not even Cerezo himself seemed very optimistic about his prospects for remaking the Guatemalan political system. When asked about his chance to win effective ruling power away from the military, promote human rights and social reform, and solve looming economic problems, Cerezo reportedly quipped, "I am a politician, not a magician!" He and the Guatemalan congress faced daunting problems. The economic recession of the early 1980s continued (Appendix, Table 1), a high level of human rights abuse continued, and the guerrilla conflict persisted despite the army's counterinsurgency war. By its third year in office, Cerezo's administration was being roundly criticized—even within his own party—for corruption and for failure to make progress on socioeconomic reforms, economic recovery, or human rights. Cerezo's greatest success came mainly in external affairs, where his endorsement of and work for the Central American Peace Accord contributed significantly to its signing in Guatemala in August 1987.[21]

HONDURAS

Honduras is an unusual and paradoxical country. By a geological quirk, its soil lacks the rich volcanic material prevalent throughout the region's other countries. Geographically isolated, with broken terrain, and very poor transportation facilities, Honduras did not develop a significant export economy in the nineteenth century and remained mainly a subsistence economy. The common people of Honduras were even poorer than their Nicaraguan, Salvadoran, or Guatemalan counterparts. Honduran history, however, reveals little mass rebellion or guerrilla warfare. Until very recently, the country was a calm eddy in Central America's troubled waters.

The reasons for this social and political stability in the face of mass poverty are several. Honduras never really developed so coherent or powerfully privileged an elite class as did its three neighbors, Nicaragua, El Salvador, and Guatemala. Of course, there have always been some rich Hondurans, but their wealth remained regionally based. Unlike the rest of Central America, coffee became a significant export crop for Honduras only after World War II.

When commercial banana production was introduced at the turn of the century, foreigners, not Hondurans, were responsible. The banana industry developed along the sparsely populated northern coast and displaced few peasant or Indian communal holdings. Indeed, though land was generally poor in quality, it was nearly always plentiful in Honduras; thus, poor peasants could usually find free or cheap land to farm. Virtually no land shortage developed until the mid twentieth century, when foreign market demands and urban population growth led wealthier Hondurans to begin a process of concentrating landownership.

These economic development patterns had other ramifications.[22] First, since there was no need to quell an angry, dispossessed, and exploited rural working class, the Honduran army remained rather weak well into the twentieth century. Second, the banana industry contributed to labor relations unlike those seen in neighboring nations. Because banana companies were foreign owned, Honduran governments were not very keen on keeping banana workers' wages down. Indeed, rising wages meant more basic consumption and thus helped Honduran entrepreneurs. Moreover, because banana production was less labor intensive than, for instance, coffee production, the companies could pay higher wages without becoming less competitive. Strikes were frequent, but Honduran governments felt less inclined to use force to suppress workers and the companies were more willing to make wage concessions than often proved true in other countries or in the production of other crops. Thus, although labor unions were not formally legalized until 1954, they had existed informally and operated fairly freely for many decades. Over the long haul, Honduras developed a much larger (and politically more potent) organized work force than other Central American countries.

In another contrast with neighboring nations, the Liberal/Conservative debate began much later in Honduras. In the nineteenth century, the country was dominated by a succession of nonideological caudillos who simply succeeded each other by force of arms. Party development began in earnest when a Liberal, Marco Aurelio Soto, was president (1876–1883). True to the Liberal vision of the era, he began efforts to modernize the nation, build a service infrastructure and state apparatus, and to attract foreign investors. By the end of the century the Honduran Liberal party (Partido Liberal de Honduras—PLH) was formed. Liberals dominated the political scene until the 1930s. Their conservative counterpart—the National party—was born in 1923, but was able to take power only when the PLH split in the 1932 election. National party caudillo Tiburcio Carías Andino was elected in 1932 and held the presidency until 1949—giving Honduras its longest period of political stability.

Following Carías's retirement, Liberal-National conflict over control of power intensified. The Liberal party's electoral strength recovered with the rapid expansion of labor union movement in the early 1950s. National party efforts to keep the Liberals out of power prompted the army in 1956 to seize power in order to end the dispute; there followed a year of military rule. When the military relinquished power, PLH candidate Ramón Villeda Morales swept the 1957 election. Villeda's government signed the Central American Common Market accords and passed several modernizing social policies, including social security, labor, and agrarian reform laws. Despite such symbols of progress, Honduras remained the poorest country in Central America.

From the mid twentieth century onward, Honduras developed problems and patterns more typical of the rest of Central America. As noted earlier, land hunger first became a real problem during this period. This was due in part to appropriation of peasant-occupied lands by larger landholders as the latter sought to take advantage of increased internal and external commodity markets. Another important cause was a sudden rise in population growth rates due to improved public health conditions and practices developed during World War II. The rapid increase in demand for land in the 1950s and 1960s led to greater tension between classes and increasing peasant mobilization.

An additional growing similarity between Honduras and other Central American nations came from the militarization of its political system. With the advent of the cold war, labor unrest in the banana plantations was commonly blamed on "Communist agitators." As part of its general regional strategy to contain communism, the United States "concluded several agreements to train and equip the loosely organized armed forces of Honduras, and since the early 1950s, over one thousand personnel [had, as of 1979] taken courses in U.S. facilities."[23] Although from the 1950s through the 1970s there was virtually no guerrilla opposition to the Honduran government, much of the U.S. military training of the era dealt with counterinsurgency and put a strong emphasis on "national security."

Not surprisingly, the increasing factionalism and conflict within and between the Liberal and National parties left a power and leadership vacuum. This vacuum, plus the growth of the military's strength, contributed to an expansion of the armed forces' involvement in politics. Whereas civilian caudillos had run the country for the first half of the twentieth century, the armed forces since the 1956 coup have ruled directly or have powerfully influenced civilian rulers from just offstage.

Honduran military rule, however, until the 1980s was rather more benign than in neighboring states. The military acted more as an arbiter between other political groups than as an agent of a ruling class. Labor, peasant, and political party organizations were generally tolerated. Catholic priests and nuns were allowed to carry the "social gospel" to the poor and to build grass-roots organizations. And especially after the birth of the Alliance for Progress and Central American Common Market, there was much talk of basic socioeconomic reforms, some directly promoted by military governments.

In 1963 Air Force Col. Oswaldo López Arellano overthrew Villeda Morales and assumed power in coalition with National party figures. The regime repressed labor and peasant activism and began to enlarge and strengthen the armed forces.

The regime's conservative economic policies, certain disadvantageous trade relations built into the Central American Common Market, and the 1969 war with El Salvador led to growing public unrest as López's presidency ended. The failure of the successor National-Liberal coalition to deal with growing national turmoil prompted López Arellano, now a wealthy general, to seize power once again. This time, with the support of labor and peasant sectors and other progressive elements, he implemented several populist programs, including a modest agrarian reform.

Military participation in rule changed character in the late 1970s. Embarrassed by a bribery scandal, López transferred power in 1975 to Col. Juan Alberto Melgar Castro, the first of two hard-line military dictators who abandoned López's populist reforms and curtailed civilian participation in national administration. Melgar was overthrown in 1978 by Col. Policarpo Paz García. Despite the rapid changes in regimes, the military strove to promote national economic development and turned away from social programs. Although the Melgar and Paz regimes largely ignored questions of social justice, they remained relatively respectful of basic human rights and permitted certain civil and political liberties. There were no death squads, no systematized tortures, and no rash of disappearances. The press remained relatively free and boisterously critical of the military regimes.

Despite their developmentalist goals, the armed forces proved quite inept as rulers and economic managers. By the late 1970s corruption scandals, deepening economic difficulties, the fall of the Somoza regime in Nicaragua, and growing pressures from spurned civilian politicians created powerful incentives for the military to abandon power. Although the Carter administration never severed military assistance to Honduras, it brought pressure on General Paz to relinquish power. Under such internal and external pressures, the military called elections in 1980 for a constituent assembly that would rewrite the constitution; in November 1981, presidential elections were held.

Liberal Roberto Suazo Córdova won a clear majority and took over the formal reins of power in January 1982. Col. Gustavo Alvarez Martínez became head of the armed forces. Prospects for a true democracy were soon clouded, both by the performance of Suazo and Alvarez, and by policies of the new Reagan administration. Washington put heavy pressure on Honduras to lend itself to U.S. efforts to overthrow the Sandinista government of Nicaragua and to curtail the activities of Salvadoran guerrillas inside Honduran territory. A U.S. military spokesman neatly summarized the U.S. appraisal of the situation: "Honduras is the keystone to our policy down there."[24] Suazo and Alvarez accepted the presence of U.S. troops on continuous "maneuvers," the construction and expansion of military bases and facilities in Honduras, and even U.S. training of Salvadoran troops. Sanctuary and overt cooperation were provided to the contra army that the United States was developing to attack Nicaragua's Sandinista government. Honduras thus became the active ally of the U.S. military strategy for Nicaragua and El Salvador,[25] leading some wags to claim the country had become an aircraft carrier—the USS *Honduras*. In exchange for all this, Honduras received hundreds of millions of dollars in U.S. assistance—especially military aid.

This military assistance program rapidly expanded the size and power of the armed forces and permitted Alvarez to overshadow and intimidate the civilian president and congress. Relations with Nicaragua deteriorated badly. By 1984 the U.S.-financed contra forces in Honduras had begun to rival in number the Honduran military and had severely disrupted public order along the Nicaraguan border. In 1983 Honduras already had death squads, whose membership included public security force and Nicaraguan exile elements; political disappearances and murders became increasingly commonplace. As repression grew and domestic political tensions rose, several leftist guerrilla groups appeared and began operations—a novelty in Honduras. Though very weak and extremely fragmented, the Honduran guerrilla movement continued to grow as the decade proceeded.

In 1984 senior armed forces officers ousted Alvarez from his command because he had deepened Honduras's role in the U.S.-Nicaragua imbroglio. Another sore spot was Alvarez's insensitivity to the military's tradition of corporate decisionmaking and his decision to permit the training of Salvadoran soldiers—until then hated enemies—at a new U.S. training facility at Puerto Castillo. In 1984 and 1985 Suazo's increasingly high-handed maneuvering to retain the presidency provoked a grave constitutional crisis. In an astounding twist of events the armed forces called labor and peasant groups into the street to confront the regime and thus force Suazo to permit elections to go forward. The stratagem worked: a Suazo antagonist, the PLH's José Azcona Hoyos, won the 1985 presidential election.[26]

In the late 1980s, Azcona's tenuous civilian government tottered forward, propped up—in one of the region's great ironies—by organized labor, the military, and the U.S. government.[27] Although still less violent than in El Salvador and Guatemala, the human rights situation continued to deteriorate despite promises by the Azcona government to clean things up. Looming economic problems and growing tensions with Nicaragua threatened Honduras with continued difficulty for the immediate future. With the loss of its former tranquility, Honduras had become much more like its violent, unstable Central American neighbors.

5

A THEORY ABOUT CENTRAL AMERICAN REBELLIONS

There are many competing theories about why a revolution has occurred in Nicaragua and major national revolts have developed in El Salvador and Guatemala in the past decade. One explanation made fashionable by President Reagan, his advisers, and Central American conservatives blames "Communist subversion" by the Soviet Union, Cuba, and (more recently) the Sandinista government of Nicaragua.[1] According to this theory, pro-Soviet Communist agents have stirred up the Central American rebellions and have supplied the rebels with the money, arms, and intelligence with which they fight their governments.[2] The National Bipartisan Commission on Central America clearly stated this thesis:

> Whatever the social and economic conditions that invited insurgency in the region, outside intervention is what gives the conflict its present character. Of course, uprisings occur without outside support, but protracted guerrilla insurgencies require external assistance. Indeed, if wretched conditions were themselves enough to create such insurgencies, we would see them in many more countries of the world.
>
> Propaganda support, money, sanctuary, arms supplies, training, communications, intelligence, logistics, all are important in both morale and operational terms. Without such support from Cuba, Nicaragua, and the Soviet Union, neither in El Salvador nor elsewhere in Central America would such an insurgency pose so severe a threat to the government.[3]

Without denying the presence of outside involvement in the Central American insurrections, other theories blame the region's rebellions on political, economic, and social processes within the region itself. Such arguments treat these domestic factors as the main causes of revolt and regard foreign involvement as a relatively less important cause or motivation for rebellions.

We reject the subversion thesis's contention that outside Marxist forces have undermined what would otherwise have been a stable state of grinding poverty. Instead, in this book, we argue that rapid changes in economic and political conditions within Central America are the main forces driving rebellion. After briefly reviewing some general theories about sociopolitical violence and revolution and some specific theories about the conflict in Central America itself, we then develop a theory to explain the origin and evolution of the recent popular insurrections in Nicaragua, El Salvador, and Guatemala and the lack of similar movements in Costa Rica and Honduras. This theory does not overlook involvement by external actors but treats it as one of many resources that rebels can take advantage of. Our theory likewise treats U.S. intervention as a factor in the struggle for power. In Chapters 6 through 8 we present evidence from many sources in a test of this theory.

RECENT RESEARCH ON CENTRAL AMERICAN POLITICAL VIOLENCE

There has been a veritable deluge of scholarship recently on conflict and revolution in Central America,[4] but little of it is explicitly theoretical.[5] Among the more explicit theories, one school has treated economic factors such as the nature of production, class relations, and economic growth and development as the driving forces of Central American turmoil.[6] Pérez Brignoli and Baíres Martínez, for example, argued that "thirty years of prosperity seem to have created internal conditions sufficient to nurture a social conflict of vast proportions."[7] Bulmer-Thomas was more specific: "The expansion of EXA [export agriculture], however, has disrupted economic and social relations in agriculture to the point where the political model underpinning EXA is called into question. Political and social stability in Central America, therefore, threatens to break down *because* of the success of export-led growth rather than *despite* it."[8]

Another school of explanation for Central America's rebellions has emphasized such domestic political factors as elites and their behavior, the disaffection of interest and pressure groups, and the decay of the state or of traditional dominance systems.[9] Other theories have stressed both domestic and international actors that organize, mobilize, and coalesce Central American oppositions.[10] Within this approach fall various studies of the Catholic church as both a domestic and an international actor involved in mobilizing opposition.[11]

Many explanations for Central America's rebellions have treated them as the result of a complex combination of socioeconomic processes and political factors (both internal and external). In some works the theory linking these economic, political, and organizational factors to turmoil is mainly implicit, rather than explicit.[12] Other complex theories have expressly linked Central American rebellions to the combined effects of social strains upon collective psychology, arguing that economic and political change created intense dissatisfaction.[13] The most promising of the complex explanations have concentrated on the development of contradictory or conflictual class relations in Central America's dependent agro-export-oriented economies.[14] This emergent school has held that the structural sources of grievances for key class groups include the following factors: historically extreme maldistribution of wealth and income, aggravated by recent rapid growth of rural and industrial proletariats and by increasing concentration of wealth (especially agricultural land), and declines of real incomes for rural and urban working classes during the 1970s. Torres Rivas explained the theory of economic contradictions:

> The international crisis of 1974/75 brought to the surface throughout the region the differentiation of the classes that had been developing since the postwar era. The popular movement grows upon confronting a bourgeoisie (capitalist class) hit hard by the international recession, thus masking the general [regionwide] crisis of the system with the particular crises of each of the bourgeoisies.[15]

Many agents—religious community organizers, political parties, labor unions, and revolutionary groups—have mobilized and organized the aggrieved. Violent regime repression of opposition demands for reform in Nicaragua, El Salvador, and Guatemala not only have failed to stem such popular demands for change, but actually have increased opposition, radicalized it, and forged revolutionary coalitions. The decay of Central American governments, their organs of social control, and the coalitions backing the regimes has helped to shift the balance of power toward opposition forces and contributed to the growth and spread of revolutionary violence. Torres Rivas again illustrated this, explaining how political and organizational factors have led to Central American rebellions:

> The counterrevolutionary State is the consequence of the bourgeoisies' difficulty in forging new alliances . . . [or] maintaining the old system of alliances . . . which in turn reinforces the repressive character of the political order. . . . The State loses the capacity first to control, and later to dismantle, popular demands for reform. The crisis of the State now becomes a crisis of the entire society and develops as the masses gradually but inevitably gain space, recognition, and influence behind the leadership of Marxist political-military groups.[16]

This trend toward a complex theory of class conflict and political factors appears to be developing into an incipient school of explanation for the nearly simultaneous rebellions in three Central American nations. This approach has important similarities to more general recent theories on the origin and development of revolutions and major national rebellions.

THEORIES OF REBELLION AND REVOLUTION

Scholars have put forward many schemes for categorizing theories of revolution, rebellion, and political violence. Despite prodigious amounts of scholarly research on these subjects during the 1960s and 1970s, major reviewers of the field agree that most approaches have had serious shortcomings.[17] Some very useful insights, however, have emerged from recent efforts to assess theories about rebellion and revolution.

The first such point is that no matter how plausible explanations based on individual psychology and perceptions may seem, theories of relative deprivation derived from the frustration-aggression literature[18] suffer from "the absence of any direct evidence concerning the relationship between perceptions, psychological processes, and political violence among individuals."[19] In other words, adequate attitudinal data across time have never been available (nor are they ever likely to be) for a variety of practical reasons. It thus remains effectively impossible to link grievances or perceived deprivation by individuals to specific outbreaks of violence involving those same individuals.

Second, various structural theories of violence and revolution have been demolished when shown to be logically inconsistent, false when tested, incomplete, or tautological.[20] A third problem is that class-conflict approaches to revolution—especially the more doctrinaire Marxian theories—often erroneously fixate upon production factors and class relations to the exclusion of important political phenomena such as the independent role of the state as a political actor[21] and the importance of organization and resource mobilization by both regime and insurgents.[22]

With these problems in mind, one can integrate several still promising theoretical approaches into a more comprehensive theory that can help us understand recent conflict in Central America. First, as Kriesberg pointed out, there must be a fundamental basis of conflict, or cause, that defines "quasi-groups or categories" of affected persons. Such groups, typically aggrieved victims of social change, serve as "recruiting grounds for organizations."[23]

What bases of conflict are most likely to lead citizens to resort to widespread rebellion? Theda Skocpol agreed with Marx that evolving class relations constitute a fundamental source of revolution:

> The Marxist conception of class relations as rooted in the control of productive property and the appropriation of economic surpluses from direct producers by nonproducers is, in my view, an indispensable theoretical tool. . . . Class relations are always a potential source of patterned social and political conflict, and class conflict and changes in class relations actually do figure prominently in successful social-revolutionary transformations.[24]

John Walton concurred with Skocpol on the likely origin of conflict but believed that her limited set of great social revolutions (France, Russia, and China) is too narrow to be of much use in studying most major outbreaks of political violence. He explored the conceptually broader and historically more common phenomenon of ***national revolts***, "protracted, intermittently violent, non-local struggles [with extensive] mobilization of classes and status groups that become recognized claimants of rival sovereignty and engage the state."[25] National revolts eventually affect policy and social development, but without the rebels actually ever coming to power to implement a revolutionary program. Walton's argument is persuasive for Central America, where three of five countries have had widespread rebellions, but where only in one country, Nicaragua, has a full-scale social revolution occurred.

Like Skocpol and Walton, Jeffrey Paige and Eric Wolf have written that a major engine of class transformation in agrarian societies (and therefore a major source of grievances) is the impact of their inclusion into the world capitalist economy through the development of heavy dependence upon export agriculture.[26] "The penetration of global capitalism into precapitalist societies [fosters] export agriculture and an internal market for the consumption of imports [so that] the peripheral economy is unevenly developed, . . . [eventually producing] a massive transformation of the indigenous economy."[27] This change harms large sectors of the peasantry and of the urban poor and middle sectors. Thus, the injury caused to specific social groups by national development under the dominant influence of export agriculture provides people with grievances. But Kriesberg argued that the presence of aggrieved citizens is in itself insufficient for political conflict to become manifest. Two additional things must happen: (1) Affected groups must become self-aware of their opposition to other groups, and (2) the aggrieved parties must develop oppositional goals. In essence, the aggrieved must organize and must focus their struggle for change upon some target—most likely the regime in power.[28]

Both Rod Aya and Charles Tilly made an important contribution to theory on revolts by pointing out that effective organization for opposition requires the mobilization of resources (e.g., cadres, cash, arms, communication, allies). They also emphasize the key role of the government, or state, in shaping rebellion. The state may become a key target or focus of opposition by the organized aggrieved, resulting in a situation of contested sovereignty. The state also shapes its opponents as it both represses them and promotes change.[29] Walton and Skocpol agreed with Aya and Tilly that political factors (organization and resource mobilization by the aggrieved, a contest over sovereignty, and the state's response to opposition's challenge) eventually determine the outcome of major rebellions.[30]

AN EXPLANATORY THEORY FOR CENTRAL AMERICAN REBELLIONS

There are several elements common to both the Central Americanists' emergent theoretical approach to the rebellions of the 1970s and 1980s and the more general theories about revolution and political violence. The following propositions attempting to explain the origin and evolution of Central America's recent rebellions have been developed from both of the areas summarized above. The propositions emphasize three elements—class relations, the role of the state, and organization and resource mobilization—with the greatest promise for explaining the last decade's turmoil in the Central American isthmus.

The expansion of speculative export agriculture (from the 1950s through the 1970s) and rapid capital-intensive industrialization (1960s–1970s) in Central America created or expanded classes or subclasses of landless agricultural wage laborers, urban subproletarians, proletarians, and such white-collar sectors as commercial and public employees.

In the absence of deliberate government efforts (such as agrarian reform or wage policies) to reduce or ameliorate inequities, Central America's rapid economic growth during the 1960s and 1970s tended to increase inequalities in wealth and income and to reduce the real wages of agricultural and urban wage laborers.

Rapidly escalating oil prices and resultant inflation, the deterioration of the Central American Common Market (in the mid- and late 1970s), and natural or economic catastrophes (e.g., the 1972 Managua earthquake, 1978–1979 common market trade disruptions) greatly reduced real income and employment among working-class and some white-collar sectors.

The grievances caused by increasing inequalities, declining real income, economic/natural catastrophes, and the political dissatisfactions of would-be competing elites led in the mid- and late 1970s to burgeoning agrarian, labor, neighborhood, and community self-help, opposition party organization, and to reformist demands upon the state and protests about public policy.

Differential regime responses to burgeoning organization and protests determined whether rebellions occurred: On the one hand, where regimes responded to demands and protests with ameliorative policies (to reduce inequalities of wealth and to permit recovery of real wages) and with low or modest levels of force or repression, protests subsided (Honduras, for example). On the other hand, where regimes rejected demands and protests for ameliorative policies and responded with sharply escalated repression by public security forces, protests and opposition organization and resource mobilization increased and rebellions occurred (Nicaragua, El Salvador, Guatemala).

Subjected to repression and refusal to reform, the aggrieved developed greater organization, formed progressively greater coalitions among regime opponents, mobilized increased economic resources from poor and wealthy regime opponents and from some external sources, forged alliances with and swelled the ranks of armed leftists guerrillas, and violently contested the regime's sovereignty. The outcome of the contest over sovereignty depended upon the relative success of the regime versus the rebels in mobilizing and maintaining domestic and external economic and material support and organization.

DISCUSSION

In Chapters 3 and 4 we showed how each Central American nation entered the 1970s with numerous common economic and social pressures toward ever-greater concentration of wealth, increased rural and urban lower-class unemployment, and decreased agricultural self-sufficiency among large segments of the rural poor. The rapid enrichment of the national bourgeoisies and the growth of the middle classes and improvement of their living standards thus held forth to the poor, via ever more sophisticated mass communications, a model of consumption that for increasingly large segments of the populace became less attainable as they became more impoverished. The theory outlined here argues that such growing inequality and rapid structural transformation of Central American societies generated numerous grievances that mobilized pressures for redress—that is, that increased class conflict.

The theoretical argument over responsibility for recent Central American rebellions has much more than mere academic interest. The difference between blaming such turmoil on outside Communist subversion or on domestic political and economic factors is very important because it affects how different actors in the region (area governments, influential social groups, international agencies, and other nations—especially the United States) react to critical problems and issues.

For both practical and ideological reasons, serious consequences flow from how such major actors as the Central American and U.S. governments understand the turmoil in the isthmus. If one believes that rebellions occur because of festering domestic inequalities and political repression (and that "subversion" is not the prime cause of revolt but a resource used by rebels), then peace in the region might best be pursued by emphasizing the promotion of social reforms. The pursuit of reforms, however, is likely to harm powerful vested interests and to provoke countercurrents of resistance. If, in contrast, one believes that rebellions stem mainly from subversion—the position taken by the National Bipartisan Commission on Central America—then military and police measures against suspected subversives will be the more likely policy choices and working for social reform will take on secondary importance. The cost of escalated repression, however, is usually paid in the tragic currency of lost life and liberty.

Ultimately, if it is our theory rather than the subversion theory that is correct, then most Central American governments and the United States have applied the wrong solutions to many problems in Central America in recent years. In the main, protests over problems of inequality have been treated with repression, which militarizes political relations and creates new sources of grievances. Because of such policy errors, the fundamental problems remain unsolved, turmoil has worsened, and unrest appears likely to continue almost indefinitely.

6

INSURRECTION AND REVOLUTION IN NICARAGUA

Understanding the roots of rebellion in Nicaragua and the rest of Central America requires close scrutiny of three decades of economic change and socio-political relations. Data resources on the five Central American nations have grown greatly since the 1950s and thus permit us to explore such matters with some success. Although the five countries manifest important differences, the similarities among their histories, cultures, and economies are great. Such similarities greatly facilitate comparing the Nicaraguan rebellion with those in El Salvador and Guatemala and understanding why Costa Rica and Honduras have not had similar uprisings. Central America's common traits fortuitously reduce otherwise uncontrollable differences that could confound a comparison of five dissimilar nations from different world regions.

Despite the importance of the issues at stake in Central America, we recognize that it is the frequent curse of political economic analysis to be unexciting. If climbing a mountain of statistics on one country risks boring some readers, scaling five such mountains could turn even the study of revolutions into tedium beyond the endurance of almost anyone. We will therefore strive to ration the quantitative data in this and the following two chapters. We beg the reader to bear in mind, however, that tens of thousands of Central Americans are killing each other because of the issues the figures illuminate. To explain the bloody politics of Central American conflict we must first lay a foundation of economic data. This chapter begins to build that foundation with information on Nicaragua, whose politics seem perpetually blighted with war and foreign intervention.

ROOTS OF CLASS CONFLICT

Under the direction of the Somozas and the stimulus of the Central American Common Market and Alliance for Progress, Nicaragua underwent rapid industrialization and expansion of commercial export agriculture during the 1960s and early 1970s. Overall economic growth statistics were impressive; per capita gross domestic product rose an average of almost 3.9 percent for the decade 1962–1971, and an average of 2.3 percent between 1972 and 1976 (see Appendix, Table 1). One gauge of the extent and speed of social change during the CACM boom is that between 1960 and 1970, real GDP per capita in Nicaragua rose by 54 percent—by far the greatest increase in the region. This jump in overall production was accompanied by other kinds of social change: Between 1960 and 1980 Nicaragua had Central America's biggest surge in urban population and manufacturing output and its biggest drop in the agricultural work force (see Appendix, Table 2).

Income

Despite such impressive growth, policies of the government prevented the benefits from this new economic activity from finding their way into the pockets of poorer Nicaraguans. Unions were generally repressed, wages—normally set by the regime—were kept low, and consumer prices rose rapidly. The data in Tables 3 through 6 (Appendix) reveal what happened to the income and living conditions of working-class Nicaraguans during this period of very rapid economic growth. Consumer prices in Nicaragua rose at a moderate average of about 3.6 percent per year between 1963 and 1972 (see Appendix, Table 3). But then the 1973 Organization of Petroleum Exporting Countries (OPEC) oil embargo and subsequent rapid escalation of oil prices set off a severe wave of inflation—from 1973 through 1977, consumer price increases averaged 10.7 percent per year.

Inflation might not have been a problem for ordinary Nicaraguans had their earnings kept pace with prices. But the wages earned by working-class people did not keep up with soaring consumer prices. An index of real working-class wages (wages corrected for consumer price increases) in manufacturing, transportation, and construction for the period from 1963 through 1979 is presented in Table 4.[1] Real working-class wages rose in Nicaragua from 1963 until about 1967. But by 1970 real wages had peaked and gone into a decade-long slide that by 1979 had eaten away over one-third of their 1967 purchasing power. Therefore, during the 1970s, employed, wage-earning Nicaraguans suffered a palpable drop in their ability to feed and shelter their families.

There are other indications that income was shifting away from working-class Nicaraguans in the 1970s. One such measure is the share of national income paid out as employee compensation (Appendix, Table 5). A decrease in the value of the index of employee compensation indicates a relative shift of income away from salaried and wage-earning workers and toward investors and entrepreneurs. During the 1960s, Nicaraguan employees' share of national income increased, but then it took a sharp drop in 1974 and 1975. Although it is somewhat risky to estimate changes beyond the 1975 end of our data, the working-class wage trends reported for Nicaragua in the later 1970s (Appendix, Table 4) strongly suggest that the employee share of the income pie most likely shrank still further.

Although unfortunately we lack an earlier bench mark for comparison, we can state that income inequality between rich and poor Nicaraguans had become very great by 1977, when the wealthiest fifth of the people earned 59.9 percent of the national income, while the poorer half were left with only 15.0 percent.[2] The devastating December 24, 1972, earthquake probably triggered this shift in income away from wage earners when it put tens of thousands of white- and blue-collar workers out of work.

Nicaragua's middle class, which experienced a decade of improving living standards during the 1960s, suffered a sharp reversal as of 1973. Middle-class employment opportunities shrank markedly in the mid-1970s as many small businesses and commercial jobs were destroyed by the Managua earthquake. Nine thousand manufacturing jobs disappeared from 1972 to 1973 (about 13 percent of the total), as did fifteen thousand service sector jobs (over 7 percent of the total). Many new jobs appeared in the poorer-paid and lower-prestige construction sector, which nearly doubled in size by 1974, and in the informal sector.[3] Those who remained employed found their salaries subjected to a stiff surtax to finance reconstruction (much of the proceeds of the surtax were being stolen by corrupt officials). The work week was also increased by as much as 25 percent, but with no increase in salary.[4]

Employment

Not only did real wages and income distribution shift, to the detriment of working-class groups during the CACM boom, but also employment opportunities in Nicaragua failed to keep up with the rapid growth of the work force. Moreover, underemployment—an inability to find full-time work or acceptance of agricultural wage labor because of insufficient farmland for family subsistence farming—was generally believed to affect from one to five times as much of the economically active population as did unemployment. Data on unemployment from 1970 through the early 1980s appear in Table 6.[5] Overall, Nicaraguan unemployment rates rose steadily from less than 4 percent in 1970 to 13 percent in 1978—more than tripling, despite rapid economic growth. Among groups hit very hard by unemployment were workers left jobless by the earthquake, and peasants forced off the land by the rapid expansion of agricultural production for export.

Wealth

During the 1960s and 1970s, Nicaragua's three major capitalist factions, which centered around the Banco de América, the Banco Nicaragüense, and the Somoza family interests, began to converge.[6] Once separated from each other by regional, clan, and political party differences, these great investor factions increasingly prospered and intertwined their investments under the CACM industrialization boom and the stimulative economic policies of the Somoza regime. Following the Managua earthquake, however, the Somoza faction became aggressively greedy and began to undermine the relative positions and profits of the other investor groups. At the same time, growing political and labor unrest caused many Nicaraguan capitalists to doubt whether the regime could continue to promote beneficial growth. Anastasio Somoza Debayle's once-growing support among the upper classes began to erode in the mid-1970s and thus prevented the development of a unified bourgeoisie.

In agriculture, concentration of land ownership increased from the 1950s through the 1970s, especially in the fertile and populous Pacific zone. High cotton prices permitted speculating largeholders to squeeze subsistence cultivators off the land and into an already oversupplied wage labor market.[7] "The process of agricultural development was a concentrator of both land and income."[8] By 1977, the 1.4 percent of farms larger than 350 hectares[9] contained 41.2 percent of the cultivated land, but roughly 60,000 campesinos had no land at all. Small farms (less than 4.0 hectares) made up 36.8 percent of Nicaragua's farms, but occupied only 1.7 percent of the cultivated land. In the 1950s

> the State favored policies oriented to preferentially support those agroindustries [belonging to the Somozas' and their cohorts]. This situation intensified in the following decade and [included] not only financial, trade, and credit policies . . . but also the use of the public budget and institutions to supply them with labor, machinery, electricity, administrators, transport, etc.[10]

In sum, both relative and absolute measures of income and wealth reveal that during the 1970s poor and middle-class Nicaraguans lost some of their share of overall national income and wealth, and suffered a sharp drop in their real earning power. Such a loss in both relative economic standing and effective income doubtless gave many Nicaraguans strong economic grievances.

POPULAR MOBILIZATION

The decline of working-class wages in the late 1960s and early 1970s was followed by the revitalization of the nation's long suppressed industrial labor movement,[11] which stepped up organization, work stoppages, and strikes in pursuit of wage gains in 1973–1975.[12] A decline of middle-class living standards due to inflation and to the effects of the Managua earthquake also spawned considerable growth of union membership and organization and a surge of strikes by public sector white-collar workers, such as teachers and health personnel. Catholic social workers, missionaries, and priests began organizing unions among Pacific-zone peasant wage laborers in the 1960s. As a tool for teaching the gospel, Catholic social promoters also organized hundreds of small groups (CEBs) among urban and rural poor people. These CEBs taught catechism and encouraged community self-help activism.[13] Peasant unions increasingly pressed for wage gains, and CEBs, for better urban services and housing. CEBs among the urban poor multiplied rapidly after the Managua quake, as did similar Protestant-organized self-help groups. The peasant union movement gained great momentum after 1975.[14]

As the economy deteriorated, especially after 1974, Nicaraguan private sector pressure organizations grew and became more boldly critical of the government. Such private sector groups increased their calls for political and economic reform. For example, the Democratic Liberation Union (Unión Democrática de Liberación—UDEL), dominated by business leaders, appeared in 1974. UDEL not only called for reform but also attempted to promote some "trickle-down" development of cooperative business enterprises to benefit poorer Nicaraguans.

New opposition political parties (Christian Democratic, Social Christian) became increasingly active in Nicaragua in the 1960s and 1970s,[15] and new anti-Somoza factions of the old Conservative and Liberal parties developed during the 1970s. Elements from the Conservative party united with the Social Christian party and the anti-Somoza Independent Liberal party in the National Opposition Union (Unión Nacional Opositora—UNO) to contest the 1967 national election. Student opposition to the regime grew rapidly during the 1970s. The Sandinista National Liberation Front (Frente Sandinista de Liberación Nacional—FSLN), the only surviving rebel group of some twenty guerrilla bands that had appeared between 1959 and 1962, greatly expanded its links to and support from university student groups during the 1970s.[16]

GOVERNMENT REPRESSION AND ITS EFFECT ON OPPOSITION

President Anastasio Somoza Debayle declared a state of siege and began a program of demobilization in late December 1974 after an embarrassing FSLN hostage-taking incident. During the resultant three-year reign of terror in rural areas (especially in the department of Zelaya), the National Guard murdered several thousand (mostly innocent) people suspected as subversives or possible FSLN sympathizers. Among the victims were many Catholic lay catechists, CEB members, and countless peasants in zones where the FSLN supposedly operated.[17] During a brief lifting of the state of siege because of Carter administration pressure, public protests against the regime rose rapidly. The government reacted by redoubling repression by the National Guard, especially in urban areas. The guard openly targeted youths from the early teens up because they were suspected of pro-Sandinista sympathies. The military and police dragged hundreds from their homes and the streets and murdered them. From 1977 on, the National Guard conducted an ever-intensifying war against the people of Nicaragua. Such repression eventually drove thousands, especially young people, to join the FSLN.

Following the January 1978 assassination of Pedro Joaquín Chamorro, bourgeois elements redoubled their activity in opposition to the Somoza regime. Key business interests such as the Superior Council of Private Initiative (Consejo Superior de la Iniciativa Privada—COSIP) joined with unions and moderate parties to support general strikes, and to form the Broad Opposition Front (Frente Amplio Opositor—FAO). Strongly backed by the United States and Nicaragua's Catholic hierarchy, the FAO strove unsuccessfully to negotiate an end to the Somoza regime before the FSLN could overthrow it militarily.[18]

Popular uprisings occurred all over urban Nicaragua between August and October 1978. On August 23, 1978, a small Sandinista unit seized the National Palace, taking more than two thousand hostages, including most members of the Chamber of Deputies. They negotiated the release of sixty Sandinistas from prison, a ransom, and safe passage out of the country. Days later, opposition leaders called a successful general strike. In September, thousands of people spontaneously attacked National Guard posts and drove the regime's troops out of several communities. These community revolts in Masaya, Rivas, Jinotega, Matagalpa, Estelí, and several parts of Managua typically occurred without significant advanced coordination by the FSLN. But the National Guard brutally crushed each uprising, one by one. The guard would concentrate its forces around each rebel town, cut off its utilities, and then brutally shell and bomb it for several days before sending troops in to recapture it. These wars against the rebellious towns inflicted catastrophic losses of civilian life and massive damage to property and public services.

The FSLN, split for several years over tactics, realized that popular outrage had doomed the regime and rendered its tactical debate sterile. The three Sandinista factions quickly reunified in 1979 under the Joint National Directorate (Dirección Nacional Conjunta—DNC) and began to build a network of wealthy and influential supporters that included a dozen prominent citizens, known as the Group of Twelve (Grupo de los Doce). When the FAO-regime negotiations collapsed in early 1979, moderate and even conservative anti-Somocistas turned to the Sandinistas as the last option to defeat the regime. In 1979 the FSLN forged the United People's Movement (Movimiento Pueblo Unido—MPU) and National Patriotic Front (Frente Patriótico Nacional—FPN) coalitions, confederations of regime opponents made up of virtually all opposition forces in Nicaragua. The MPU and FPN, under the military leadership of the FSLN, were committed to the defeat of the Somoza regime. In May 1979 an FSLN-led provisional government was formed in San José, Costa Rica, to formally embody the opposition's revolutionary claim to sovereignty.

By opening its military ranks to all regime opponents and by forging broad alliances, the FSLN availed itself of extensive financial, organizational, and human resources within Nicaragua for the final offensive against the regime. Its military ranks flourished, ballooning from less than 500 troops under arms in mid-1978 to between 2,500 and 5,000 by June 1979. Other key resources mobilized by the revolutionary coalition in 1979 included effective control over several parts of northern Nicaragua, sanctuary for bases and political operations in Costa Rica, diplomatic support from France and various Latin American regimes in the Organization of American States (OAS), and some external financial and arms support. FSLN agents purchased Belgian automatic rifles from private arms dealers in the United States and took delivery at a base camp in Honduras. Cuba, Venezuela, Panama, and Costa Rica cooperated in delivering a shipment of Western-made arms via Costa Rica for the final offensive of June 1979. Whenever FSLN forces entered a community in combat, many local residents would spontaneously fight alongside them or assist them in other ways, thus vastly enhancing the guerrillas' numerical strength and capabilities. This massive and direct popular combat participation inestimably strengthened the insurgents.

OUTCOME OF THE CHALLENGE TO SOVEREIGNTY

The FSLN and opposition coalition's unity, material resource base, popular support, military capacity, and external support all grew rapidly in late 1978 and 1979. The FSLN-MPU/FPN coalition's revolutionary government in exile in 1979 took advantage of enthusiastic support from Costa Rica, where it enjoyed political sanctuary and popular sympathy and where the FSLN had secure bases. Within Nicaragua, FSLN troops enjoyed massive voluntary popular support and assistance in combat against the National Guard.

The decline of the Somoza regime's strength in 1978 and 1979 presents a clear contrast to the opposition's growth. Nicaragua's population had risen in spontaneous revolt against Anastasio Somoza Debayle's government in dozens of incidents in late 1978. By late 1978 the regime had lost the support of virtually all social classes and interest sectors, save portions of Somoza's Liberal Nationalist party (Partido Liberal Nacionalista—PLN) and the National Guard. PLN and regime supporters—many very corrupt and anxious to escape with as much of their wealth as possible—began to abandon Nicaragua in late 1978 and early 1979. Neighboring Honduras and Costa Rica were soon flooded with Mercedes Benz autos driven out by Somoza cohorts and their families. The flow of desertions from Somoza's closest collaborators became a flood after National Guard troops casually murdered ABC reporter Bill Stewart before the network's own cameras on June 20, 1979. The tyrant's associates sensed that that horrible television footage had stripped away their last pretense of legitimacy outside Nicaragua.

The Carter administration had announced its opposition to Somoza's continued rule, a key loss of a traditional external prop for the regime. The United States cut off new aid to Nicaragua in the 1979 budget and prevented pending deliveries by some of Somoza's arms suppliers. Although the U.S. government wanted Somoza out of office, it also tried very hard but ineffectually to prevent the Sandinistas from winning power. Elsewhere in the hemisphere, the Organization of American States and numerous Latin American regimes had openly sided with the opposition by 1979. The cornered National Guard fought tenaciously against the Sandinistas and Nicaraguan people, but was progressively encircled and pushed back toward Managua during the seven-week final offensive. Having looted the national treasury of dollars for himself and his associates, Somoza ultimately gave

THE TRIUMPH. FSLN troops in a liberated military vehicle arriving at Somoza's bunker in Managua, July 1979 (photo by Thomas Walker).

up and left Nicaragua for Miami on July 17, 1979. When the guard collapsed two days later, the Sandinista-led rebel coalition took power.

THE REVOLUTION

The revolutionary government faced an incredible array of problems. The war had killed 50,000 people—almost 2 percent of the populace. (An equivalent loss to the United States would be 4.5 million, or well over seventy-five times the U.S. death toll in the entire Vietnam War.) There was also an estimated $1.5 billion in property loss, all-important export and domestic staple food crops had gone unplanted, and the new government had inherited $1.6 billion in international debts from the old regime. To its great chagrin, the new government realized that it would have to assume and pay Somoza's debt in order to remain creditworthy in international financial circles. There were also serious long-standing problems of public health, housing, education, and nutrition, all of which had been exacerbated by the war.

The revolutionary coalition led by the Sandinistas sought to destroy the Somoza regime and its economic power base, to replace the old regime's brutality and inequality of treatment of Nicaraguans with a fairer, more humane, and less corrupt system, and to reactivate the war-damaged economy. The Sandinistas themselves wanted to move the economy toward socialism in order to improve the lot of the lower classes, to built a participatory democracy under their own leadership, and to integrate all Nicaraguans into the national social and political system. Others in the coalition disagreed about much of the Sandinistas' revolutionary program and hoped to wrest power from the FSLN or at least share power with it. Such profound differences over the ends of the revolution quickly established the lines of political conflict in revolutionary Nicaragua and shattered the anti-Somocista alliance.

U.S.-Nicaraguan Relations and the Contra War

The Sandinistas' main long-term concern was a fear that the United States might try to reverse the course of the Nicaraguan revolution, as it had done in the cases of other reformist or revolutionary Latin American governments (Guatemala in 1954, Cuba in 1961, the Dominican Republic in 1965, and Chile in 1973). Although the Carter administration had criticized and opposed Somoza, it had also worked tenaciously to keep the Sandinistas from power. For example, the United States had supported the FAO-Somoza negotiations of 1978, approved a $66 million International Monetary Fund loan to the Somoza regime in early 1979, and attempted to persuade the OAS to send "peacekeeping" troops to Nicaragua in June 1979. At the time of the FSLN victory, the CIA had sent DC-8 jets disguised with Red Cross markings to Managua to evacuate Somoza's officer corps to Miami.[19] Even before the Sandinistas came to power, President Carter had authorized the CIA to fund certain segments of the press and labor movement.[20]

The Carter administration offered the new regime a nervous hand of friendship in the form of diplomatic recognition, emergency relief aid and the release of suspended loans from prior years' aid packages in 1979, and a new $75 million loan commitment in 1980. In 1979–1980 the Sandinistas had fairly good working relations with U.S. Ambassador Lawrence Pezzullo but felt increasingly apprehensive about U.S. links to the several thousand national guardsmen who had escaped to Honduras and the United States. In fact, the United States was becoming increasingly involved in organizing the ex-Somocista forces, which were beginning to conduct terrorist activities in Nicaragua from their refuge in Honduras.

The behavior of the incoming Reagan administration simply confirmed the Sandinistas' worst fears. During his campaign, candidate Reagan had promised to try to reverse the Nicaraguan revolution, and his advisers had talked of "destabilizing" the Sandinista government. The 1980 Republican platform had "abhor[red] the Marxist-Sandinist takeover" in Nicaragua and called for cutting off all aid. As soon as Reagan took office in 1981, he claimed (with very little evidence) that Nicaragua was the main source of arms for the rebel movement in El Salvador. President Reagan immediately cut off the balance of the $75 million loan, as well as wheat purchase credits approved by President Carter.

The United States then began a policy of steadily escalating harassment, pressure, and aggression against Nicaragua. One aspect of that policy was indirect military pressure via massive aid to build up the Honduran military, continuous "maneuvers" in Honduras of from one thousand to several thousand U.S. troops, and intensive aerial, seaborne, and covert espionage of Nicaragua. Another aspect was constant U.S. efforts to isolate Nicaragua diplomatically from its neighbors in Central America. These pressures, sweetened with large amounts of U.S. aid, persuaded both Honduras and Costa Rica to provide sanctuary to anti-Sandinista rebels. The United States also succeeded in blocking progress toward an agreement among Central American nations negotiated by the Contadora nations (Mexico, Panama, Colombia, and Venezuela). The United States successfully pressured multilateral lending and development agencies to cut off credit to Nicaragua, and on May 7, 1985, the United States embargoed trade with Nicaragua. Reagan administration spokespersons and the Department of State conducted a publicity campaign—as energetic as it was inaccurate—to discredit and defame the revolutionary government of Nicaragua and to exalt those of the Sandinistas' enemies who might prove most malleable for U.S. purposes.

The centerpiece of the Reagan administration's strategy for Nicaragua was a military and political effort to topple the Sandinista regime. In 1981 Reagan gave the CIA $19.8 million to organize and train in Honduras an exile army of anti-Sandinista counterrevolutionary elements. This force, whose nucleus consisted of former National Guard officers and soldiers and political allies of the former dictator, became known as the "contras." By 1982 attacks across the Honduran border had become almost daily. Contra forces regularly sabotaged bridges and other economic targets and had taken almost a thousand civilian and military lives within Nicaragua by the end of that year.

By the following year five major groups made up the contra forces; the most important among them were the Honduras-based Nicaraguan Democratic Force (Fuerzas Democráticas Nicaragüenses–FDN) and the Costa Rica-based Revolutionary Democratic Alliance (Alianza Revolucionaria Democrática—ARDE) and two Miskito Indian groups. In 1983 the contras began extensive guerrilla operations within Nicaragua, especially in the rugged terrain of the northeast and southeast. The CIA added to the destruction caused by the contras by blowing up Nicaraguan oil storage tanks and pipelines and mining harbors on both coasts. The CIA also supported the contras with intelligence, funding, and training (including a comic-book-style manual on sabotage for contra foot soldiers and a more sophisticated training book for contra leaders, *Psychological Operations in Guerrilla Warfare*, which recommended political assassinations of pro-Sandinista civilians and the deliberate creation of martyrs from among anti-Sandinista ranks.[21]

By 1985 the contras had amassed some 15,000 persons under arms, but had achieved no significant successes against the Nicaraguan military. They had, however, established a clear record of economic sabotage, atrocities against civilians, and had taken some 13,000 lives. In the mid-1980s, the U.S. Congress was proving

THE CONTRA WAR. Peasant children in a feeding program at a war refugee agricultural self-defense resettlement camp (photo by Steve Cagan). Infrastructural damage: A food storage facility destroyed by the contras (photo by Thomas Walker). Repatriated contras who had laid down their arms in 1985 in accordance with the Nicaraguan government's amnesty program declared late in 1983 (photo by Steven Cagan).

to be an increasingly unreliable funding source for the contra war and had placed legal restrictions on U.S. efforts to topple the Sandinistas. As a consequence, the Reagan administration made increasing efforts to fund and assist the contras covertly. These efforts included operations (some of them only marginally legal and some flatly illegal) by the National Security Council's Col. Oliver North, by private actors, and by other executive-branch agencies.

When the Iran-Contra scandal broke in October 1986, placing further U.S. funding to the contras in doubt, the Reagan administration pressed the contras to intensify their offensive within Nicaragua. Supported by a legal CIA-run military supply operation in 1987, this offensive brought the war to its destructive peak and raised the death toll to over 26,000 by 1989. Despite the great increase in combat operations within Nicaragua, the contras' military successes remained very limited. After the Central American Peace Accord was signed in August 1987, the contras eventually entered negotiations with the Sandinista government (1988) and the war began to wind down.

A contra political directorate had been organized by the United States in the early 1980s to present a more palatable public front that might facilitate continued funding by Congress. However, this unified front proved quite unstable and broke apart more than once. In its last form, the contra directorate was called the Nicaraguan Resistance (Resistencia Nicaragüense—RN), and was feuding internally even as it negotiated with the Sandinistas. Although there had been considerable contra exfiltration to Honduras and most contra units had virtually disbanded by early 1989, the new Bush administration called for continued U.S. aid to help hold them together. Direct U.S. aid to the contras by 1989 had totaled over $400 million.

The Revolutionary Government

What kind of government was it to which the Reagan administration reacted so antagonistically? The FSLN consolidated its political dominance over the new government by early 1980, while maintaining other coalition members on the junta, in the cabinet, and Council of State (Consejo de Estado). Though it was clear that the FSLN's nine-man DNC held ultimate veto power over the nature of the government and its programs, the Sandinistas created a pluralist system in which representatives of the upper-class minority were encouraged to participate. Upper-class, business, and various political party interests, while present in the coalition, were not allowed to dominate policy and therefore became increasingly antagonistic toward the FSLN. The regime maintained a dialogue with major business interests through their principal representative, the Superior Council of Private Enterprise (Consejo Superior de la Empresa Privada—COSEP),[22] and with a coalition of parties that had taken on the role of opposition to the regime.

The Sandinistas sought to build their own brand of democracy, one that emphasized popular participation in formulating and implementing public policy and the distribution of services and programs to the great mass of poor Nicaraguans. At first scornful of national elections because the dictatorial old regime had always manipulated them, the revolutionary government announced its intention in mid-1980 to postpone national elections until 1985. Immediately after the rebel victory, however, local elections took place all over Nicaragua. The Sandinistas also encouraged the widespread formation of grass-roots organizations of women, workers, peasants, youth, children, and neighborhoods. Through these organizations hundreds of thousands of Nicaraguans debated and voted on issues, worked collectively to solve local problems, took part in carrying out national health and literacy campaigns, petitioned their government, and met with officials, elected officers and representatives to governmental bodies and national organizations. The formation of labor unions was also encouraged, and organized labor grew rapidly. Labor's demands for higher wages, however, soon ran afoul of government needs for economic austerity and the FSLN desire for dominance within the movement.

The Sandinistas argued from the first that the new system must tolerate diversity of political opinion, not only because they had come to power as part of a coalition, but also because they were trying to maintain a mixed economy that required the cooperation of the privileged classes and because the international climate required political pluralism for the survival of the revolution. When the junta added new pro-Sandinista groups to the Council of State in 1980, several other party groups cried foul and began to coalesce into an open opposition to the government. The climate for political opposition within the revolution remained open, but not completely free. Other parties suffered from constraints on their press coverage and public activities under the State of Emergency decreed in response to the contra war in 1982, and proregime crowds (*turbas*) sometimes harassed critics of the regime, especially between 1982 and 1984.

The Council of State debated and passed election and party laws that had been heavily influenced by the opposition. The government set national elections for president and National Assembly (to replace the junta and Council of State) in November 1984. Most restrictions on parties and the press were lifted for the campaign; equal, free, and uncensored access to government radio and television was provided; and a vigorous campaign ensued among seven parties. International observers and the press[23] overwhelmingly agreed that the election occurred without fraud or intimidation by the FSLN, though it was marred by the decision of one conservative coalition not to participate, and by the effort of another party's presidential candidate to drop out late in the campaign. U.S. pressure—part of the U.S. campaign to discredit the revolution in the U.S. and abroad—played a major role in dissuading these groups from taking part in the election. Daniel Ortega Saavedra, DNC member and coordinator of the junta, was elected president, with 63 percent of the total vote. Opposition parties divided about one-third of the National Assembly.

Despite the external attack and obstruction by their U.S.-backed enemies, the Sandinistas were quite successful in beginning their revolution.[24] They shaped a new governmental system, reactivated and reshaped much of the war-ravaged economy, and implemented numerous social programs. Health services were dramatically expanded both in curative and preventative medicine, and national vaccination and health education campaigns significantly lowered rates of polio, malaria, and infant mortality. A massive literacy crusade raised literacy rates from slightly over 52 percent to about 87 percent. Agrarian reform programs promoted increased national self-sufficiency in food production, formed thousands of cooperative agricultural enterprises, and distributed hundreds of thousands of acres of farmland to individuals and cooperatives.

The growth of the contra war, however, forced the government to reorganize itself in order to defend the revolution—which, ironically, also meant the postponement of many of its central social and economic programs. By 1987 over half of the national budget went for military expenditures and the armed forces had been expanded to 60,000 regulars and over 100,000 militia. (Pentagon experts normally recommend a ratio of about 10 government troops to contain 1 guerrilla or irregular troop.) Evidence of the shift in government priorities soon became tangible for Nicaraguans. Social reforms, medical, health, and educational programs and public service development all suffered noticeably from the heavy military spending burden. Medical care deteriorated, garbage pickup and water service in Managua were curtailed, schools began to go without supplies and repairs, buses and taxis rusted for lack of parts and repairs. From 1979 through 1983 we noticed in our periodic visits to Nicaragua that the regime had made evident material progress in recovery from the 1972 earthquake and the 1977–1979 war. From 1984 on, each visit showed new signs of physical decay and reversals of earlier progress.

Human Rights

The human rights performance of the revolutionary government was far from perfect, but was unusually good for a revolutionary regime and vastly superior to that of Somoza and the other governments of northern Central America. The government moved swiftly to prevent its own supporters and forces from perpetrating human rights abuses in the chaotic days after seizing power. It established a new Sandinista Police and Sandinista Popular Army and worked to curtail abuse of authority by their officials. It humanely treated thousands of captured National Guard troops and officials, who were investigated, tried for their crimes, and sentenced. International human rights agencies have criticized for unfair procedures the Special Tribunals, which tried the 6,300 former guardsmen, but these special courts dismissed charges against or acquitted 22 percent of the prisoners. Despite the heinous crimes of which some prisoners were convicted, none was executed. By 1985 more than half of those sentenced had completed their sentences, received a pardon, or had been released on appeal.[25]

Despite the correct suspicion that the opposition newspaper was receiving CIA funding to publish antigovernment propaganda,[26] the regime allowed *La*

Prensa to operate for almost three years without precensorship. During that period, however, the government closed the bitterly critical paper several times, for two to three days on each occasion, for publishing false information or criticizing the revolutionary government in violation of the press law. Under the mounting pressure of the contra war, the revolutionary government in 1982 decreed a State of Emergency that suspended most civil guarantees and implemented prior press censorship. All media, including FSLN's own *Barricada* and the proregime *El Nuevo Diario*, as well as independent radio news programs, underwent prior censorship of news content thereafter. Censorship eased substantially and many other civil rights were restored in 1984 before the national election, but an expansion of the war in 1985–1986 led to reinstitution of many restrictions in 1986. The government closed *La Prensa* indefinitely in June 1986 for supporting U.S. aid to the contras,[27] but permitted it to reopen without precensorship after the Central American Peace Accord was signed.

Two other areas of human rights proved most problematic for the revolutionary government. In 1982 the growing contra war prompted relocation of eight thousand Miskito Indians from their homes in the war zone along the Río Coco to inland camps. Poorly handled by the regime, the relocation angered many Miskito, caused thousands to flee, and led many to join two anti-Sandinista guerrilla groups. "The external conflict created a context in which Miskito demands for self-determination were seen by the Sandinistas as separatist and related to U.S. efforts to overthrow the government by arming indigenous insurgents and by attempting to turn world opinion against the Sandinistas through false accusations of 'genocide.'"[28]

With such perceptions, military and judicial authorities in the Atlantic zone did abuse Miskito rights, further worsening tensions in the area.[29] (We must insist here that all credible observers concur that the Reagan administration's often repeated charge of a "genocide" of the Miskito is false.[30]) By late 1983 the government realized the gravity of its errors. It began autonomy talks with Atlantic Coast indigenous peoples, aimed at increasing local self-determination, and in 1985 it permitted the Miskito to return to their homes. Tensions subsided and Miskito support for the contras had all but disappeared by late 1986.

The practice of religion remained generally free in Nicaragua under the revolution, but the government became increasingly intolerant of those who expressed antiregime political goals through religious practice or groups. The government admitted many foreign missionaries of various sects and permitted churches to take part in the literacy crusade of 1980–1981. Many Catholics and numerous Protestant congregations, having provided much of the logistical support to the FSLN during the insurrection, ardently supported the new government and its policies. The hierarchy of the Catholic church, however, strongly and increasingly opposed Sandinista rule, and Church-regime conflict became overt by 1982. Certain Protestant sects' missionaries were denied entry to Nicaragua, and pro-FSLN groups on one occasion occupied properties of one sect before being evicted by the police.[31]

Relations between the government and Catholic church eroded rapidly during and after the trip of Pope John Paul II to Nicaragua in 1983. Each side apparently acted deliberately to provoke the other during the planning and execution of the visit. Archbishop Miguel Obando y Bravo became the leading figure of the internal opposition to the Sandinistas by 1984. Since then Obando (elevated to cardinal in 1985) and the Nicaraguan Council of Bishops have steadily sharpened their criticism of government policy. The Iran-Contra hearings in the United States in 1987 revealed that Cardinal Obando had even received laundered financial support from the CIA. For its part, the Sandinista government has punctuated its escalating criticism of the Church's political role with efforts at dialogue.[32] The Sandinistas expressed their displeasure by periodically closing Catholic Radio and by deporting a dozen foreign-born priests active in opposition politics. Finally, in 1986, when Bishop Pablo Antonio Vega and Father Bismarck Carballo (a spokesman for the Archdiocese of Managua) endorsed the $100 million aid package for the contras being considered by the U.S. Congress, they were exiled.[33] Following the signing of the Central American Peace Accord in August 1987, however, these and other priests were permitted to return to Nicaragua.

In summary, assailed by increasing domestic criticism, worsening economic woes, and the continued contra war, the revolutionary government's human rights performance began to deteriorate in 1982. Things improved noticeably around the 1984 election, but suffered clear reversals and further decline after 1985. By 1986, Nicaragua's eroded human rights performance received more criticism by human rights organizations. Repression of government critics and opponents remained much less violent than in Guatemala and El Salvador, but had clearly become more pronounced than before. International human rights observers cited the Nicaraguan government for intimidation, harassment, and illegal detention of opponents, independent union leaders, and human rights workers, as well as for press censorship, curtailment of labor union activity, and poor prison conditions. The human rights climate improved again in late 1987 and early 1988, but eroded somewhat in mid-1988 when domestic opposition elements staged a series of demonstrations. By late 1988, however, the human rights climate improved again as the government offered concessions to the opposition and announced national elections for early 1990.[34]

The Economy

Economic policy reflected moderation and pragmatism and varied greatly from models followed by other Marxist-led governments. The revolutionary government renegotiated the terms of the international debt it inherited from the Somoza regime. It also sought and obtained hundreds of millions of dollars in grants and "soft" loans from various governments and international organizations—mainly in the West. And though it confiscated the properties of the Somozas and their cohorts, it preserved and sought to encourage a private sector that accounted

RELIGION AND REVOLUTION IN NICARAGUA. Lay "Delegates of the Word" being trained by a prorevolutionary priest to teach the social gospel (photo by Thomas Walker). Junta Coordinator Daniel Ortega (under the second "A" in "Nicaragua") and other government officials participating in the open session of the 1981 Central American Congress of the Student Christian Movement (photo and copyright by Tommie Sue Montgomery, 1981).

for between 50 and 60 percent of GDP. Within two years, the economy had recovered much of its prewar level of production. Agrarian reform did not take a radical form with heavy emphasis on state farming, but rather was responsive to peasant demands for individual or cooperative smallholdings.[35] Although it made many errors of execution of agrarian policy, the government adopted credit and pricing policies that encouraged key sectors of private export agriculture—the largest farmers—to keep producing. U.S. pressures to curtail Western credit to and trade with Nicaragua led ultimately to increasing reliance on the Eastern bloc for credit (Appendix, Table 7), other aid, and trade in the mid-1980s.

Despite such progress, Nicaraguan capitalists felt quite insecure under the revolutionary government and were generally reluctant to invest. Among factors contributing to their sense of insecurity were the business sector's lack of control over the political system and the Sandinista leadership's Marxist philosophy. Another was the substantial change in the rules of the economic game that came about when the revolutionary government nationalized the import-export sector, a key source of profits and of control over the business environment. Moreover, the industrial sector suffered from a general decline of the Central American Common Market due to the exhaustion of the growth potential of the CACM's import-substitution development model, from a general worldwide economic recession, and from the U.S. credit and trade embargoes.[36]

The Sandinista government quickly adopted several policies to benefit the majority of poor Nicaraguans—wage increases, food price subsidies, and expanded public services in health, welfare, and education—but in the middle run, such policies were undermined by new exigencies. As economic austerity needs became more pressing, the newly expanded labor movement was legally prohibited from striking. (In fact, despite this prohibition, many strikes took place and were generally tolerated.) Because taxes could not cover the array of services being attempted, the government borrowed heavily abroad. As the contra war forced the government to spend more and more on the military, security and social welfare spending could no longer be financed simultaneously out of existing tax and foreign credit revenues. In order to maintain continued critically needed foreign credit and with the external debt at over $5 billion by 1986, the revolutionary government had to enact further severe austerity measures to curtail imports (sharp currency devaluations, reduction of food subsidies and social program spending) in 1985 and 1986.

Because of the war, some government economic mismanagement, austerity measures, and declining public and private investment, consumer prices soared (Appendix, Table 3), popular living standards and services deteriorated, and shortages of many products grew rapidly between 1985 and 1989. Interestingly, a major cause of the rapid acceleration of the economic crisis in 1986–1988 was apparently the sharp reduction in Soviet bloc economic assistance registered in 1986–1987 (see Appendix, Table 7). As the economy went increasingly out of control, inflation reached 1,200 percent in 1987. Despite draconian economic measures—including a harsh austerity program, restructured pricing, elimination of subsidies, and the establishment of a new currency—implemented in 1988 and early 1989, hyperinflation continued and the economic situation grew still worse.[37]

CONCLUSIONS

Rapid economic growth in the 1960s and 1970s worsened living conditions for the majority of working-class Nicaraguans. This mobilized many people into the political arena in the mid-1970s in search of better working and living conditions or modest reforms. When the Somoza regime brutally cracked down on its critics, the repression caused alliances to be forged among a broad front of opponents, radicalized their originally narrow demands into revolutionary ones, and united the opposition behind the once-weak FSLN. The new rebel coalition marshaled progressively greater resources, whereas those of the regime deteriorated, leading the revolutionaries to power.

The beginning of the revolutionary transformation of Nicaragua in July 1979 was a moment of Central American history no less important than the National War of 1857 or the establishment of the Panama Canal. When the Sandinistas consolidated their domination over the revolution, they catalyzed powerful internal and external political forces into more drastic actions in the isthmus. Internal opposition to the FSLN's program developed, and the United States mobilized and financed an armed counterrevolution from abroad. Although the United States badly wounded Nicaragua socially and economically, it clearly failed to weaken the FSLN's political position or to significantly threaten the regime militarily.

U.S. reaction has distorted, if not blocked, the Nicaraguan revolution and has at the same time profoundly altered the political landscape of much of the rest of Central America. Chapter 7 reveals that although the Salvadoran and Guatemalan national revolts share important structural and political origins with the Nicaraguan revolution, their outcomes have been altered by external intervention. In El Salvador, the injection of U.S. assistance into the conflict in 1980 made a decisive difference in the resources available to the regime. In Guatemala, by the mid-1980s, both internal elites and the United States moved toward cautious political reform in order to mobilize resources against the rebel coalition.

7

NATIONAL REVOLTS IN EL SALVADOR AND GUATEMALA

Despite the differences in national histories, economies, culture, and regime types, the development of national revolts in El Salvador and Guatemala bears a striking resemblance to the onset of the Nicaraguan insurrection.

El Salvador

ROOTS OF CLASS CONFLICT

Income

The economy of El Salvador grew rapidly in the 1960s and 1970s. GDP per capita—a measure of overall economic activity in proportion to population—rose an average of 2.1 percent per year during the 1962–1971 decade, and even increased slightly for the 1972–1978 period to 2.3 percent per year. As noted for Nicaragua, however, the benefits of general economic growth in the Salvadoran economy were very unevenly distributed. Data on consumer prices in El Salvador, which inflated at an average of about 1.5 percent per year for the 1963–1972 decade, are presented in Table 3 (Appendix). Rising oil prices, however, drove consumer prices rapidly upward to an average of 12.8 percent per year from 1973 through 1979.

Did wages, set by the government, rise enough to compensate for this surging inflation? The evidence demonstrates clearly that they did not. An index of real working-class wages in agriculture, manufacturing, transportation, and communication in El Salvador is presented in Table 4 (Appendix). It reveals that real wages rose steadily in the 1960s and early 1970s, but declined sharply in 1974 and 1975, climbed again briefly in 1976, then skidded down even more steeply from 1977 to 1980. Salvadoran workers, thus, lost at least one-fifth of the real purchasing power of their income between 1973 and 1980. Moreover, the base of income of Salvadorans was very low in real terms. Expressed in constant 1986 dollars, per capita GDP in 1960 ($772), 1970 ($950), and 1980 ($1,044) was consistently the second lowest in Central America. The reader should bear in mind that such averages do not reflect the maldistribution of income. Thus for individuals in the poorer half of the population, the disposable annual income probably ranged from $100 to $125, while food and clothing costs were little less than in the United States. Obviously, then, officially set wages for those lucky enough to be employed throughout the CACM boom period steadily lost effective purchasing power.

Employment

Did employment opportunity increase or decrease during the CACM boom? Despite the rapid industrialization and productivity growth of the Salvadoran economy, the capital-intensive production of consumer goods generated relatively few new jobs for the growing work force—just the opposite of what it was intended to do. Moreover, changes in the agrarian economy pushed hundreds of thousands of peasants off the land, also swelling joblessness. Estimates place unemployment in El Salvador at around 16 percent in 1970. By 1978 the unemployment level was estimated to have risen to 21 percent. After 1980 unemployment rose even more sharply because of the impact of the war; nervous investors closed some plants and disrupted Central American trade forced others to close. All expert observers of the Salvadoran economy concur that unemployment rose markedly during the 1970s, both in the countryside and in the cities.[1]

Wealth

In El Salvador during the 1970s, wealth became concentrated in fewer hands.[2] During the 1950s and 1960s much of the nation's best agricultural land had been converted to capital-intensive cultivation of export crops (in particular cotton) at the expense of subsistence-farming tenants, squatters, and smallholders. During the 1960s, pressure upon the land increased dramatically—the overall number of farms grew by 19 percent, but the land under cultivation shrank by 8 percent. The 1965 agricultural minimum wage law caused the number of *colonos* and *aparceros* (peasants cultivating for subsistence a plot of land donated by the owner) to drop to one-third of the 1961 level by 1971, and the amount of land so employed to drop to one-fifth of the earlier level.[3]

Thus, in the 1960s a dramatic change in Salvadoran rural class relations greatly increased rural poverty. There was a sharp increase in rental and ownership of tiny (less than 2.0 hectares) farms. From 1961 to 1971 the amount of land in rented small plots and the number of renters rose roughly 75 percent. The overall number of small plots of less than 2 hectares rose by one-third, but the amount of land in them rose by only one-fifth, so that the average size of all smallholdings shrank from 0.84 hectares to 0.79 hectares. Despite the increase in the number of small plots, the growing number of newly landless peasants swamped that change—the share of campesinos without land rose from 12 percent in 1961 to 41 percent in 1971. The largest farms (over 50 hectares) shrank in number by 4 percent and in extent by 14 percent.

Apparently many large farmers sold off part of their holdings for capital to invest elsewhere. It has been reported that members of this rural bourgeoisie invested heavily in the fast-expanding industrial sector during the 1960s and 1970s. They invested in technologically modern, mechanized, capital-intensive industries that generated large profits. Industrial production and industrial worker productivity grew rapidly while real industrial wages and levels of employment actually declined.

According to experts on the Salvadoran economy, workers' share of the burgeoning national income deteriorated while production and investment became more centralized.[4] Major coffee growers invested roughly four times as much in industry as any other Salvadoran group, and attracted joint ventures with about 80 percent of the foreign capital invested in the country. Moreover, while the total output of Salvadoran industry more than doubled between 1967 and 1975, the number of firms actually producing goods diminished by as much as 10 percent. Orellana estimated that for the 1971 to 1979 period, wages and salaries received 44 percent of national income, while capital received 56 percent of national income as profit, dividends, interest, and rent.[5] Montgomery argued: "The old saying that 'money follows money' was never truer than in El Salvador. . . . These investment patterns not only contributed to an ever-greater concentration of wealth, but confirm that the traditional developmentalist assumption that wealth . . . will 'trickle down' in developing nations is groundless."[6] Orellana agreed: "The majority of Salvadorans, excluded from the benefits of that growth, were prevented from adequately satisfying their basic needs."[7]

Although El Salvador's capitalist elite apparently grew both relatively and absolutely wealthier during the mid-1970s, this pattern changed abruptly in 1979. The Nicaraguan revolution's impact on El Salvador's economy, plus the onset of extensive domestic popular mobilization and political unrest within El Salvador itself in 1978, brought about a sharp decline in investment and economic growth, beginning in 1979 (see Appendix, Table 1). The recession also stemmed partly from falling coffee prices and partly from the breakdown of Central American trade due to the exhaustion of the potential of the CACM import-substitution growth model. El Salvador's 1974–1978 average annual GDP growth rate of 5.3 percent was sharply reversed. The Salvadoran economy experienced a 3.1 percent *decline* in overall production and a 5.9 percent drop in GDP per capita in 1979. In 1980 the economic contraction deepened, with GDP per capita falling 11.7 percent. This severe recession not only harmed the interests of El Salvador's coffee producers and industrialists but also brought massive layoffs among their employees.

In summary, the development model followed by the Salvadoran state under the Central American Common Market increased overall production as well as the share of national wealth controlled by the national capitalist class. Employment and real wage changes reveal that not only did the Salvadoran working classes become relatively poorer during the 1970s, they became absolutely poorer, and markedly so. The purchasing power of working-class wage earners in El Salvador dropped sharply, beginning in 1973. Joblessness and underemployment rose steadily during much of the 1970s and accelerated late in the decade. When one considers the miserable earning power of the average poor Salvadoran, these facts compellingly demonstrate how severely the standard of living of most Salvadorans deteriorated during this period. Such declines in living conditions, measured for most people by such fundamentals as how much food they could put on the table each day, constituted powerful sources of political grievances among large numbers of Salvadorans.

POPULAR MOBILIZATION

Although the military's PRUD-PCN party always controlled the national government, new opposition parties from across the ideological spectrum appeared during the 1960s.[8] An early sign of growing political opposition was the appearance of two reformist parties: the social democratic National Revolutionary Movement (Movimiento Nacional Revolucionario—MNR) in 1959 and the Christian Democratic party (Partido Demócrata Cristiano—PDC) in 1960. The Democratic National Union (Unión Democrática Nacionalista—UDN), a coalition of leftist elements, formed in 1967.[9] The PDC and MNR briefly formed a legislative coalition with dissident deputies from the ruling PCN in the late 1960s. This coalition anticipated a major reform push by the National Opposition Union (Unión Nacional Opositora—UNO), an electoral coalition of the PDC, MNR, and UDN. UNO's presidential candidate, José Napoleón Duarte, apparently won the 1972 election but was denied the office by fraud. UNO reportedly also won the 1977 presidential election, but was again defrauded of victory.

A simmering stew of organizations (from unions to self-help organizations to peasant leagues), many promoted by the Church and by the new political parties, developed rapidly during the late 1960s and the 1970s. The number of cooperatives rose from 246 to 543 between 1973 and 1980.[10] Labor union membership among proletarians and middle-class workers rose steadily from the late 1960s, reaching 44,150 in 1970 and 71,000 by 1977; several unions, especially those of public employees, became more militant in their wage demands.[11] The number and frequency of strikes rose dramatically in 1974 in response to badly deteriorated wages; such disputes diminished in 1975–1976 as wages improved briefly, then escalated again rapidly in 1977–1978 as inflation ate away living standards (see Figure 7.1).

Development programs sponsored by the Catholic church, PDC, and even the U.S. Agency for International Development (USAID) swelled the number of working-class organizations in El Salvador during the 1960s and early 1970s.

Catholic Christian base communities spread widely through urban and rural poor neighborhoods. In the 1970s the CEBs became increasingly involved in making political and economic demands on behalf of the poor. Numerous peasant organizations also developed during this period, in part encouraged by proposals for modest land reform during the regime of Col. Arturo Armando Molina (1972–1977). Peasant leagues began to press the government for land reform and for higher agricultural wages. The United Popular Action Front (Frente de Acción Popular Unida—FAPU), a coalition of labor unions, peasant organizations, university student groups, a teachers association, and the Communist Party of El Salvador (Partido Comunista de El Salvador—PCS), was formed in 1974. FAPU was the first of several such coalitions that would eventually build a very broadly based network of opposition.

Five Salvadoran guerrilla organizations formed between 1970 and 1979 to challenge the PCN regime militarily (see Appendix, Table 8). Each guerrilla group also forged a coalition with unions and other popular organizations between 1974 and 1979. The formation of these five coalitions greatly enhanced opposition capability and resources by permitting increased use of strikes and mass demonstrations and by generating other material resources for the armed opposition.

GOVERNMENT REPRESSION AND THE OPPOSITION

After 1970, the response of El Salvador's PCN military regimes to rapidly swelling popular mobilization became increasingly repressive.[12] A rightist paramilitary organization with direct ties to public security forces, the Nationalist Democratic Organization (Organización Democrática Nacionalista—ORDEN), formed in the late 1960s. ORDEN, whose acronym spells the Spanish word "order," recruited tens of thousands of peasants from among former military conscripts. Its purposes were to suppress peasant organization and to serve as an anti-Communist militia. ORDEN soon began to fulfill its grisly promise. It attacked and killed striking teachers in 1968 and thereafter became increasingly involved in violent repression. One of ORDEN's common techniques was to murder persons involved in organizing workers, peasants, or political opposition to the regime.

As the first guerrilla actions began to occur and labor and peasant organization membership grew after 1973, regular security forces became much more overtly repressive. In 1974 National Guard and ORDEN forces murdered six peasants and "disappeared" several others affiliated with a Church-PDC peasant league. On July 30, 1975, troops killed at least thirty-seven students protesting the holding of the Miss Universe pageant in San Salvador. Regular government troops in the capital massacred an estimated two hundred of several thousand UNO supporters as they protested fraud in the 1977 presidential election. From 1975 on "death squads," a label that McClintock characterized as a misnomer employed deliberately to disguise political terror by regular security forces and ORDEN,[13] became increasingly active. Beginning with the public assassination of opposition legislator and labor leader Rafael Aguinada Carranza in 1974, death squads assassinated and kidnapped dissidents, Catholic social activists, and priests and attacked church property. Eighteen Catholic clergy and religious personnel, including Archbishop Oscar Arnulfo Romero, were murdered between 1977 and 1982.[14]

Levels of political repression in El Salvador reached such heights in the late 1970s that official mortality statistics began to reflect the curve of terror. After falling wages led to sharply increased labor disputes in the 1977–1979 period, two separate indicators of violence showed dramatic increases (see Figure 1). The government's own annual tally of violent deaths, reported in official statistical abstracts,[15] rose from normal background levels of an average of 864 murders per year for 1965–1966 to 1,837 in 1977, and then skyrocketed to 11,471 violent deaths in 1980. The other index in Figure 1 is based on the number of political murders per year, reported by a Catholic church human rights agency.[16] Its data record a rise from an average of about 14 political murders per year between 1972 and 1977 to 299 per year for 1977–1978 and to 1,030 by 1979; the number then shot up to 8,024 for 1980, and 13,353 for 1981.

Statistics and graphs do not convey much of the intensity and nature of governmental abuse of human rights in El Salvador. The following violations became commonplace: searches of persons and residences on a massive scale; arbitrary, unmotivated, and unappealable arrests by secret police/military agencies; widespread and systematic use of physical and psychological torture; violent kidnappings; arbitrary and indefinite retention (often without charges) of prisoners; use of illegally obtained "confessions" extracted through torture or intimidation; official refusal to provide information about detainees; judicial corruption; extremely poor prison conditions; systematic impunity for human rights violators; government antagonism toward humanitarian, human rights, and relief agencies; and intimidation and harassment of prisoners or released prisoners and of their families. Among commonplace types of torture used by the military and police of El Salvador are the following:

> Lengthy uninterrupted interrogations during which the prisoner is denied food and sleep; electrical shocks; application of highly corrosive acids to the prisoner's body; hanging of prisoners by the feet and hands; hooding prisoners [for long periods]; introduction of objects into the anus; threats of rape; disrespectful fondling and rape; threats of death; simulation of death of the prisoner by removing him from the cell, blindfolded and tied, late at night, and firing shots [toward the prisoner but] into the air; all manner of blows; . . . [and] threats of rape, torture, and murder of loved ones of the prisoner. Among the thousands of murdered detainees, the signs of torture reach uncommon extremes of barbarism: dismemberment [of various types], mutilation of diverse members, removal of breasts and genitals, decapitation . . . and leaving of victims' remains in visible and public places.[17]

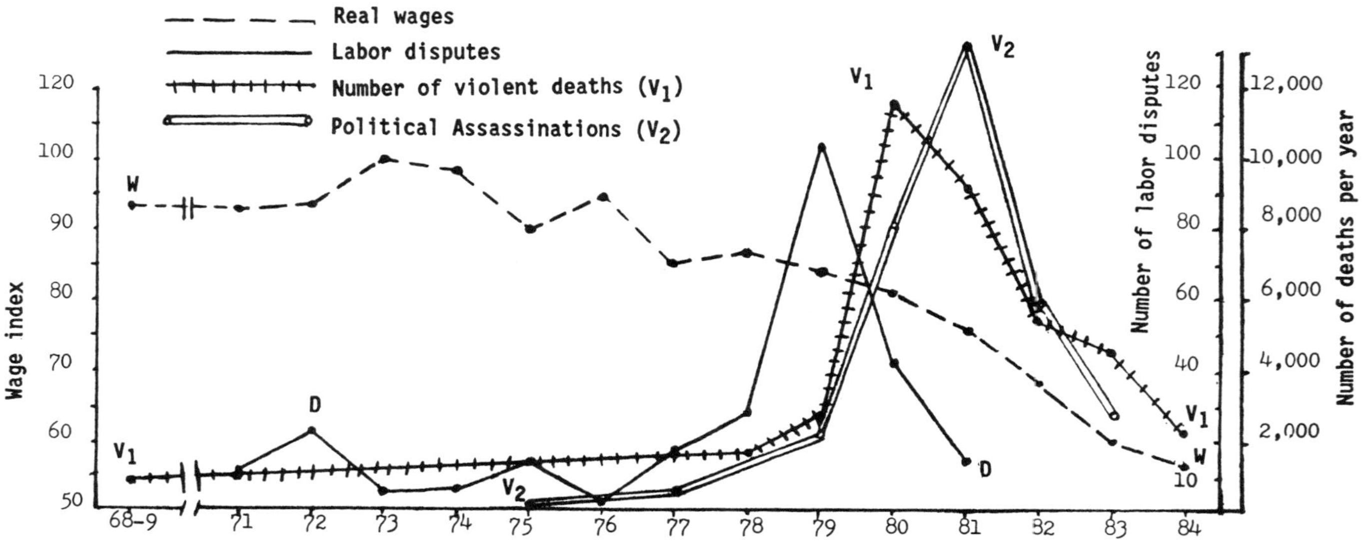

Figure 1. Real wages, labor disputes, and political violence, El Salvador, 1968–1984.

The rapid rise of such government repression in the mid-1970s was followed by the formation of four large opposition coalitions; each linked several labor, peasant, and student groups to one of the guerrilla organizations. FAPU formed in 1974, the Revolutionary Popular Bloc (Bloque Popular Revolucionario—BPR) in 1975, the 28th of February Popular Leagues (Ligas Populares 28 de Febrero—LP-28) in 1978, and the Popular Liberation Movement (Movimiento de Liberación Popular—MLP) in 1979. By joining together and allying with armed rebels, the opposition coalitions' constituent groups committed themselves to revolutionary action. Together these confederations could mobilize hundreds of thousands of supporters into demonstrations and strikes and could raise funds and recruits for the guerrillas. Guerrilla groups also raised large war chests by kidnapping wealthy Salvadorans for ransom. After mid-1979 arms flowed to the guerrillas from private dealers in Costa Rica; other arms came through a sympathetic Nicaragua for a short period during 1980 and early 1981.

The October 15, 1979, coup temporarily allied several former opposition parties with reformist military and business factions. The junta created by the coup failed to curtail the rapidly escalating official violence, however. Rightist elements soon took over the junta and expelled the reformers. This caused the social democratic MNR and the majority faction of the Christian Democrats to break with the junta.

Further unification of the opposition occurred quickly in early 1980: The five guerrilla groups joined together into the Farabundo Martí National Liberation Front (FMLN), in order to increase coordination of their political and military actions. Opposition forces then forged the Revolutionary Coordinator of the Masses (Coordinadora Revolucionaria de Masas—CRM) in January 1980 and continued massive strikes, protests, and guerrilla warfare. Several parties and mass coalitions, including the MNR and much of the PDC, then united into the Revolutionary Democratic Front (FDR). The FDR and FMLN soon allied to form the joint political-military opposition organization FMLN-FDR, which increasingly coordinated overall opposition revolutionary strategy, had some 4,000 troops and 5,000 militia, and controlled several zones of the country. The FMLN-FDR adopted a platform for a revolutionary government, began planning programs for the anticipated new regime, and established governmental structures within their zones of control.[18] In recognition of this clear and potentially effective challenge to the sovereignty of the junta, Mexico and France recognized the FMLN-FDR as a belligerent force, increasing the rebels' legitimacy. The FMLN-FDR's representatives operated openly in Panama, Nicaragua, Mexico, Colombia, and, ironically, the United States.

OUTCOME OF THE CHALLENGE TO SOVEREIGNTY

Momentum in the contest over sovereignty was shifting toward the Salvadoran opposition in 1979 and 1980. The rebels had progressively built a massive and

FMLN REBELS. An FMLN platoon in eastern El Salvador in 1985 (photo by Tommie Sue Montgomery). Female guerrillas in northern Morazón Province, 1988 (photo by Steve Cagan).

cooperative popular base, acquired considerable financial resources, and had several thousand men and women under arms. The October 15, 1979, reformist coup linked the major opposition parties, a reformist military faction, and key middle-sector proponents of democracy in an effort to implement major structural reforms and curtail violence by the security forces. Within weeks, however, rightist elements gained ascendancy within the junta while regime violence actually escalated. This subverted the reformist opposition's tentative accession to power via the October coup and blocked its reform attempts.

The restructuring of the junta in early 1980 closed one middle (and less violent) path to change and drove much of the moderate center-left (the MNR and a majority of the PDC) into an alliance with the armed opposition. On January 30, 1980, Guillermo Ungo and other moderates resigned from the junta and cabinet. When the junta was reconstituted with more conservative elements of the Christian Democrats and government violence continued, the FDR formed (April 1980), followed by the FMLN (October 1980). By late 1980, guerrilla troops had seized effective control of huge areas of Morazán, La Unión, and Chalatenango provinces, so that "1981 opened with the army badly stretched and the undefeated FMLN poised for a major offensive."[19]

The government, in contrast, found its condition and support in disarray. The first junta itself was divided; the agenda of centrist MNR and PDC members for social reform was blocked by the more conservative military members. The junta had little support from the mass organizations and was opposed by most of the private sector. When the PDC joined the junta in 1980, the major organization representing Salvadoran capital, the National Association of Private Enterprises (Asociación Nacional de Empresas Privadas—ANEP) was so outraged that it began to boycott participation in the government. Rightist elements within and outside the military attempted several times to overthrow the regime. The poor performance of the armed forces—with only 15,000 ill-trained men—on the battlefield throughout 1980 suggested that the collapse of the regime was imminent.

The decision of the U.S. government to provide military aid to the failing Salvadoran armed forces profoundly altered the balance of forces between the regime and insurgents. The provision of military aid and advice and of economic assistance during the waning days of the Carter administration began the rescue of the Salvadoran regime. U.S. technical assistance and financing for the government and armed forces escalated rapidly under the Reagan administration. Carter's modest 1980 military assistance grant to El Salvador was $5.9 million. By 1985, U.S. military aid to El Salvador had reached the sum of $533 million. By fiscal year 1989, the U.S. aid total (military plus civilian) had risen to $3.55 billion; 1989 aid levels were $292.5 million for economic assistance and $96.5 million in military assistance.[20]

The Reagan administration, which heavily supported the PDC's Duarte, helped contain rightist opposition to the government and assisted with programs from agrarian reform to constituent assembly elections.[21] The U.S. military assistance (training, arms, munitions, aircraft, and intelligence) held the Salvadoran army together long enough to increase its size and capability so that it could effectively counteract the FMLN. Unlike what had occurred in Nicaragua, U.S. aid in El Salvador rescued the official armed forces and prolonged the conflict.

> The principal reason for the extended nature of the war was the capacity of the junta to hold its piecemeal military apparatus together . . . to ward off guerrilla offensives [and hold] the population in a state of terror. . . . It could only have achieved this or, indeed, survived for more than a few weeks with the resolute support of the U.S., which Somoza was, in the last instance, denied.[22]

The development and nature of the Salvadoran government after 1979 depended heavily upon the interaction among several major forces—hard-liners in control of the armed forces, major business interests, extremely rightist anti-Communist ideologues of the sort represented by Roberto D'Aubuisson and his Nationalist Republican Alliance party (Alianza Republicana Nacionalista—ARENA), and the Carter and Reagan administrations. The United States championed the cause of José Napoleón Duarte's faction of the PDC as the only acceptable political force to provide a legitimizing facade to the struggle against the armed opposition. Backed by the immense financial, technical, and political resources of the United States, Duarte was installed in the presidency and the PDC took a majority of the legislative seats via the 1984 presidential and 1985 legislative elections—both of dubious quality.[23] Although detested as a "Communist" by the Right and distrusted by the military, Duarte with his U.S. backing was indispensible to both because they needed U.S. aid to avoid losing to the rebels. U.S. pressure upon the military and right was sufficient to protect the Duarte/PDC civil government but could neither control radical rightist forces nor compel them to permit social reform. In a very real sense, Duarte formally held the office of president without ever really coming to power.

U.S. presence in El Salvador, then, created a very unstable and artificial coalition among highly incompatible elements. The Duarte government exercised no effective control over the security forces or the war.[24] Duarte's early initiatives to negotiate with the FMLN-FDR were effectively blocked by disapproval of both the Salvadoran military and the United States. Both wished to win the war rather than negotiate any type of shared power with the opposition. The constitution written in 1982–1983 effectively barred the most needed aspects of agrarian reform—probably the only program that might have removed some of the social pressures that led to the rebellion to begin with. The government was unable to muster support from the business community or conservative parties for badly needed economic austerity programs, and the PDC's allied labor unions, Duarte's main base of mass support, became increasingly frustrated and reluctant to cooperate with the regime in the late 1980s. The inefficacy and growing corruption of the PDC, aggravated by internal divisions, led to the party's defeat by ARENA in the 1988 legislative elections. On March 19, 1989, moderate-appearing ARENA candidate Alfredo Cristiani won the presidential election, with party strongman Roberto D'Aubuisson discreetly in the background.

COSTS OF THE STALEMATED CIVIL WAR

The situation in El Salvador during the early 1980s was a bloody stalemate. The rebels held their own against and adapted to increasingly powerful and sophisticated military pressure until 1984–1985. The FMLN showed little sign of weakening; indeed, FMLN troop strength reached about 10,000 by 1984. However, U.S. training, aid, and intelligence helped the regime's forces steadily gain ground in the mid-1980s as their transport, logistics, and tactics improved. By 1986 government troop strength had risen to 52,000 from the 1980 level of 15,000. In 1985–1986, rebel strength in the field apparently shrank by as much as half, to about 5,000, where it remained roughly static into the late 1980s. This was partly because the growing government air power had curtailed the size of the guerrilla-controlled zones and because of an FMLN strategy shift.[25]

The war ground on into the late 1980s, however, and civilian casualties in rebel-held zones continued to escalate. In 1988 and 1989 the guerrillas revealed new capacity to operate effectively in urban areas. When the ARENA-led congress refused to postpone the March 1989 presidential election in response to an FMLN offer to return to peaceful civic competition, the FMLN attempted to disrupt the election by causing widespread power outages and disruption of transportation.

A dispassionate summary of some of the horror of El Salvador's civil war appears in Table 9 (Appendix). Some 42,000 people died between 1980 and 1982; another 30,000 have died since then. Virtually all objective observers blame at least 80 percent of these deaths on the military, the police, and ORDEN.

Intensifying pressure from a Reagan administration worried about continued U.S. Congressional support caused the Salvadoran military, police, and ORDEN to curtail sharply the numbers of deaths and disappearances in 1983 and 1984. Despite such efforts—in themselves revealing how much of the repression emanated directly from the security forces—increasing combat operations kept the casualty rate up in the mid-1980s. By 1989 some 70,000 Salvadorans had died in the revolt or repression. More than one in six had fled abroad. Even for those untouched by personal losses, the war, migration, and capital flight deepened the nation's depression and increased human misery. From 1980 through 1987 the economy slowed down by almost 10 percent of its 1980 per capita production level (see Appendix, Tables 1 and 2).[26] Moreover, the civilian government remained so weak that as of 1989 no perpetrators of human rights violations had ever been punished. "After all of Washington's human-rights pressure against El Salvador's death squads, no army officer has ever been prosecuted for a human rights abuse."[27]

The Central American Peace Accord, signed in Esquipulas, Guatemala, in August 1987, raised some hopes for a negotiated settlement of the Salvadoran war, but new obstacles kept appearing in the path toward peace. Among hopeful signs were the government's dialogue with opposition parties and the decision of the FDR (the allies of the FMLN) to return to civic life and contest the 1988 and 1989 election. On the negative side of the ledger, however, was the fact that the government's post-Esquipulas cease-fire talks with the FMLN were quickly cut off. Indeed, immediately after the Central American Peace Accord was signed, combat intensified and human rights violations rose sharply in El Salvador. Further, as noted earlier, an early 1989 FMLN offer to participate in the 1989 presidential election if the voting could be delayed by six months was rebuffed by the new ARENA majority in the legislature and by the army. Many observers believed in early 1989 that without a negotiated settlement of the war soon, the conflict and human rights abuses could well escalate—especially under an ARENA president and legislature.

Guatemala

ROOTS OF CLASS CONFLICT

Income

Under the economic guidance of the military-business partnership, Guatemala, too, experienced the same kind of rapid growth in overall economic output seen in Nicaragua and El Salvador. Per capita GDP grew at an average of 3.0 percent from 1962 through 1971, and at an average of 2.6 percent from 1972 through 1980 (Appendix, Table 1). During the CACM boom, per capita GDP in constant 1986 dollars rose from $1,020 to $1,732 between 1960 and 1980, a 70 percent increase and the second highest growth rate in Central America (Appendix, Table 2).

As in Nicaragua and El Salvador, however, the growth of the Guatemalan national economic pie did not mean increased income available to the poor. The average annual change in the consumer price index (CPI) from 1963 through 1972 was only 0.7 percent, but rose to 12.3 percent per annum for 1973–1979 (Appendix, Table 3). It can be seen in Table 4 (Appendix) that real wages did not keep up with inflation. Working-class wages peaked in 1967, then declined throughout the 1970s. In 1979 the effective purchasing power of real working-class wages had declined by over one-fourth of 1967 levels.

Income distribution also became markedly more unequal during the CACM boom. Between 1970 and 1984 income distribution became more and more concentrated in the hands of the wealthiest fifth of the population, whose share of national income rose from 46.5 to 55.0 to 56.8 percent for the years 1970, 1980, and 1984, respectively. The income share earned by Guatemala's poorest fifth of the population shrank from 6.8 to 5.5 to 4.8 percent for the same years.

The share of the middle three-fifths of income earners also shrank, from 46.7 percent in 1970 to 39.5 percent in 1980 to 38.4 percent in 1984.[28]

Employment

Official unemployment statistics for Guatemala (Appendix, Table 6), which we can safely assume understate the true rate of joblessness, reveal a steady growth of unemployment even during the years of most rapid CACM-induced growth. Official unemployment rates rose from 4.8 percent in 1970 to 5.5 percent in 1980, and then nearly doubled to 10.0 percent by 1984. Estimated underemployment rates rose from 24.5 percent in 1973 to 31.2 percent in 1980 to 43.4 percent in 1984.[29]

Wealth

Data on wealth distribution have proven more difficult to obtain for Guatemala than for the rest of Central America, but recent studies permit certain inferences.[30] Land has long been very unequally distributed in Guatemala. The agrarian census of 1950 reported that farms smaller than 5 *manzanas* (roughly 3.5 hectares) made up 75.1 percent of the farms but only occupied 9.0 percent of the cultivated land. The 1.7 percent of farms larger than 64 *manzanas* (45 hectares) made up an astonishing 50.3 percent of the cultivated land.[31] The 1979 agricultural census revealed that inequality of landownership in Guatemala had increased, becoming the most extreme in Central America and the second most extreme ever reported in Latin America. The rapid growth of rural population reduced the amount of arable land per capita from a 1950 level of 1.71 hectares/capita to less than half that amount (.79) by 1980.[32]

In the late 1970s Indian agrarian unemployment began to rise while wages deteriorated. This change was accompanied by reports that communally and privately held land in the Indian highlands was being appropriated by Ladinos (mestizos). This concentration of landownership caused people to migrate from those regions to the cities or to public lands newly opened for colonization in the Petén and Izabal. Numerous reports, however, indicate that many smallholders in these departments were being driven off their new plots, especially by military officers and politicians who amassed much land in those zones.[33] To add to the increasing poverty of Guatemala's Indian peasants, the 1976 Guatemalan earthquake devastated the western highlands, sorely harming the living conditions of tens of thousands of rural poor.

Worker productivity in manufacturing grew steadily from the 1950s through the 1970s, yet, as already noted, both real wages and the working- and middle-class shares of national incomes declined sharply during the 1970s. The main beneficiaries of increasing productivity were both foreign and national investors.[34] During the same period the ownership of the means of industrial production became steadily more concentrated in a decreasing number of larger firms, while private sector pressure group organization became steadily more extensive and sophisticated.[35] In some industries modernization of production and growing concentration of ownership displaced many workers.

Although Guatemala's upper classes prospered during most of the 1970s because of the CACM industrialization boom and the relatively high coffee prices of that era, conditions began to deteriorate in 1981, when per capita GDP began a real decline, which continued through 1985. Among factors causing economic contraction in the early 1980s were declining commodity prices, the effect on trade of political unrest elsewhere in Central America, and capital flight. Thus, Guatemala's sharp general recession (as distinct from deteriorating real working-class wages) began around 1981 and deepened sharply in 1982. This slump, lagging four years behind a similar slump in Nicaragua and two years behind the one in El Salvador, seriously eroded the economic position of Guatemalan economic elites and made them critical of the economic management of the regimes of Generals Romeo Lucas García (1978–1982), Efraín Ríos Montt (1982–1983), and Oscar Humberto Mejía Víctores (1983–1986).

POPULAR MOBILIZATION

Reformist elements had promoted important changes under Guatemala's democratic governments of 1944–1954, but after the 1954 coup they suffered badly. The National Liberation Movement (MLN) regime and the armed forces embarked upon a program of demobilization that attacked and decimated the ranks of reformist politicians, unionists, and Indians who had supported the Arévalo and Arbenz governments. Marxist guerrilla opposition to the regime first appeared in 1962 (see Appendix, Table 8), but suffered a severe setback from the heavy general repression and from an intense counterinsurgency campaign in the late 1960s.[36]

Popular mobilization was rekindled in Guatemala during the 1970s as real wages fell and income distribution worsened, but still lagged behind levels in Nicaragua and El Salvador—probably because of heavier regime repression and the problems involved in organizing an ethnically more divided society.[37] The decline of manufacturing wages in the early 1970s was followed by a marked increase in unionization and industrial disputes during the government of Gen. Eugenio Kjell Laugerud García (1974–1978) (see Figure 2). When Laugerud momentarily eased repression of the labor movement in 1978, there was a wave of strikes. The 1976 earthquake's damage to lower-class housing had caused the mobilization of slum dwellers into two confederations. These groups pressed for housing assistance and in 1978 organized a transport boycott to protest increased bus fares.

Another factor mobilizing political participation during the 1960s and 1970s was the social Christian movement. The Christian Democratic party promoted hundreds of agrarian cooperatives and a labor union movement during the 1960s in an effort to build a constituency and organizational base. As in El Salvador and Nicaragua, Christian base communities appeared throughout much of poor rural and urban Guatemala during the early 1970s. CEBs helped organize community and labor groups among Guatemala's long quiescent Indian populace as the 1970s came to an end.

From 1970 until 1986 the Guatemalan presidency remained firmly in the grip of high-ranking military officers, who ruled through the rightist Institutional Democratic party (PID) and National Liberation Movement (MLN). Despite military rule and repression, an explosive proliferation of political parties, factions, and coalitions occurred in Guatemala during that period. Led by the Christian Democrats, reform-oriented political parties of the center and left called for new policies and tried to win power through elections. The opposition was denied presidential election victories three times (1974, 1978, 1982) when the military regimes fraudulently manipulated election returns. Elections so clearly meant next to nothing that popular confidence in the political system ebbed. Abstention from elections rose steadily from 44 percent of registered voters in 1966 to 64 percent in the 1978 national election.[38] When the manipulation of the 1982 presidential election by incumbent president Lucas became publicly known, younger army officers overthrew the Lucas regime and installed Gen. Efraín Ríos Montt as president. They intended that Ríos begin a process of return to civilian government, but he failed to do so.

GOVERNMENT REPRESSION AND THE OPPOSITION

Guatemalan regimes had employed high levels of repression against labor union activists, students, peasant groups, Indians, opposition parties, and other dissidents during the counterrevolutionary period of the late 1950s. Somewhat relaxed during the early 1960s, such repression escalated sharply during the 1966–1970 administration of Julio César Méndez Montenegro (the first civilian president since 1954). In 1966 there appeared both private and public security force death squad terrorism, which consistently took dozens of lives a month. An aggressive 1968–1970 counterinsurgency campaign by the army decimated the Revolutionary Armed Forces (FAR) and the Edgar Ibarra Guerrilla Front (Frente Guerrillera Edgar Ibarra—FGEI) guerrilla movements. During the regimes of Col. Carlos Arana Osorio (1970–1974) and his successor Laugerud García, terror against unions, parties, students, peasant organizations, and cooperatives gradually increased.

Even against this high "background" level of political violence, repression of popular opposition escalated to extreme levels in the late 1970s.[39] The 1978 election further stimulated opposition activity, especially to protest a fraudulent vote count that put the candidate of the military's PID, General Lucas García, in the presidency. The government of Lucas sharply escalated repression: It killed many people in response to popular protests about increased bus fares in 1978; death squads and the security forces assassinated tens of thousands of people between 1978 and 1982, including dozens of national and local leaders of the Democratic Socialist, Christian Democratic, and United Front of the Revolution parties. Hundreds of union leaders, university faculty, and student leaders also died or disappeared during the Lucas government.

General Lucas increased repression severely and rapidly (see Figure 2). Since 1960 the U.S. Embassy has tallied Guatemalan political murders. The vast bulk of these murders have been committed by government security forces and rightist death squads.[40] The average political murder rate—drawn from an index based primarily on urban areas—rose from about 30 per month in 1971 to 75 per month in 1979 and then soared to a peak of nearly 303 per month by 1982.[41] The number of rural killings by the army in counterinsurgency operations is thought by some to be much higher, although no reliable numerical measures exist.

As in El Salvador and under the Somozas in Nicaragua, repression of opposition failed to suppress mobilization and eventually generated even more intense opposition. In the countryside, peasant organizations led by the Peasant Unity Committee (CUC) stepped up organizing, and staged a major strike against sugar planters in 1980. In 1978 and 1979 the regrouped FAR and a new revolutionary group made up predominantly of Indians, the Organization of the People in Arms (ORPA) renewed armed actions in the western highlands. Soon afterward the Guerrilla Army of the Poor (EGP), also with strong indigenous support, resumed combat against the regime in the highlands. Estimates placed the number of guerrilla troops at around 4,000 by 1982; the rebels' popular support was widespread.

Confronted with apparently massive support for the guerrillas among the large indigenous population, the army sharply escalated rural repression. After the fraudulent elections of 1982 and the coup that installed Gen. Efraín Ríos Montt as president, the Guatemalan army began a rural counterinsurgency campaign in Indian zones that Ríos's press secretary Francisco Bianchi justified in the following terms: "The guerrillas won over many Indian collaborators. Therefore, the Indians were subversives, right? And how do you fight subversion? Clearly, you had to kill Indians because they were collaborating with subversion. And then they would say, 'You're massacring innocent people.' But they weren't innocent. They had sold out to subversion."[42] The army committed numerous massacres of entire villages and many atrocities against suspected guerrilla sympathizers. The army forced the relocation and concentration of Indians, many of whom were pressed into work on modern, army-owned farms producing vegetables to export, frozen, to the United States. The military formed army-controlled, mandatory "civil self-defense patrols" involving virtually all adult rural males. There are estimates that place the death toll from the rural counterinsurgency program as high as 150,000 persons between 1982 and 1985. U.S. Embassy violence statistics have tended not to register such massacres of Indians and other rural dwellers in the counterinsurgency program because embassy staff cannot easily verify the incidents.[43] At

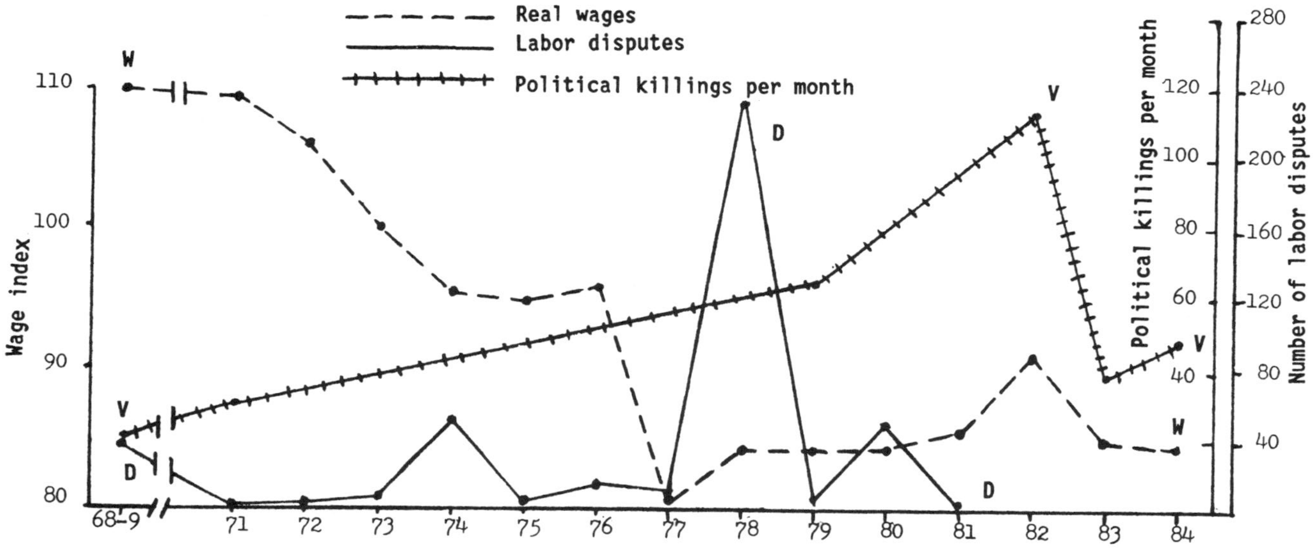

Figure 2. Real wages, labor disputes, and political violence, Guatemala, 1968–1984.

least 500,000 persons, mostly Indians, have become internal or external refugees because of the counterinsurgency war that many anthropologists view as genocidal.[44]

Met with such repression, Guatemalan opposition groups attempted to forge coalitions to enhance their power and resource base.[45] The Democratic Front Against Repression (Frente Democrático Contra la Represión—FDCR) appeared in 1979. It included numerous unions and the PSD and FUR. Two years later, several of the FDCR's more radical elements—including the peasant federation CUC—split away from the FDCR and formed the January 13th Popular Front (Frente Popular 13 de Enero—FP-13). In 1982 both the FP-13 and the FDCR endorsed yet another coalition effort led by a group of prominent regime opponents. This third group was the Guatemalan Committee of Patriotic Unity (Comité Guatemalteco de Unidad Patriótica—CGUP).

The nation's guerrilla groups united into the Guatemalan National Revolutionary Union (Unidad Revolucionaria Nacional Guatemalteca—URNG) in 1982 and issued a revolutionary manifesto challenging the regime's sovereignty. As late as 1989, however, the URNG had still failed to establish further formal links to other popular organizations or to political parties because the process of return to civilian rule had either kept or coaxed such groups back in the legal political arena. Labor unions, for example, were very reluctant to form any sort of political links that might jeopardize their legal status—even to legal political parties.[46]

Thus it appears that revolutionary coalition building stagnated as the regimes of Ríos Montt and Mejía Víctores began a slow and cautious transfer of minimal executive and lawmaking power to civilians. Rightist terrorism in urban areas was sharply cut back after 1982, despite the intensification of rural counterinsurgency. The electoral registry was reformed and a new voter registration undertaken. In 1984 elections were held for a constituent assembly, which began drafting a new constitution. Once the constitution was finished, elections for president, congress, and municipalities were held in late 1985. Although the parties of the far left did not participate in the 1985 elections, centrist parties did take part. Even the social democratic PSD, which rightist terrorism had driven underground a few years before, tested the legal political venue once again. Though held against a backdrop of three decades of brutal and bloody demobilization, the election itself was generally free from the rightist terror against opposition parties. The Christian Democrats, led by presidential candidate Vinicio Cerezo Arévalo, won the presidency and a majority of the congress in clean elections in November and December 1985.[47]

Representatives of Guatemalan political parties admitted that they took part in the 1984 and 1985 elections and the constituent assembly because they believed the military seriously intended to reduce its role in governing.[48] Although doubts remained until the elections themselves were over, as the polling date drew nearer in October 1985, civilian political circles reported increasingly frequent signs of the military's determination to permit an open and fraud-free election. The military regime's opening to civilian politicians in the mid-1980s—especially its curtailment of terror against the centrist opposition and refusal to engage in electoral fraud in 1985—thus helped prevent the opposition parties from allying with the revolutionary Left. The marriage between the democratic center and leftist guerrillas in neighboring El Salvador had been a key step in the radicalization of the opposition.

Many civilian politicians openly affirmed, however, that the 1985 election might well be Guatemala's "last chance" for a peaceful transformation of the regime. They implied that should the military fail to move toward democracy or should it block substantial social reform by a new civilian government, it would almost inevitably drive centrist forces to ally with the armed Left and to pursue the path of violent revolution. In comparison to turnout in earlier elections (e.g., 1982's 46 percent), there were sharp increases in voter turnout in the elections of 1984 (78 percent) and 1985 (69 percent), especially in urban areas. This increase in electoral participation reflected widespread popular hope for peaceful change, at least among the urban populace, which had experienced somewhat lessened violence and increased political freedom.

The August 1987 Central American Peace Accord presented an additional opportunity to promote peaceful reconciliation of Guatemala's smoldering insurgency and to build political consensus. However, the Cerezo administration's cease-fire talks with the URNG, held in Madrid, were immediately suspended. The required National Reconciliation Commission was criticized as inefficacious by some of its own members, and dialogue between the government and other national political and economic forces was limited. The Guatemalan guerrilla war heated up in late 1987 as both the URNG and the army sought to improve their positions. Combat operations in early 1989 continued at a level that completely belied the military's claim of virtual victory over the URNG. In sum, the Esquipulas Accord produced little progress toward either peace or national reconciliation in Guatemala.[49]

POSSIBLE OUTCOME OF THE CONTEST OVER SOVEREIGNTY

Because the Guatemalan military regime instituted a process of political reform, the armed leftist opposition was isolated from a broader political coalition. Meanwhile, the army's brutal rural counterinsurgency program increasingly denied guerrillas access to their Indian supporters. Moreover, the military's retreat from executive power and the election to the presidency of Christian Democrat Vinicio Cerezo increased the government's domestic and external legitimacy. The increased legitimacy brought the new government additional economic and political resources that—at least initially—rallied popular support. The military's retreat from formal executive and legislative power has also strengthened the armed forces' hand against its armed opposition by mollifying many of its critics and by permitting the military to concentrate more on security matters. Although guerrilla troop strength does not appear to have ebbed since 1982, the political reforms of 1984–1986 (whether superficial or substantive) strengthened the government's position.

In the short run, therefore, the momentum in the struggle over sovereignty in Guatemala shifted toward the regime and armed forces. Major political blocs, at least temporarily, cast their lot with the civilian regime, leaving the revolutionary opposition without a broad political base among the urban Ladino population. Counterinsurgency since 1982 has exacted a high toll from indigenous supporters of the guerrillas,[50] partially isolating the URNG forces from its major group of sympathizers. Should President Cerezo complete his term in 1991 and along the way have implemented some reforms and curtailed terrorism by the security forces, support for the URNG could ebb. However, at the halfway mark of Cerezo's presidency, there was extensive criticism of the PDC government's failure to address the problems afflicting the poor. There was also a resurgence of terrorism against centrist political forces in 1988 that could renew pressures for further revolutionary coalition building.

As of early 1989, the Cerezo government remained unable to implement significant reforms in economic or human rights policy.[51] The armed forces appeared able to veto initiatives on human rights and repeatedly blocked efforts to prosecute previous human rights violators. Business groups, opposition parties, and labor criticized Cerezo for indecision and policy errors, and the administration itself was becoming increasingly factionalized. The prospects for continued stability under the new civilian-led government were clouded, especially given growing signs of restiveness within the armed forces.

Conclusions

Economic and political processes in Guatemala and El Salvador bear considerable resemblance to those in Nicaragua in several ways. Eroding popular living standards contributed to growing opposition mobilization in both countries. Military regimes in both countries responded to increased mobilization by escalating repression, hoping thus to demobilize both real and perceived opponents. This sharp intensification of repression was followed in both countries by opposition efforts to forge broadly based coalitions and to employ new resources against the incumbent regimes, and by a process of radicalization of opposition.

The parallels among the three cases do not continue much further, however. El Salvador's newly forged revolutionary coalition was stalemated when the United States threw its vast resources into the struggle to counterbalance the insurgents. Even without massive U.S. assistance to the regime, Guatemala's divided opposition failed to coalesce into a revolutionary alliance when the military introduced political reforms in the mid-1980s. Although further unification and radicalization by the opposition could certainly occur in Guatemala in the future, the strategy of conservative reformism apparently succeeded, in the short run at least, in keeping the opposition divided and weak.

8

MAINTAINING STABILITY IN COSTA RICA AND HONDURAS

Costa Rica and Honduras suffered important negative effects from the Central American Common Market growth boom, but—at least until the late 1980s—both escaped the violent instability of the rest of the region. Among the reasons for this relative stability were public policies that partly alleviated some of the effects of declining popular living standards and that avoided brutal political repression.

SOURCES OF CLASS CONFLICT

Economic growth in both Honduras and Costa Rica was accelerated by the investment and industrialization booms associated with the Central American Common Market (see Appendix, Table 1). Costa Rica's per capita gross domestic product rose at an average annual rate of 3.4 percent during the 1962–1971 decade, and at an annual average of 2.6 percent from 1972 through 1979. Per capita GDP in constant 1986 dollars almost doubled, from $1,332 to $2,222 between 1960 and 1980. Among Central American nations, Costa Rica had the largest share of its work force (16 percent) in manufacturing by 1983. By 1987, Costa Rica (at 23 percent) ranked second in the isthmus in terms of manufacturing contribution to domestic production (see Appendix, Table 2). The agricultural sector work force shrank from 51 percent to 29 percent between 1960 and 1980. Commerce, services, and the government sector all expanded in Costa Rica as the nation rapidly modernized and urbanized.

Honduras was the nation of Central America least altered in social and economic structure by the common market. In the late 1970s, Honduras still reminded many observers of what the rest of the region had been like several decades before. Honduras' economic performance was certainly the least successful of the five CACM nations in terms of overall growth. Much of its new investment went into agriculture. Honduras' agricultural sector remained the largest in the isthmus (Appendix, Table 2), having only declined from 70 percent to 63 percent of the work force between 1960 and 1980. Even though its work force in manufacturing more than doubled (from 6 to 13 percent) between 1950 and 1983, the Honduran manufacturing sector remained the smallest in Central America.

Despite its relative slowness within the region, Honduras did experience a sustained period of overall economic growth. Per capita GDP growth averaged almost 1.5 percent per year between 1962 and 1971. As a consumer but not an exporter of manufactured consumer goods, Honduras quickly developed trade imbalances with other CACM nations and particularly with neighboring rival El Salvador. These trade imbalances and resulting economic difficulties worsened sharply after the 1969 war with El Salvador. These setbacks helped depress Honduran economic growth, which slowed to only 0.4 percent from 1972 through 1979. Overall, however, per capita GDP (in constant 1986 dollars) in Honduras rose from $575 in 1960 to $886 by 1980, a 54 percent increase.

Income

Our theory about the onset of rebellion in Central America (Chapter 5) holds that severe declines in real working-class wages and living conditions play an important role in mobilizing many people into labor, political, and protest organization and activity. Because many urban and rural wage earners in Central American societies live on earnings that give them little or no margin of safety or surplus, a drop in their real earnings (wages corrected for inflation) can have catastrophic effects on their ability to survive. A rapid erosion of life chances can be a powerful impetus to join political or labor groups seeking redress of such problems.

Wage data on Costa Rica and Honduras reveal that wage workers in both countries lost ground relative to other income earners in the mid-1970s, but recovered much of their purchasing power by 1978–1979. The index of working-class wages in Table 4 (Appendix) shows that Costa Rican workers' wages fell in 1975 and 1976, but recovered and then began to exceed earlier levels significantly by the late 1970s. Wages dropped again in 1982 but began an immediate recovery in 1983–1984. In Honduras, wages fluctuated somewhat but experienced no sustained declines like those occurring in Guatemala, El Salvador, and Nicaragua at the same time. Honduran working-class wages fell in 1974 and 1975, recovered in 1976, fell again in 1977, and then rose to above 1973 levels again in 1978 and 1979. Real working-class wages in Honduras declined again in 1981, recovered in 1982, and dropped again in 1983 and 1984. In sum, while working-class earnings and living standards did decline in Honduras and Costa Rica during the mid-1970s, they were less severe and sustained than those in neighboring countries, apparently because the governments of both countries permitted real wage rates to recover much of their earlier purchasing power.[1]

Income Distribution

Another way to examine the amount of economic class disparity in Honduras and Costa Rica is to explore shifts in the distribution of income among classes. One measure of changing income inequality pattern during the 1970s is the share of national income paid out as employee compensation. A decrease in the level of employee compensation would indicate a relative shift of income away from salaried and wage-earning workers and toward investors and entrepreneurs. Data on both Honduras and Costa Rica in Table 5 (Appendix) reveal that between 1970 and 1975, the employee-compensation share of all national income fluctuated somewhat, but tended to increase. Costa Rican levels remained well above the 1962 index-year level. Honduran employee compensation improved markedly in the early 1970s. If we assume that the working-class wages indices reported in Table 4 (Appendix) suggest trends beyond the end of the data in Table 5 (Appendix), we may conjecture that the wage and salary income share in Honduras and Costa Rica continued to rise after 1975.

Various studies[2] indicate that during the 1960s and early 1970s, Costa Rican public policy had redistributed income toward the middle three-fifths of the populace, mainly at the expense of the richest fifth.[3] Unfortunately, there are no comparable data on income distribution available for Honduras.

In summary, Costa Rica and Honduras present a clear contrast to Nicaragua, El Salvador, and Guatemala in both relative and absolute income trends. In the former two, wages fluctuated during the 1970s and early 1980s, but tended toward cycling back up after sharp declines—at least to recover lost purchasing power within a year or two. As shown in Chapters 6 and 7, however, in the latter three countries real and relative income for working-class citizens suffered sustained and severe declines.

Wealth

Honduras and Costa Rica also diverge sharply from the marked increases in class inequality observed to have occurred in Nicaragua, El Salvador, and Guatemala during the 1970s. Although both nations were members of the CACM and experienced the rapid energy-driven consumer price increases of the mid-1970s, data reveal that these factors affected wealth distribution in Honduras and Costa Rica less than in the rest of the isthmus.

Costa Rica's social democratic political system and low military expenditures brought that nation into the 1970s with an extensive social welfare system that attenuated the impact of inflation on popular living conditions. Data comparing Costa Rican spending on social programs to that of other isthmian nations appear in Table 10 (Appendix). In the 1970s and early 1980s Costa Rica's ratio of spending for social services versus defense was between four and five times greater than that of its nearest competitor among the other Central American countries. The positive effects of these policies on living conditions are evident in Costa

Ricans' higher levels of literacy, greater longevity, and lower mortality rates.[4] As noted above, income distribution in Costa Rica became modestly but measurably less unequal during the 1960s and 1970s, helping to prevent the rapid movement of wealth toward the upper classes, as occurred in Nicaragua, Guatemala, and El Salvador.

In Costa Rican agriculture, concentration of landownership grew steadily in the 1960s and early 1970s, but the availability of some colonizable land until the late 1960s and the still-growing banana industry absorbed much of the surplus agricultural work force. Moreover, during the 1974–1978 period, Costa Rica developed an aggressive and successful land reform program that distributed land to numerous peasants and staved off the deterioration of living standards for many.[5] Additionally, the growth of employment opportunities in the urban service and manufacturing sectors absorbed a substantial proportion of the surplus agricultural population and prevented the sharp growth of rural unemployment and poverty.

Honduras, the least industrialized nation in the CACM, underwent the least dramatic changes in socioeconomic structure in the first two decades of the CACM. During the 1970s, therefore, Honduras experienced wealth and income inequality increases less severe and rapid than those affecting Guatemala, El Salvador, and Nicaragua.[6] As noted above, working-class wages tended to recover from inflation in the late 1970s and income distribution did not sharply disfavor wage and salary earners. Honduran governments vigorously encouraged the growth of export agriculture in the 1960s and 1970s, and colonizable agricultural land continued to be available until the late 1970s. Both of these factors helped to prevent a rapid growth of rural unemployment. Because of widespread peasant organization and mobilization during the 1960s and 1970s, the government began an ambitious agrarian reform program.[7] From 1975 to 1979 the Honduran program distributed some 171,480 hectares to roughly 10 percent of Honduran landless and land-poor campesino families.[8] Although the agrarian reform distributed only about one-fourth of its goal and has been widely criticized as insufficient and co-optative, it was nevertheless a major transfer of wealth toward campesinos. Since 1980, peasant organizations, facilitated by the 1970s reform legislation, have invaded much additional land, in what amounts to an informal or quasi-legal redistribution program.[9]

POPULAR MOBILIZATION

In Costa Rica popular mobilization also appears to have increased markedly during the 1970s.[10] Indeed, many communal self-help organizations there were organized by social promoters employed by the government itself. Although the union movement (including industrial workers, service workers, and white-collar public employees)[11] was highly divided among competing, party-affiliated confederations, union membership grew during the 1970s.[12] Industrial disputes rose sharply during 1975–1976 when wages went down, but subsided when wages recovered strongly in the late 1970s (see Figure 3). Wage disputes rose again in 1982 after real wages fell sharply in 1982, but leveled off in 1983 and 1984 as working-class earnings once again recovered purchasing power.

The political party system of Costa Rica remained stable in the 1960s and 1970s; the social democratic National Liberation party (PLN) remained strongest but alternated in power with a coalition of moderately conservative parties under the Unity banner. Radical left parties won a few seats to the Legislative Assembly, but remained weak outside the union movement. The Catholic church was generally quiet during this era. Overall, mobilization of demands by a broad array of Costa Rican groups increased, and there was some terrorism by tiny conspiratorial groups often connected to foreign conflicts.[13] The traditional Unity coalition of conservative parties was reorganized under the banner of the Social Christian Unity party (Partido de Unidad Social Cristiano—PUSC) in 1985. In sum, although there was increased organizational activity, no dramatic increase in opposition organization or coalition formation developed in the late 1970s or the 1980s,[14] and no significant challenge to the sovereignty of the Costa Rican state occurred.

In Honduras,[15] popular mobilization generally increased during the 1960s and 1970s.[16] The greatest growth in unionization came among peasant wage workers and landless peasants organized into land occupation movements by several federations. The Catholic church took a modest role in mobilizing such rural activism in the 1960s but generally retreated from it in the 1970s. The Liberal party remained out of power during military rule from 1963 through 1981. The National party collaborated with the first López Arellano regime in the 1960s but was frozen out afterward. Two small new centrist parties developed during the 1970s. These were the Christian Democratic Party of Honduras (Partido Demócrata Cristiano de Honduras—PDCH) and the Innovation and Unity party (Partido de Inovación y Unidad—PINU). When elections resumed in 1979, however, neither PINU nor the Christian Democrats had captured a major share of the support of the Liberal or National parties. Business and private sector organizations also multiplied and became more active in pressing policy demands upon the state during the 1960s and 1970s.

Several small leftist guerrilla groups appeared in Honduras during the 1970s and early 1980s (see Appendix, Table 8).[17] In 1960 a pro-Castro splinter from the Honduran Communist party (Partido Comunista de Honduras—PCH) formed the Morazán Front for the Liberation of Honduras (Frente Morazanista para la Liberación de Honduras—FMLH), a guerrilla group sporadically active in the 1960s and early 1970s. In 1979 the FMLH reappeared. In 1978, the PCH spun off more dissidents who formed the Popular Movement for Liberation (Movimiento Popular de Liberación—MPL), known as the "Chichoneros." The MPL's most spectacular action was the taking hostage of eighty San Pedro Sula business leaders in 1982. The Lorenzo Zelaya Popular Revolutionary Forces (Fuerzas Populares Revolucionarias "Lorenzo Zelaya"–FPR), founded by a pro-Chinese faction of the PCH, appeared in 1981 and conducted various acts of urban political violence.

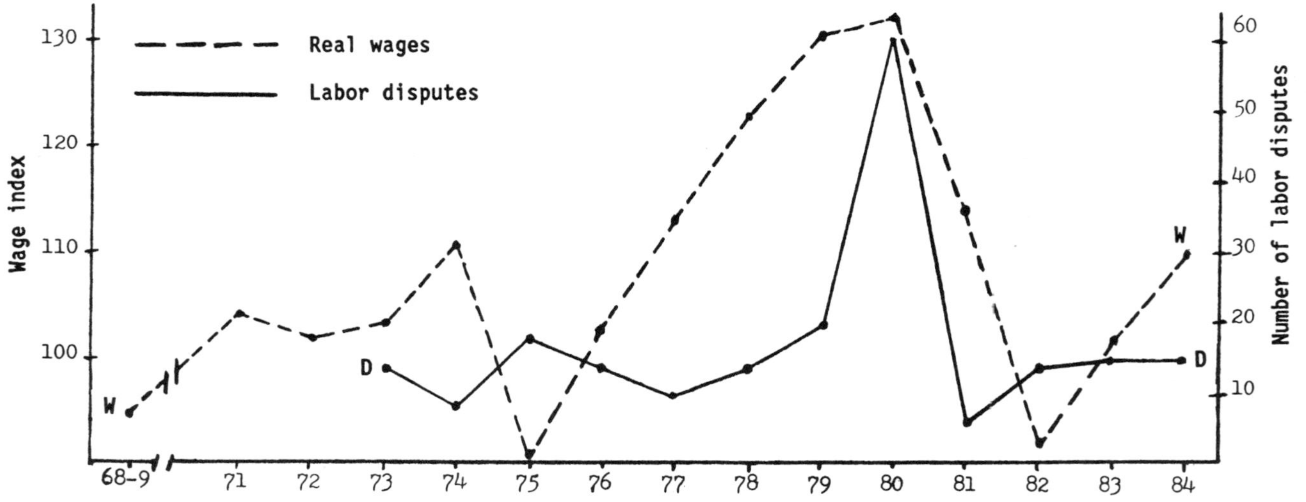

Figure 3. Real wages and labor disputes, Costa Rica, 1968–1984.

The Revolutionary Party of Central American Workers of Honduras (Partido Revolucionario de Trabajadores Centroamericanos de Honduras–PRTCH), the Honduran branch of a regional revolutionary group, was founded in 1977. In 1983 the guerrilla groups formed the National Directorate of Unity (Dirección Nacional de Unidad–DNU) to coordinate their activities on the revolutionary left. Overall, despite the rise of armed opposition, insurgent violence in Honduras remained at a very low level compared to that of neighboring nations.

Overall, then, the levels of popular mobilization of various sorts increased in Costa Rica and Honduras during the 1970s. Indeed, in both nations some violent political participation occurred in protest of regime policies, and in Honduras the violence reached the level of incipient guerrilla struggle by various leftist factions. In neither nation, however, was legitimate mass mobilization repressed to the point of triggering armed resistance as a last resort, as had been true in Nicaragua, El Salvador, or Guatemala.

GOVERNMENT RESPONSE TO POPULAR MOBILIZATION

The response of Central American regimes to popular mobilization in the 1970s varied substantially. We have already seen the violently repressive responses of the Salvadoran, Guatemalan, and prerevolutionary Nicaraguan regimes to swelling popular organization and protest. Although they were very different regime types, Costa Rica and Honduras responded in a strikingly different fashion from the other three Central American governments.

Costa Rica kept an open, constitutional regime characterized by electoral honesty and considerable popular access to public officials. Costa Rican officials generally responded to mobilization of demands by accommodating pressure group initiatives of many sorts. Even when such demands escalated to include civil disobedience, demonstrations, strikes, and riots, the government generally responded with study and compromise to defuse conflict. For instance, violent civil disturbances—land invasions in the early 1970s, the Limón riot of 1979, and banana workers' strikes in 1980, 1981, 1982—were met with very modest official force, so that deaths were very rare.[18] Efforts to somehow accommodate those pressing the demands were also made—the government negotiated with protesters or strikers, formed panels of inquiry, or made conciliatory policy gestures.

In the early 1980s, Costa Rica experienced a severe economic crisis. As living standards of a majority of Costa Ricans plummeted, public approval of the government declined. Nevertheless, efforts to forge a militant general nationwide labor confederation failed. Voting for leftist parties—long considered a bellwether of protest—actually declined in the 1982 and 1986 national elections. Costa Rica's more radical party and labor groups became increasingly divided in the early and mid-1980s. Polls revealed that even in the midst of a severe recession, most citizens remained loyal to the regime.

Honduras remained under military rule most of the time from 1963 through 1982. During the early 1970s the second military government of Gen. Oswaldo López Arellano (1971–1975) accommodated burgeoning campesino mobilization and developed a populist agrarian reform program. López was deposed for the second time in 1975 by a conservative faction of the armed forces led by Col. Juan Alberto Melgar Castro. Labor repression then increased, marked by a massacre of fourteen protesters at Los Horcones in 1975. In an astounding departure from what would have happened in neighboring nations, army officers implicated in the massacre were tried in civilian courts, convicted, and imprisoned.[19]

Violent regime repression of opponents (illegal detentions, disappearances, and murders) rose significantly in Honduras in the early 1980s, but still remained quite moderate by Central American standards. For instance in 1982, a year when Guatemala and El Salvador each had over ten thousand political disappearances and murders, Honduran human rights activists reported a total of only forty assassinations and "permanent disappearances."[20] Political parties, unions, peasant leagues, and a free press operated openly. They no doubt helped to restrain human rights violations by vigorously denouncing government abuses of authority.[21]

Honduran security forces took numerous measures to curtail armed opposition, including forming rural militias called Civil Defense Committees (Comités de Defensa Civil—CDCs) in several areas, and stepped up counterinsurgency efforts. Right-wing elements, apparently involving some Nicaraguan exiles and enjoying military complicity, began to murder and to kidnap and torture suspected subversives and critics of the government in the early 1980s. By 1982, "extrajudicial action [had become] standard operating procedure for the Honduran armed forces in dealing with violent opposition. The methods include[d] disappearances, torture, use of clandestine detention centers, and . . . execution of prisoners."[22] Although human rights violations increased markedly in the early and mid-1980s,[23] they remained well below levels observed in El Salvador and Guatemala.

One key aspect of the Honduran case was the process by which the armed forces returned formal power to civilians. Despite the growing institutional strength of the military during the 1960s and 1970s, the Honduran armed forces did not become nearly as repressive or aggressive in expanding their power within and hold over the state apparatus as did neighboring militaries. As the punishment of military officials for the Los Horcones massacre revealed, the Honduran military had not placed itself completely above accountability to the law and constitution. The growth of popular unrest in the mid- and late 1970s, disaffection among the military's traditional National party allies, blatant corruption of the military regimes, and pressures from the Carter administration combined to persuade then-president Gen. Policarpo Paz García to hold elections for a constituent assembly in 1980, an action supported by the senior officer corps.

When the Liberal party captured a near majority of the constituent assembly in 1980, the military permitted the Liberals to draft the new constitution. No one was surprised, however, that Paz retained military ascendancy by holding the provisional presidency. Confounding the expectations of many observers, however, the armed forces permitted both traditional parties (including the Liberals' social-democratic Left) and the two new groups (PINU and the Christian Democrats) to take part in a generally free and open 1981 election. Moreover, again contrary to widespread expectations, the military did not rig the 1981 elections on behalf of its longtime National party allies. Liberal candidate Roberto Suazo Córdova won a clear majority in a clean election, and General Paz relinquished the presidency in early 1982.[24]

Despite the evident frailty of the civilian government, the rapid, U.S.-financed growth of Honduran military power, and an upsurge in repression by the security forces in the mid-1980s, civilian rule wobbled on. One of the most striking weaknesses of the Honduran government's prospects for democracy, surprisingly, was President Suazo himself. In an apparent attempt to retain power, he precipitated a constitutional crisis in 1985. Suazo failed in his effort, but the resultant chaos led to the adoption of a Uruguayan-style combined party primary–presidential election in 1985 in which the majority party's front-runner would take office. This brought about the confusing result that José Azcona Hoyos, the leading Liberal candidate, became president in 1986, despite having won fewer total votes than the leading National party candidate, because the Liberal candidates together drew the most popular votes. The prospects for the survival of civilian government in Honduras appeared very questionable in the late 1980s. Among continuing threats to civilian, constitutional rule were economic strains, increased repression, desultory elite commitment to democracy, and increased popular unrest over Honduran support for U.S.-backed anti-Sandinista rebels (the contras).[25]

SUMMARY AND CONCLUSIONS

During the 1970s, both Costa Rica and Honduras at least partly ameliorated the growing inequalities affecting working-class victims of rapid economic change, while employing either a low or a moderate level of repression. There are, however, important differences between the two cases that bear further attention. First, although political repression was very low in Costa Rica, it was substantially higher in Honduras under both the military governments of the late 1970s and the Suazo and Azcona governments in the 1980s. Such repression notwithstanding, the Honduran security forces voluntarily transferred nominal control of executive and legislative power to a constitutional regime, a political reform of symbolic significance to Hondurans. Second, the public policies of Costa Rica and Honduras during the 1970s differed sharply in specifics, but the net effect in both cases was to permit working-class wages to recover previous purchasing power after declines, and to shift some wealth and income to certain lower-class groups.

Thus, although Costa Rica and Honduras were quite different, in each case key political elites and the state made modest concessions to working-class needs and restrained (at least some of the time in Honduras) draconian efforts to curtail political mobilization. Of course, it is still quite possible that Honduras's fluctuating repression could escalate and ultimately feed general opposition to the civilian government. As of 1989, however, the united leftist political-military organizations still lacked a base of support from a broad general coalition of other political groups.

9

POWER, DEMOCRACY, AND U.S. POLICY IN CENTRAL AMERICA

In the introduction to a paper he gave at a U.S. Department of State conference on Central America in March of 1979, one of the authors asserted that Washington's

> apparent definition of interest [in Central America]—and certainly its strategies for achieving them—are outdated, shortsighted and fundamentally flawed. . . . U.S. goals . . . are short-termed, reactive, and excessively concerned with stability and, hence, the maintenance of an elite-dominated status quo. These policies pose a grave threat to long-range U.S. interests by contributing to the continuation of socially unjust systems and thereby increasing the probability of civil and regional conflict and stimulating an ever-growing feeling of anti-Americanism among the peoples of the region.[1]

A decade later, if anything, U.S. behavior toward the isthmus in the ensuing period has dramatically underscored the validity of that pessimistic observation. The U.S. defense of the forces of status quo in El Salvador, Guatemala, and Honduras, its promotion of counterrevolutionary reaction in Nicaragua, and its recent preference for military rather than negotiated solutions have contributed significantly to an unprecedented escalation in violence. By 1989 that violence had taken between 200,000 and 300,000 lives (mainly civilians), displaced millions, left countless others jobless, orphaned, or physically or psychologically maimed and had nearly ruined the economies of the region. Although U.S. policy was not the only cause of the Central American tragedy, it has been a very important contributing factor to the onset and evolution of the violence.[2]

In the preceding chapters we have presented specific information about U.S. policy towards the individual countries. This chapter emphasizes the nature and problems of U.S. policy in the region. Although the tactics and style of U.S. policy towards Central America occasionally change, its overall objective remains remarkably constant. That objective is to protect U.S. economic and security interests by keeping as much influence as possible over events and policies in Central America. The traditional U.S. way of assuring such influence has been through the maintenance in power of friendly, "moderate"—read pro-U.S., traditional, elite-dominated—regimes.

In the twentieth century the United States went from the policy of the big stick, in the first three decades, to that of the good neighbor, under Franklin D. Roosevelt and Harry Truman. This was followed by cold war interventionism, under administrations from that of Dwight Eisenhower through that of Gerald Ford. Interventionism was then interrupted by a tenuous promotion of human rights during the first years of the Jimmy Carter presidency, but resumed at the end of the Carter administration and continued throughout that of Ronald Reagan. Throughout those nearly ninety years, however, a major concern has been with maintaining control in "our backyard." Even in times of lofty rhetoric about good neighborliness, the Alliance for Progress, human rights, or democracy, U.S. policies clearly revealed an overarching concern with maintaining stability and control.

One colorful but troubling example of the U.S. preoccupation with control and security is that of President Franklin Roosevelt, who described Anastasio Somoza García of Nicaragua as an "S.O.B.," but maintained cooperative relations with the dictator because he was "*our* S.O.B." President John F. Kennedy promoted the Alliance for Progress to encourage economic and social development and democracy in order to undercut the appeal of communism in the hemisphere. Often at cross purposes with promoting democracy and development, however, was the simultaneous increase in U.S. military aid and training throughout Latin America. Intended to increase the counterinsurgency capability of Latin America armed forces, the military aid helped soldiers topple several democratic regimes and abuse human rights. President Carter, despite his evident concern for human rights, tried hard in 1978 and 1979 to keep the Sandinistas out of a new government in Nicaragua. He even attempted to preserve Somoza's brutal National Guard and corrupt Liberal Nationalist party intact after the dictator's departure.

THE PROBLEM OF POWER

Any serious discussion of the problems of U.S. behavior in Central America should address the critical relationship between power and democracy. Power is the basic currency of politics. Simply put, groups within a given polity generally receive benefits and attention from their government and political system in rough proportion to the amount of power they can bring to bear on that system. The powerful receive the most; the powerless, little or nothing. Charles W. Anderson argued that the traditional "power contenders" in Latin American society—the Church, the military, the rural and urban economic elites—allow new groups to enter and receive benefits from the political system only when these groups demonstrate their own "power capabilities."[3]

Power capabilities vary from group to group. The Church exercises authority through the traditional belief systems and moral suasion. The military has a near monopoly of the means of violent coercion. Economic elites use their economic resources for influence. In contrast, lower-class groups have far fewer resources. To some extent they can wield power by organizing, and by carrying out strikes, protests, and the like. But the incontrovertible fact about Central America is that the majority of the people—illiterate or semiliterate peasants, urban and rural workers, and slum dwellers—usually lack the organization that would give them real power capabilities. When they attempt to develop power through peaceful collective activity and organization, they are often seen as subversive, labeled "Communist," and violently repressed. Accordingly, because Central America's poor majorities have held little power, public policy has usually remained unresponsive to their social plight. We have seen how this lack of responsiveness has generated grievances, and how repression was applied, thus causing violence to become the people's recourse of last resort.

It is the gross disparity in power between a relatively small privileged group—the upper class and emerging middle sector—and the underprivileged and impoverished majority that lies at the root of the Central American crisis of the late twentieth century. As we noted in earlier chapters, power relationships in the five countries have deep historical roots. It is no accident that Costa Rica, the country that developed the most egalitarian society, and Honduras, which—due to its status as an economic backwater—never developed a highly cohesive and exploitative elite, have been least affected by recent turmoil. Conversely, it is also not surprising that Guatemala, El Salvador, and Nicaragua, the countries with the greatest historically rooted power disparities, have experienced the highest levels of violence. The elites in those three countries, long accustomed to their lopsided monopoly of power, have so far shown little inclination to share power or to make the sacrifices needed for the genuine development of all sectors of society.

DEMOCRACY

There is no doubt that democracy is one of the most powerful bases of legitimacy for contemporary governments. Seldom do we find a regime of any type anywhere in the world that does not claim to be democratic. The problem lies in the fact that there is much disagreement over the meaning of the term *democracy*. Socialist theorists tend to stress economic and social criteria, whereas those from the industrially developed West emphasize political—often narrowly procedural—characteristics. In the United States, one definition with which few would quarrel is that democracy is "government of, by, and for the people." However simple this definition may sound, it sets forth two conceptual elements fundamental to democratic theory: first, that the system should be as participatory as possible, and, second, that it should facilitate the general well-being.[4]

In the 1980s the United States has promoted "civilian rule" and proclaimed the birth of "democracy" in its client states, Guatemala, El Salvador, and Honduras, and condemned its alleged absence in the revolutionary state of Nicaragua. However, if we honestly apply the criteria set forth in the last paragraph, it is very difficult to sustain those conclusions.[5] All four countries have held nationwide, internationally observed elections. And it is true that, except in the case of El Salvador, they have been internationally acclaimed as procedurally clean. But democracy requires much more than simply holding procedurally correct elections or establishing civilian rule. A critical issue is popular participation in elections and in other political affairs.

The 1985 Guatemalan and the 1982, 1984, and 1989 Salvadoran elections were held against a background of state-sponsored terror that had taken tens of thousands of lives and had disarticulated most mass-based civic and political organizations. By default, candidates ranged from center to far right and media outlets genuinely critical of the system were nonexistent. Citizen participation was confined largely to the formal act of voting by most citizens, and to campaign involvement by a tiny minority of center and right-wing party activists. In Nicaragua, however, there was no program of state-sponsored terror. On the contrary, many organizations representing the poor majority had been encouraged to develop, grow, and make demands on their government. The major international human rights organizations all concur that the practice of systematized torture, murder, and disappearance of political opponents—massively institutionalized in Guatemala and El Salvador—was not a problem in Nicaragua. Though the right-wing Coordinadora Democrática coalition chose not to participate in Nicaragua, three parties on the right as well as three on the left challenged the Sandinistas. What is more, the antiregime Nicaraguan media (including *La Prensa* and Radio Católica), though lightly censored, carried a sharply anti-Sandinista message to the voters, as did the six participating opposition parties in extensive uncensored free time-slots on state-sponsored radio and television.

The U.S. application of the term *democracy* in Central America is also called into question if we ask in each case, Is this a government "for the people"? In whose interest does it rule? By 1984, the social achievements of the Nicaraguan government were so significant that even the Kissinger Commission felt obliged to admit that "Nicaragua's government has made significant gains against illiteracy and disease."[6] Had it chosen, the commission might also have mentioned advances in agrarian reform, housing, social security, and the status of women. Even after the contra war forced the diversion of large amount of funds out of the social and into the military budget, the Sandinistas continued as best they could to combat pressing social problems. Eventually, by the late 1980s, however, most such programs had been weakened due to the high cost of defense.

In El Salvador, Guatemala, and Honduras, in contrast, although some reforms were proclaimed on paper, few real advances were made. Some would attribute this to a lack of will on the part of elected governments. More likely it is because in those three countries, the centrist civilians who were nominally elected never really came to full power. At best, they became the formal officeholders, but the elite-oriented military establishments continued to function as the real "regimes" or to exercise veto power over key policy matters.

The difference between titular "government" and real "regime" is not simply a matter of academic semantics: it is absolutely central to any informed judgment of whether or not a political system is truly democratic. If, as appears to be true in Guatemala, El Salvador, and Honduras, elections produce governments without power to govern in behalf of the people, then to call those countries democracies is inappropriate.

MOBILIZATION

The decades following World War II were marked by a growing awareness that something was seriously wrong in Latin America. Those who viewed mass poverty as rooted in an extremely unequal distribution of power began advocating a greater diffusion of power. In the 1940s and 1950s, social democratic and Christian democratic parties talked of "penetrating" the masses, of creating and fortifying party-oriented labor, peasant, and neighborhood organizations that would unify and express the interests of the masses. From the 1950s onward, educators such as Paulo Freire of Brazil, aware that mass empowerment would require the emergence of a socially, politically, and linguistically literate citizenry, began promoting, through adult education, consciousness-raising programs that encouraged poor people to examine and question their social condition.[7]

In the wake of the victory of the Cuban revolution in 1959, the United States was jolted into a period of support for reform in Latin America. Thus the Alliance for Progress was created in 1961.

The Peace Corps, inaugurated the same year, promoted community development throughout the Third World, and particularly in Latin America, by mobilizing, educating, and empowering poor people to solve their own problems. For a while, thousands of idealistic U.S. citizens lived among and worked with Latin America's urban and rural poor and promoted collective self-help programs.[8] Inspired by the old saying that it is better to teach a hungry person to fish than simply to give him a fish, Peace Corps community action promoters helped poor communities form legal community action committees, which, in turn, elected their own leaders, identified needs felt in the community, and tried to mobilize resources to address those needs. Through community action, thousands of schools, soccer fields, clinics, roads, bridges, housing projects, and small electrification and potable water projects were built. Ultimately, many hundreds of thousands, perhaps millions, of ordinary Latin Americans experienced a surge in democratic participation.

Before long, however, a strong reaction set in. Ill-equipped or disinclined to respond to the legitimate demands of newly articulate poor people, and annoyed in some cases that community groups ignored or bypassed traditional politicians, some Latin American elites came to see the community action movement as a nuisance or a threat. Local elites chided Peace Corps volunteers for associating with what the latter often called "those Communists"—the poor people in the community action organizations. Eventually, when the central governments, too, conveyed their displeasure to U.S. diplomats, the Nixon administration officially terminated Peace Corps involvement in community action. This graphically illustrates how the maintenance of good relations with pro-U.S. regimes was far more important to Washington than was the continuation of efforts to promote the democratization of Latin American society through increased popular participation.

Others also became interested in popular participation and mass mobilization. Programs similar to community action were started by the Costa Rican government, for example. However, the most extensive government-sanctioned mobilization effort occurred in revolutionary Cuba. Spurred into action, at least in part, by an awareness of an impending CIA-sponsored counterrevolutionary invasion, Fidel Castro and his associates began to mobilize the Cuban people early in 1961. A huge literacy crusade, with significant politically socializing content, was begun, and common citizens were encourage to form grass-roots Committees for the Defense of the Revolution. By the time the United States launched the Bay of Pigs invasion in April 1961, Cuba was prepared to resist. Because of revolutionary mobilization, the counterrevolutionary effort to topple Castro failed dismally.

Clearly the most extensive mobilizing activity in the hemisphere in the 1960s was begun by the Latin American Catholic church. Even in the 1950s, some important Latin American Church figures such as Dom Helder Câmara of Brazil had begun calling for social justice and an uplifting of the oppressed majority. By the end of that decade and the beginning of the next, they found a powerful ally in the Vatican as Pope John XXIII embarked on his pivotal aggiornamento, or updating, of the Catholic church. Part of this process of change, as expressed in pronouncements of the Second Vatican Council, was the new focus on the problems of Latin America, by then the largest single segment of world Catholicism. This, in turn, stimulated Latin American Catholics to engage in an even deeper examination of the human problems of their region.

The high-water mark of such concern came at the Second General Conference of Latin American Bishops at Medellín, Colombia, in 1968. Focusing on the problems of poverty and exploitation in Latin America, the bishops used a form of structural analysis not unlike the "dependency" explanation we discussed in our second chapter.[9] As we noted in Chapter 4, they argued that Catholic clergy should make a preferential option for the poor and that, in order to carry out this option, priests and nuns should create Christian base communities (CEBs), or grass-roots organizations, in which people of all classes would discuss the social problems of their community or country in light of the social gospel. In addition, natural community leaders or lay delegates of the word would be trained to preach the social gospel and act as community organizers.[10]

The impact of Medellín on Latin America in general, and especially on Central America, was greater than anyone might have dreamed in 1968. No doubt to the astonishment of many conservative bishops who had perfunctorily signed the high-sounding Medellín declarations, thousands of priests and nuns—and even a few bishops—began implementing the ideas of the conference almost immediately. By the 1970s, extensive grass-roots mobilization was taking place through newly created CEBs in the four countries of northern Central America. Poor people by the tens, possibly hundreds, of thousands were becoming aware of themselves as human beings made in the image of God and having a right to be treated by their government and employer with dignity and justice. Though the objectives and tactics of the CEB movement were nonviolent, the elite-dominated governments of the region predictably viewed them as highly subversive. Again the label "Communist" was applied and, eventually, tens of thousands of Catholics, including dozens of priests and nuns and even one archbishop, died in the repression that was mounted to reverse their mobilizing effort.

By the mid- to late 1970s, the social mobilization process had become massive and extremely widespread throughout northern Central America. Peasants had mobilized into unions and federations and created cooperative organizations concerned with production and marketing. Urban workers had expanded the labor movement. Teachers, medical personnel, students, and women had all become more organized and active. As we noted in earlier chapters, the Honduran regime chose to accommodate or, at worst, only mildly repress the mobilization process. Such relative moderation is probably one of the major reasons why Honduras avoided open insurrection. In Nicaragua, Guatemala, and El Salvador, however, the much more entrenched and powerful elites chose violent demobilization rather than accommodation as the tactic for dealing with newly articulated popular demands. In all three countries, repressive violence begot responding violence, as previously moderate citizens in increasing numbers opted for insurrection or guerrilla warfare. In Nicaragua, the process of mobilization, repression, and insurrection ultimately led to the victory of the revolutionary coalition in 1979. In Guatemala and El Salvador, in contrast, the unprecedented scale and cruelty of state-sponsored terrorism (with heavy U.S. material support for the Salvadoran regime in the 1980s and for the Guatemalan regime from the early 1960s through 1977) curtailed or reversed the process of civilian mobilization and stalemated the rebels on the battlefield.

The process of mobilization that had brought about the Nicaraguan revolution continued and was encouraged by the new government thereafter. Prior to the victory, Catholics from the Christian base movement had joined with nationalist Marxists from the FSLN and others to organize a variety of grass-roots organizations. These included the Rural Workers' Association (Asociación de Trabajadores del Campo–ATC), the Sandinista Workers' Federation (Confederación Sandinista de Trabajadores–CST), the Association of Women Confronting the National Problem

(Asociación de Mujeres Frente a la Problemática Nacional–AMPRONAC), the Civil Defense Committees (Comités de Defensa Civil–CDCs), and the Sandinista Youth (La Juventad Sandinista).[11] After 1979 the CEB movement also continued and other grass-roots organizations, such as the National Union of [small] Farmers and Ranchers (Unión Nacional de Agricultores y Ganaderos–UNAG), emerged. By 1984, the U.S. Embassy in Managua estimated that between 700,000 and 800,000 Nicaraguan citizens—around half of the adult population—were in such organizations.[12]

The grass-roots organizations performed a variety of functions. They helped defend the revolution. They were a device for political socialization. They helped mobilize volunteer participation to carry out several ambitious social programs. And, most important, they provided an avenue for political and governmental participation, which ordinary people had never experienced previously. The local organizations held internal elections, discussed the community's most pressing needs, organized to solve those needs, successfully petitioned their government for everything from material and financial support to major changes in government policy, and named representatives to local, regional, and national planning boards of government economic and social service entities.[13] Sometimes such organizations abused their power or engaged in petty corruption, but overall they gave many ordinary Nicaraguan citizens the first opportunity in their lives to participate meaningfully in the political process.

In addition to the grass-roots organizations, the Sandinista-led government used education as a vehicle for advancing participation and democracy in Nicaragua. Relying in large part on the techniques of Catholic educator Paulo Freire and the labor of tens of thousands of volunteers, the revolutionary government carried out a basic literacy crusade within its first year in power. The drive significantly lowered rates of adult illiteracy and won Nicaragua the United Nations (UN) prize for the best literacy crusade of the year. Thereafter, continued attention was paid to maintaining and increasing literacy and generally improving the educational level of all Nicaraguans. In addition to building the skills of the work force and socializing Nicaraguans to support the revolution, a central motive for the heavy emphasis on education was to "empower" the people—to create a citizenry capable of intelligent self government.[14]

Costa Rica is the only other country in Central America where significant and sustained governmental efforts have been made to mobilize the populace. In the 1960s and 1970s the Costa Rican government promoted hundreds of local citizen self-help organizations through its National Community Development Directorate (Dirección Nacional de Desarrollo de la Comunidad–DINADECO) and through health, education, welfare, agricultural, and housing agencies. There developed many community development, nutrition, health promotion, and economic groups (especially cooperatives) that engaged thousands of citizens in making demands on the political system and in working together to solve local problems.

GRASS-ROOTS MOBILIZATION. A protest march in San José, Costa Rica (photo by John Booth). Adult education in Nicaragua as depicted in a revolutionary mural (photo by Thomas Walker).

THE ROOTS OF U.S. POLICY IN CENTRAL AMERICA

The United States has real, legitimate, and widely agreed upon security interests at stake in today's turbulent Central America. Virtually all agree that it is in the interest of the United States that no Soviet bases, troops, advanced weapons, or nuclear arms be present in the isthmus, and that no country in the region form a military alliance with the Soviet Union. It is in the interest of the United States that Central American societies enjoy sufficient economic prosperity, democracy, and political stability that their citizens not be driven massively into exile or refuge. It is in the interest of the United States that Central American nations be at peace among themselves, and that their military forces be neither excessively large nor out of balance with each other. An arms race or increased intraregional conflict might cause a war in Central America, spark direct U.S. military intervention there, or threaten the security of the Panama canal or important trade routes.

Many critics of U.S. policy in Central America believe that U.S. actions over the past three decades have actually harmed rather than advanced these interests. In order to understand how this has come about, we must review the roots of U.S. policy.

U.S. interests in Central America have evolved over time and have sometimes been subject to intense debate within the United States. During the nineteenth century, encouraging trade, coping with massive British naval power, and transit across the isthmus were important U.S. concerns. As U.S. sea power supplanted British dominance in the late nineteenth century and as the United States rapidly industrialized, the desire to establish and control a transisthmian canal led to U.S. intervention in Panama in 1903. Once canal construction and operation were under way, the United States used troops in Panama and Nicaragua to assure a canal monopoly and protect the canal itself. U.S. diplomats (sometimes assisted by the marines) energetically and often heavy-handedly promoted U.S. business and geopolitical interests throughout Central America in the early twentieth century. During World War II, the United States, through cooperative security arrangements with Central American governments, sought to protect the Panama Canal from Axis interference.

Since World War II, U.S. interests in Central America have continued to focus upon economic and security concerns. A desire to contain Soviet-inspired communism has often been a major force driving U.S. policy. Contrary to common belief and despite the boom brought about by the common market, U.S. investments in Central America remained quite modest compared to those in most other parts of the world. Nevertheless, promotion of a "healthy business climate" in Central America has also heavily influenced U.S. policy choices.

From the U.S. perspective, the effervescent mobilization that has taken place in Central America throughout the second half of this century has been problematical. Although a cause for hope for millions of poor people and a step toward true, socially rooted democracy, mobilization worried some of Central America's entrenched elites. They viewed the process with alarm and responded with state terror to discourage participation. Hearkening to their cries of "Communist subversion," Washington, too, joined the fray. It is interesting to consider why the government of the United States—whose people tenaciously defend their own right to participate in myriad civic and interest organizations—allied itself with the privileged minority in Central America in its campaign against participatory mobilization. Perhaps the most basic reason for this behavior is that U.S. policy—especially in our backyard—often responds more to domestic political fears, misperceptions, and rhetoric in the United States than to careful analysis of the situation in the isthmus.

As a capitalist country, the United States has made consistent efforts to promote capitalism and to protect U.S. business interests both at home and abroad. Policymakers in the White House, State Department, and Congress have tended to formulate national security—especially in Central America and the Caribbean—as much in terms of nurturing business interests and trade as along military and geostrategic lines. Radical and even merely reformist political doctrines, commonly (but often incorrectly) labeled "Communist" by local elites, have usually been viewed as anathema to U.S. interests.

Since the early twentieth century, the impulse to contain this "threat of communism" to the United States and to capitalism has motivated conservative politicians and cowed and intimidated their critics. U.S. politicians fear to be depicted by their adversaries as having "lost ground" to communism. Since World War II, and especially since the Cuban revolution, the fear of Soviet-inspired communism in our backyard has shaped U.S. policy in Central America. Thus even U.S. politicians and policymakers sympathetic to the need for socioeconomic reform and democracy have supported demobilization in Central America when pressures for reform have been labeled "subversive" by Central American elites or by interested U.S. observers.[15]

Much of the U.S. preoccupation with communism in Central America, however, has been tragically ill-founded and largely inappropriate.[16] (We will examine communism in Central America below.) Ill-advised or not, the strong belief in the threat of communism held by most U.S. administrations since the 1940s has been transmitted to Latin American military establishments as part of the doctrine of national security. This doctrine, in turn, has served to justify a systematic and widespread demobilization campaign in Central America.

As taught in war colleges and military training centers around the hemisphere, the doctrine of national security is a product both of U.S. anticommunism and Latin American elaboration. It originated in an elaborate national security apparatus (CIA, National Security Council, and so forth) created in the United States in the late 1940s. In 1950, National Security Council document "NSC-68" described an expanding Communist menace and urged huge increases in military expenditures. Even though George Kennan, the originator of the concept of containment of communism, by then felt that the threat described in "NSC-68" was exaggerated, that document nevertheless became the blueprint for U.S. behavior in the early part of the cold war. Its ideas were spread to Latin America through training programs that the United States expanded or initiated with virtually all of the military establishments of the hemisphere.

Latin America in the 1950s and 1960s was fertile ground for the growth and elaboration of cold war concepts of national security. Though local Communist parties were weak and there were few, if any, obvious external threats to the security of any of the elite-based governments, the privileged classes and their military allies found it very convenient to interpret popular mobilization and protest as subversive and part of a grand, Moscow-controlled plot. In this setting, national security ideas from the United States were quickly adapted, elaborated, and refined into a full-fledged ideology, complete with training centers, native military philosophers, literature, and even meetings held annually by the Latin American Anti-Communist Confederation.

The ideology that emerged was geopolitical. National and international politics were seen as a zero-sum game between communism and the "free world." Whether in foreign or domestic affairs, a loss of territory, allegiance, or influence for one side was seen as a gain for the other. Internal politics became a battlefield. The whole issue of social, economic, and political justice was largely irrelevant or seen as a point of entry for threatening ideological influences.

The national security doctrine was also inherently elitist. Its believers argued that the military is uniquely capable of understanding the national good and, therefore, has the right to run the state and make decisions for society as a whole if, in the judgment of armed forces leaders, civilian politicians are not doing a good enough job. Democracy was directly equated, in the doctrine, with a visceral anticommunism. Accordingly, strange as it may seem, the harshly authoritarian anti-Communist "national security states" created under this ideology were often described by their apologists as "democratic."

All opposition to national security states—and most forms of civilian organization except those on the right—were viewed as subversive and "Communist" or "Communist inspired." The most brutal forms of demobilization and atomization of civilian society were accepted as appropriate. It is an open question whether the extremes of brutality engaged in by the Latin American military were just a product of U.S. advice and assistance gone awry in the hands of local zealots, or were willfully promoted by U.S. personnel. Even if the latter were true, one should still ask whether U.S. presidents and high-level officials were aware of and fully understood the nature of the programs being carried out at lower levels.

Unfortunately, there is ample circumstantial evidence to indicate that U.S. advisers were often deeply involved in promoting Latin American demobilization programs. The armies, national guards, and police of virtually all countries in Latin America received extensive U.S. training, advice, and technical and material assistance during the periods of intense demobilization. The tactics, devices, and patterns of torture, murder, and disappearance employed by security forces and government-sanctioned death squads were remarkably similar from country to country. But more ominous than that, their methods were practically identical to the those used by the U.S. CIA and its operatives in the late 1960s in Vietnam in Operation Phoenix, which, according to the estimates of U.S. and South Vietnamese government officials, featured the execution without trial of between twenty and forty thousand Vietnamese civilians suspected of being part of the support base of the Vietcong.[17]

By the late 1960s and early 1970s, countries such as Brazil, Uruguay, and Guatemala, with the most brutal demobilization programs—complete with death squads, torture, murder, and disappearance—also happened to be ones in which the U.S. Agency for International Development's benignly titled Office of Public Safety had established very close links with local security forces.[18] In the early 1970s these links became a public scandal in the United States and throughout the world. The U.S. Congress investigated the links between U.S. government programs and state-sponsored terror in Latin America. In 1974, Congress formally terminated U.S. police and internal security aid programs and ordered the U.S. Department of State to submit yearly reports on the human rights performance of all states to which the U.S. government supplied aid.

But these measures did not solve the problem. In practice, State Department human rights reports seemed to be influenced and colored more by the status quo–oriented policy goals of Washington than by the objective reality of the countries supposedly being described.[19] And though some of the most objectionable U.S. links were discreetly terminated, state-sponsored terror and direct or indirect U.S. material aid to rights-violating regimes and forces continued. Starting in 1982, the Reagan administration began successfully petitioning an increasingly red-baited Congress to make exceptions to the 1974 prohibition against U.S. assistance to police and internal security forces for El Salvador, Guatemala, and Honduras.

COMMUNISM IN CENTRAL AMERICA

Because so much U.S. policy turns on the question of communism in Central America, it is essential to explore in some detail the meaning and influence of communism. It is true that most Central American insurgents and many of the area's intellectuals find Marxist and, in some cases, Leninist analysis to be useful in understanding the reality around them. Nevertheless, it is misleading to equate the intellectual acceptance of those analytical tools with a commitment to a Communist agenda or political subservience to the Soviet-oriented international Communist movement. Most Central Americans are far too pragmatic and nationalistic to accept such control.

Indeed, Soviet-oriented communist parties have fared poorly in Central America. Communists, socialists, and anarchists—many of them European exiles—influenced Central American intellectual life and labor movements in the early twentieth century. The communists, followers of Karl Marx, received a boost over their leftist competitors because of the Soviet revolution in Russia. Although always targets of repression, communists gained leadership roles in Central American labor movements in the 1930s. The Soviet alliance with the West during World War II gave the region's tiny communist parties and their more successful unions a brief political opening the early 1940s. Although repression of the left resumed in most countries after 1945, brief exceptions occurred in Costa Rica in the 1940s and Guatemala in the early 1950s, where communist elements were junior partners with more conservative parties in government coalitions.

Communist parties fared poorly because of the Soviet practice of limiting the flexibility of local parties to pursue national solutions. Rigid attempts to justify the Stalin-Hitler pact of 1939 discredited communists in Central America, as it did their copartisans in the United States. Soviet insistence in later years that Latin American communists seek accommodation with local dictators tarnished their already poor image. Moscow so restrained local communist parties that, in the 1960s, less patient advocates of sociopolitical reform resigned in disgust and emulated Castro's successful insurgency.

Throughout most of the history of their existence, therefore, the small, Moscow-oriented communist parties of Central America have generally been viewed with mistrust and even contempt by local nationalists—including most other Marxists. Most Central American revolutionaries and intellectuals remember that the Cuban communist party, in its determination to follow Soviet orders to peacefully coexist with Fulgencio Batista, actively opposed Fidel Castro until just a few months before the rebel victory. Costa Ricans are well aware that their local communist party, the region's largest, backed the regime of strongman Rafael Calderón Guardia in his effort to manipulate the 1948 election fraudulently. That episode sparked the civil war of 1948 in which anti-communist rebel social democratic forces were eventually victorious. Since then the Costa Rican communists have never won more than five of the fifty-seven seats in the legislature, and in the last decade their representation has fallen to only three.

Nicaraguans remember that the communist-led labor movement collaborated with the Somoza dictatorship in the 1940s. They recall that the original founders of the FSLN broke away from the pro-Soviet Nicaraguan Socialist party precisely because the latter offered no national solutions to Nicaragua's problems. They also recall that only just before the FSLN victory did the local Communists join the rebel cause. Even in El Salvador, local Communists joined the insurrectionary effort just shortly before the would-be "final offensive" of late 1980 and early 1981. In Nicaragua after the rebel victory, none of the Moscow-oriented Communist parties played more than a peripheral role in the new government. Furthermore, in the election of 1984, the three Communist parties, which had lambasted the FSLN for allegedly selling out the revolution to conservative forces, garnered a pitiful combined vote representing barely 3.8 percent of the total.[20] From 1984 onward, Nicaragua's traditional Communists remained in the opposition, acting more as an irritant to the FSLN than as a source of brotherly support.

In summary, for fifty years, traditional Communist parties in Central America have exercised their greatest influence on labor movements and in brief periods of limited participation in rule in Costa Rica and Guatemala. However, at their strongest they have remained weak, conservative, and generally unpopular.

In comparison to the ideology, intentions, and significance of traditional Communist parties, those issues with respect to Central America's Marxist revolutionary movements are more complex. Most of the principal leaders of Nicaragua's FSLN, El Salvador's FMLN, and Guatemala's URNG are Marxist-Leninists. They share a strong predilection for socialism's emphasis on distributive justice as an answer for the injustices they see in their societies. They have adopted a revolutionary strategy similar to that implemented by Castro in Cuba—guerrilla warfare against regime and armed forces—supplemented by tactical alliances with other social and political forces. Marxist-Leninist rebels have gained popular support and power largely because of the repressiveness of the regimes of Nicaragua, El Salvador, and Guatemala. In Nicaragua, the Sandinistas built their base of popular support and their broad coalition because they became the only viable alternative for reform for individuals and mobilized groups brutally attacked by the Somoza regime. Moderate, centrist options for reform and redress of grievances were foreclosed in El Salvador and Guatemala by brutal repression, driving many to swell the ranks of Marxist-led guerrilla movements.

Marxist-Leninist rebels have regarded Cuba as a friend and ally and received some, albeit limited, Cuban aid in their struggles. Soviet and Eastern bloc assistance to these insurgents has been limited, in keeping with Moscow's skepticism about their chances for success. Once the Sandinistas won power in Nicaragua, however, their links to the Soviet bloc became overtly friendly and Moscow became more cooperative. After the West refused Nicaragua military assistance in 1979, the Sandinistas turned to Cuban and Soviet arms and advice for reorganizing their security forces, all the while anticipating increased U.S. hostility. As U.S. pressure on and antagonism toward Nicaragua mounted in the early and mid-1980s, Nicaragua rapidly strengthened its links to the Eastern bloc to counter an expected invasion, fend off the contras, and replace embargoed Western aid, trade, and credit.

Despite such links of necessity, the Sandinistas have been pragmatic in almost all their policies. Instead of imposing Soviet-style Stalinist centralism and one-party political monopoly of the revolution (as Castro did in Cuba), they remained committed to a mixed economy and political pluralism. Indeed, reforms in 1988 and 1989 have constituted a very strongly market-oriented austerity program and a reaffirmation to build an electoral democracy. Thus, although the Sandinistas have never tried to hide the fact that they find some elements of Marxist and Leninist analysis useful, in their first decade in power they dramatically demonstrated by means of their social, economic, and political policies that they were pragmatic and nationalistic rather than orthodox Communists.

Though Nicaragua's critics make much of the friendly relationship that the Sandinista government developed with the Socialist bloc, that link should be put in perspective. Nicaragua increased, not only its ties to the Eastern bloc, but also ties with many non-Communist regimes. Nicaragua increased trade, aid, and diplomatic relations with governments as disparate as those of Brazil, Canada, Chile, France, Libya, the People's Republic of China, the Scandinavian countries, and Spain. It is true that Nicaragua frequently votes with the USSR in the United Nations. But Nicaragua sometimes abstains (e.g., on votes on Afghanistan and the Korean Airlines shoot down) or votes against the USSR on important UN issues (e.g., the matter of sending a peacekeeping force to Lebanon). Indeed, Vanderlaan's careful examination of Nicaragua's UN voting record from 1979 through 1985 revealed that, although Nicaragua often voted against U.S. positions and with positions backed by the USSR, it agreed almost as often with the majority of Latin American countries. In fact, it was in agreement with Mexico even more frequently than with the USSR.[21] Likewise, although it is true that Nicaragua eventually came to rely almost exclusively on the Socialist bloc as a supplier of military equipment, it should also be remembered that the Sandinistas first asked the United States to help standardize its military equipment and that, in spite of Pentagon endorsement of that idea, the Carter administration—facing a conservative, cold war opponent in the 1980 election campaign—chose the politically safe option of rejecting that request.[22]

Like the Sandinistas, other Central American insurgents appear to be Marxist-Leninists with respect to revolutionary strategy, but pragmatic and nationalistic in concrete policy matters. They recognize that U.S. influence in the isthmus would probably doom any purely Communist regime or government, especially one that allowed Soviet troops or missiles within its borders. Moreover, evidence of the failure of Stalinist political and economic centralism abounds throughout the socialist world in this era of *glasnost* and *perestroika*. To assume that the Sandinistas or Central America's other Marxist rebels would ape failed systems seems unrealistic indeed.

The United States has been intently worried about communism in Central America for four decades, but its concerns about the influence of Communists has often been exaggerated. Communist parties have been weak. Marxist-Leninist guerrillas have not prospered in Honduras and Costa Rica, where regimes were not excessively repressive. The excessive concern of the United States about communism has led to misguided and counterproductive policies—especially in the form of assisting repressive regimes in their campaigns of demobilization.

DEMOBILIZATION IN CENTRAL AMERICA

Though there has been some death squad activity in Honduras since the early 1980s, systematic programs of mass demobilization in Central America have occurred largely where traditional elites were the most powerful and entrenched—

Guatemala, El Salvador, and Nicaragua under the Somozas. In Guatemala and El Salvador, demobilization took the form of state-sponsored terror. In Nicaragua it came in two forms: state-sponsored terror prior to the Sandinista victory of 1979, and U.S.-sponsored contra terror from 1981 onward. Whatever the form, the objective seems to have been constant—to atomize and make docile the ordinary citizenry of Central America. This would promote and facilitate rule by traditional, conservative, pro-U.S. elites or, where necessary, their replacement with friendly, if ineffective, reform-oriented moderates.

The demobilization process—or at least the U.S. link to it—has its longest and most brutal history in Guatemala.[23] It started immediately after the U.S.-sponsored overthrow of elected reformist President Jacobo Arbenz in 1954. Scant hours after Carlos Castillo Armas was imposed as president, a mysterious Committee Against Communism—comprised, in fact, of CIA personnel—seized Guatemalan government, political party, and labor and peasant union documents and began compiling what would soon become known as the Black List. Before the year was out, the names of an estimated 70,000 individuals connected with the former government or with grass-roots or political organizations from that era were included on that list of suspected Communists. That August, the Castillo Armas government issued a Law Against Communism, which declared, among other things, that anyone included on the Black List or "register," as it was formally called, was henceforth banned from public employment and subject to indefinite imprisonment without trial.

Though the Black List ultimately became a death list, this did not happen immediately. The major reason appears to be that the Arévalo and Arbenz governments had been reasonably successful in their attempt to train the Guatemalan security forces to respect human rights. However, in the ensuing decade the U.S. government became increasingly involved in Guatemalan affairs, blocking a return to democracy in the early 1960s and providing ever-escalating doses of security assistance, advice, and training. Meanwhile, previously nonviolent politicians, frustrated by the closing of the democratic option, turned inevitably to open rebellion. By the late 1960s, the insurgents and the opposition in general were labeled "terrorists" and a program of state-sponsored "counterterror," was begun. Featuring the torture, murder, and disappearance of thousands of suspected Communist subversives, this demobilization program was carried out both directly by uniformed security forces or indirectly by government-sanctioned death squads.

By the early 1970s, the rural areas had been "pacified." Terror now moved to the cities, as Gen. Carlos Arana Osorio, former coordinator of the rural pacification effort and now president, began eliminating alleged "subversives" (e.g., party leaders, intellectuals, media persons, and labor organizers) among the urban population. The mid-1970s brought a period of eerie calm. But soon, as corrupt military officers began taking over traditional Indian lands and peaceful Indian protests were met with violence, the whole cycle began again. Indians came to support reemerging guerrilla groups, and the regime responded with unprecedented terror in rural areas, particularly in the early 1980s.

It is true that from the 1977 through the mid-1980s, the United States cut off military aid to the Guatemalan regime because of human rights abuses. However the significance of that fact is more apparent than real. Military training continued, and under the Reagan administration, some U.S. material aid to the Guatemalan military, aid that previously had been listed as military, was relabeled nonmilitary. What is more, Israel—the biggest recipient of U.S. aid in the world—took up much of the slack as a supplier of military equipment and training to the Guatemalans during this period.

It was at the end of the cycle of demobilization of the early 1980s that the Guatemalan military—increasingly isolated from its former allies and faced with looming economic disaster—decided to return at least nominal control of the executive and legislative branches to civilians. Washington approved of the Guatemalan armed forces' plan to allow the formal transfer of power to a civilian president and congress and energetically supported the election of 1985. The Reagan administration had been frustrated by the refusal of the U.S. Congress to authorize funds for direct military aid to the unsavory Guatemalan regime and clearly saw the need to improve the image of that regime.

In Guatemala's transition to civilian rule since Vinicio Cerezo Arévalo's inauguration in January 1986, however, there has been much less than meets the eye. Moderate Cerezo had to promise before taking office not to prosecute military personnel guilty of human rights violations. Although rights abuses have continued, no one has yet been prosecuted, and Cerezo has not allowed the International Red Cross to open a Guatemalan office. Moreover, powerful economic groups successfully fought proposed socioeconomic reforms, and some business interests conspired unsuccessfully with right-wing radicals within the military to overthrow the regime. Thus, throughout his administration, Cerezo had only very limited power. Needed reforms did not take place. Rising popular discontent was met once again with an escalation of state-sponsored terror. In the absence of any real movement toward a genuine redistribution of power, the prospects for democracy in Guatemala appeared bleak.

As we noted earlier, El Salvador, too, suffered a process of demobilization in the 1970s and 1980s in which the United States played a major role. Admittedly, demobilization was nothing new to that country. Tremendous violence against poor people had been carried out by the military on behalf of Salvador's elite in the early 1930s, when the effects of the world depression had set off mass-based pressure for reform. The "Slaughter" (*la Matanza*), had taken the lives of around 30,000 people. But the violence of the late twentieth century achieved new levels of cruelty and carnage that were estimated by normally cautious U.S. media sources as having exacted a toll by 1988 of at least 70,000 dead and 500,000 displaced.[24]

The demobilization campaign was clearly a response to the unusual burst of mobilization of the early to mid-1970s. At first the campaign was carried out at relatively low, but nonetheless well-publicized, levels by the military regimes of Arturo Molina and Humberto Romero. The international attention focused on these abuses, however, made it impossible for the normal flow of U.S. military assistance to continue to the regime in the early part of the vocally human rights–oriented Carter administration. However, when the Somoza regime was overthrown by revolutionaries in Nicaragua, a sense of urgency swept Washington and a decision was made almost immediately that military aid to El Salvador, the next country likely to "fall," would have to be resumed. Such an apparent reversal of policy, it was suggested, could be made palatable only if a civilian-military, reformist government were to come to power. Washington viewed the most acceptable civilians as the Christian Democrats.[25] Meanwhile, reformist elements in the Salvadoran armed forces, private sector, and opposition parties that shared Washington's concern with blocking a revolutionary outcome began plotting to oust General Romero.

The coup d'état that would largely fulfill the wishes of both the U.S. government and these Salvadoran groups took place on October 10, 1979. The civilians who filled positions on the first civilian-military junta and in the government following the coup were reformist social democrats, Christian Democrats, and unaffiliated moderates. But the junta was rapidly transformed. Conservative interests blocked the reformists, and human rights abuses by the armed forces actually accelerated. Less than three months later, the first civilians resigned in protest over the powerlessness of their role. Their positions were then filled by individuals from the conservative wing of the Christian Democratic movement, and hard-liners from within the military replaced moderate officers in the junta.

Meanwhile, U.S. military aid to El Salvador was resumed immediately after the October coup. Despite much fanfare about moderation and reform, torture, murder, and disappearance soared to heights never seen during the previous two military regimes.[26] In February 1980, U.S. Chargé d'affairs James Cheek met with Christian Democrats in the government and urged that El Salvador institute what he called "a clean counter-insurgency war." This war could be facilitated, he argued, by giving the armed forces much greater leeway in dealing with suspected subversives. Though some Christian Democrats were cool to the idea, Cheek's suggestions were fully implemented in March through the promulgation of Decree 155, which imposed a harsh state of siege and gave the military draconian powers in dealing with civilians.[27]

Throughout the rest of the Carter administration and for several years into the Reagan period, grass-roots party and interest organizations were systematically dismantled, with almost total disregard for human rights. In public statements, U.S. officials blamed the tens of thousands of killings, first, on "violence of the right and the left," and later, when that rhetoric wore thin, on the work of "right-wing death squads." The government and even the military were falsely depicted in the United States as composed of moderates earnestly trying to bring historically endemic violence under control.

Eventually pressure mounted in the U.S. Congress to reduce the shocking level of human rights abuse in El Salvador. In 1982 and 1983, with congressional approval for further military aid hanging in the balance, the Reagan administration sent a series of emissaries to San Salvador to pressure the Salvadoran government and military and to curtail the killings.[28] As a result, for the next several years—though the aerial bombardment of civilian populations in rebel-controlled areas actually escalated—the so-called death squad killings declined. But by then, the demobilization had been largely accomplished. The leadership and much of the membership of most grass-roots party and interest organizations to the left of the conservative minority of Christian Democrats who had stuck with José Napoleón Duarte had been killed, driven underground, or forced into exile. The two opposition newspapers had been terrorized into extinction. And the Catholic church, having suffered the martyrdom of Archbishop Romero and numerous clergy and lay activists, had been cowed into a much less critical posture.

Against this background of terror, elections were held in 1982, 1984, 1988, and 1989. The electorate on those occasions did what people normally do in elections held amidst a demobilization campaign—they voted overwhelmingly for what they perceived to be the focal point of power. In 1982, with terror at its apogee, parties of the extreme right won the bulk of the votes and a majority of seats in the constituent assembly. U.S. pressure brought a slackening in the violence, and Washington essentially forced the right-dominated constituent assembly to appoint a moderate figurehead, Alvaro Magaña, as interim president. In 1984, with terror somewhat curtailed, Salvadorans cast their presidential vote for the U.S.-funded and endorsed center-right Christian Democratic candidate, José Napoleón Duarte, who, as reformist ex-mayor of San Salvador, was a popular figure. But Duarte's ability to rule effectively and promote reforms was completely hamstrung by the constitution written by the rightist-dominated constituent assembly and by the overweening power of the armed forces.

By the time of the 1988 legislative elections, President Duarte was dying of cancer and his administration had proven to be as corrupt as it was powerless. In the wake of the signing of the Esquipulas peace accord in August 1987, death squad terror once again escalated as the right attempted to sabotage its implementation, at least in El Salvador. Not surprisingly, the voters in the 1988 legislative and 1989 presidential elections abandoned the Christian Democrats and moved sharply to the right. With the election of ARENA candidate Alfredo Cristiani as president in March 1989, prospects for real democracy and social reconciliation in El Salvador in the foreseeable future appeared very bleak.

Nicaragua, as we noted above, suffered demobilization both before and after the revolutionary victory of 1979. The first wave was conducted by the Somoza regime from 1975 through July 1979. The second was carried out by U.S.-backed contras from 1981 through 1989. Together, these demobilizing activities had resulted in the death of over 75,000 people as of 1989; around 50,000 in the earlier period and more than 26,000 in the latter. Though some of the deaths counted here were those of combatants, the bulk were civilians.

The barbarity of the Somoza regime in its efforts to pacify Nicaragua and perpetuate itself in power is so well documented that it need not be belabored here.[29] What is important, however, is the close relationship that existed between the U.S. government and Somoza's National Guard. In 1979 Somoza's guard had more U.S.-trained personnel than any other military establishment in Latin America, not just proportionally, but absolutely.[30] More Nicaraguan officers and men had been trained in the United States or at the U.S.-run School of the Americas in Panama than officers of any other Latin American country, including a comparative giant like Brazil, with almost forty times the population of Nicaragua. What is more, U.S. military aid and the training of Nicaraguan military personnel ceased fully only after guard massacres of civilians in several cities in September 1978. As in the case of Guatemala, Israel immediately picked up the slack, supplying the guard with badly needed automatic weapons and other military equipment. In addition, U.S. military attachés remained in Nicaragua until a few months before Somoza fell, and, as we noted earlier, the CIA used cargo planes disguised with Red Cross markings to spirit many of Somoza's officer corps into exile in the confused first days of the rebel victory.

The instrument the Reagan administration chose for the demobilization of Nicaragua under the revolution was the contras. Conceived and originally funded as result of National Security Decision Directive Number 17 signed by President Reagan in late November 1981, the original contra army was comprised almost entirely of Somoza National Guard officers and men. Though the lower ranks of the contra army eventually came to be composed mainly of youth who had never served in the guard, the bulk of the contra officers corps continued to be comprised of ex-Guardia officers throughout.[31]

The tactics of demobilization employed by the counterrevolutionaries and their U.S. handlers shifted over time from 1981 through 1989. At first, there was a naive belief that the contras might serve as a catalyst around which disgruntled Nicaraguans would rally and overthrow their government. Some in the CIA clearly believed that the contras could serve as authentic and ultimately successful guerrillas. However, when the contras in their first two years followed their Guardia instincts and behaved like crude terrorists rather than like a guerrilla vanguard, the CIA became alarmed and commissioned its famous manual for contra officers, *Psychological Operations in Guerrilla Warfare.*[32] Although criticized in the United States for its instructions on the selective assassination of government officials and for its cold-blooded ideas on the hiring of professional gunmen to create martyrs from among the opposition at antigovernment rallies, the overall thrust of the document is actually one of relative moderation. The manual was intended to teach the contras to focus their terror narrowly and intelligently. Though selective assassination was advocated, the contras were not to terrorize the population as

DEMOBILIZATION. Scene at a Somoza National Guard body dump on the outskirts of Managua in the summer of 1979 (photo courtesy of *Barricada*). Views of two regime/death squad body dumps in El Salvador: "La Puerta del Diablo," about three miles southeast of the capital, May 1982, and "El Playón," approximately twenty miles west of the capital, March 1983 (photos and copyright by Tommie Sue Montgomery, 1982, 1983).

a whole. Instead they were to behave respectfully and thus win a civilian base, which, in the long run, would help them isolate and defeat the Sandinistas.

A few contra units actually seem to have followed the tactically sound CIA advice. Pockets of civilian support developed in remote, lightly populated regions in the central departments of Boaco and Chontales and in the north. But by and large, the contras failed to achieve the discipline desired by the CIA and behaved quite brutally.[33] This, coupled with their widespread image in Nicaragua as U.S. mercenaries and as the direct linear descendants of Somoza's hated Guardia Nacional, meant that by the mid-1980s it was clear to most informed observers that the contras could never rally enough popular support to overthrow their government.

After the mid-1980s, the contras became steadily less successful militarily and more isolated from the population. As CIA awareness of their limitations for toppling the FSLN from power grew, contra tactics changed. The idea of spawning a guerrilla-led popular insurrection against the Sandinistas was abandoned. The new strategy was to employ terror and sabotage to disrupt the economy, government, and social life of the nation. Terror and sabotage against human and material infrastructure—which, in fact, had been practiced by most contra units from the start—became the principal and most effective instrument of demobilization. Contra units attacked (1) rural social service infrastructure such as schools, health clinics, day care centers, and government food program storage facilities; (2) economic infrastructure such as cooperative or state farms, sawmills, tobacco drying facilities, bridges, power lines, and trucks; (3) cooperative or grass-roots organizations such as the small farmers association (UNAG); and (4) persons employed by, associated with, or receiving benefits from those three. In addition, starting in the mid-1980s, the contras began planting powerful antitank mines on remote rural roads, an action resulting in the destruction of vehicles of all types and the death and mutilation of hundreds of civilians. The purposes of these activities seem to have been to destroy the rural economy of Nicaragua and hence to inflict economic hardship on all citizens of that agriculturally dependent country, to cut off the delivery of innovative government social services to remote rural populations, to disrupt grass-roots organizations such as the peasants'(UNAG) and rural workers' (ATC) associations and village CDSs, and to force heavy government defense spending in order to undermine social services, cause inflation, and seed popular discontent with the Sandinistas.

The terror and sabotage campaign of the late 1980s bore fruit. Social services were curtailed throughout the country and cut off completely in some remote rural areas. Nicaraguan agricultural output declined, the economy went sour, and inflation went through the roof. Membership in grass-roots organizations, which had climbed early in the contra war (1982–1984), stagnated in 1985 and 1986. Mass organization membership then declined sharply in 1987 and 1988, as discontent over the economic situation rose and finding ways to make ends meet occupied more and more of the time of ordinary Nicaraguans. As opposition protests and union resistance to austerity programs grew in 1986–1987, the government itself repressed its opponents and curtailed civil liberties. In sum, the use of the contras as a direct and indirect device for demobilization in Nicaragua was showing some success by the late 1980s.

Further evidence can be seen in the results of a June 1988 opinion survey of 1,123 Managua adults, conducted under the auspices of the Interamerican Research Center, an international polling firm that runs polls throughout Central America.[34] When asked to name the party with which they identified, slightly less than 30 percent chose the FSLN. Clearly, Sandinista popularity had declined since the party's 63 percent showing in the 1984 election. What is both intriguing and a telling comment on Reagan administration attempts to portray its Nicaragua policy as concerned with promoting democracy, however, is that in the same opinion survey, the opposition parties (perhaps seen by Nicaraguans as somehow associated with U.S. policy) registered a *combined* identification rate of only 10 percent. Furthermore, U.S. policy was opposed by 85 percent of those questioned. In other words, Reagan's promotion of surrogate war in Nicaragua had led to declining support for the Sandinistas. At the same time, however, it had failed spectacularly to generate support for other political parties—indeed, the public appeared badly alienated from the opposition.

As this was written in early 1989, the U.S. counterrevolutionary strategy for Nicaragua was in complete disarray. The contras had entered into a period of severe and probably irreversible decline. Their on-again, off-again, U.S. military funding, which eventually totaled over $400 million, ran out in 1988. The Central American peace agreement signed in August 1987 led to their ejection from Costa Rica and made it harder for them to keep their camps in Honduras. In March 1988 the besieged contras negotiated a temporary cease-fire with the Nicaraguan government and entered further negotiations toward a full settlement. Although those talks broke down in mid-1988, most contras withdrew to Honduras and began to disband, much to the dismay of their U.S. backers. In February 1989, a further accord among the Central American presidents to dismantle contra camps in Honduras appeared to be the final nail in the contras' coffin.

CONCLUSION

U.S. policy in Central America has been not only ill advised but, more important, counterproductive to the interests of the United States as well as to those of the peoples of the isthmus. Responding more to domestic political pressures in the United States and to outmoded conceptions of security and economic interests than to the concrete reality of Central America, U.S. policy has jousted with a vastly overblown threat of communism for more than four decades. As a result, the United States has sided with a tiny exploitative elite in demobilizing strategies that have taken the lives of between 200,000 and 300,000 people. In the case of Nicaragua, U.S. policy has actually helped increase Soviet influence.

Furthermore, U.S. policy has done violence to both the concept and the practice of democracy in the region. Power and democracy go hand in hand. As long as the vast majority of the peoples of Central America are kept powerless by being deprived of avenues of participation, U.S. security will be undermined by turmoil in the isthmus and true democracy will remain an empty dream.

10

CENTRAL AMERICA AND ITS UNCERTAIN FUTURE

Forecasting the future is never an easy task, especially when the subject is a region in flux, such as Central America. Both of the authors of this volume have been "burned" at one time or another in specific predictions about that region.[1]

Accordingly, it is with humility and some trepidation that we now venture to predict. In this spirit, we will try to avoid prognostication based on recently emerging trends and instead root our predictions in those clear patterns and apparent truths identified in earlier chapters as having emerged out of decades or centuries of Central American history. Though we will occasionally express what we feel should be done, we will try not to blur the boundary between normative prescription and historically based prediction.

PROSPECTS FOR PEACE

The problem of reducing and ultimately eliminating violent conflict in Central America can be viewed from both a short- and a long-term perspective. In the long run, lasting peace will be achieved only through the creation of more just societies, ones in which economic disparities are reduced and something approximating genuine democracy, based on avenues for free and meaningful participation by the majority of the citizenry, becomes a reality. The history of the five major Central American countries, as reviewed in earlier chapters of this volume, makes this point quite clear. The countries plagued by endemic violence—Guatemala, El Salvador, and Nicaragua—are precisely those that not only suffer from tremendous economic inequities but also have been ruled traditionally by powerful elites that have stubbornly refused to allow effective grass-roots participation or meaningful social and economic reform. The other two countries—Costa Rica and Honduras—though very different from each other, enjoy relative peace precisely because they were free of one or both of the violence-producing characteristics of their neighbors.

Since the time of the Spanish Conquest, Costa Rica was set apart from the others by the fact that it had a relatively more just society, higher levels of meaningful participation, and a normally flexible elite willing to bend and make accommodations when necessary. Out of this mixture, genuine democracy and responsible government eventually emerged quite naturally. Honduras, though even poorer and more socially backward than its three immediate neighbors, perhaps for that reason never developed the type of unbending and cruelly exploitative elite that emerged in Guatemala, El Salvador, and Nicaragua. In this sense, backwardness may have been a blessing, for instead of using violence and repression as the preferred tactic for dealing with grass-roots mobilization and accompanying demands for social justice, the relatively weak elites of Honduras normally have been forced to rely on tolerance and the rhetoric of reform. Though meaningful democracy is still a distant dream for Honduras, violence at least has been kept at relatively low levels.

If we are correct in these historical observations, it would seem reasonable for us to predict that Costa Rica is likely to continue to enjoy domestic peace, Guatemala and El Salvador will probably undergo continuing conflict or periodic spasms of violence, whereas Honduras and Nicaragua could go either way. Let us take a closer look.

Costa Rica

The probability of violent conflict in Costa Rica would appear to be remote. Elite flexibility, a participatory democratic system, and a relatively egalitarian society make violence both unattractive and unlikely. We should warn, however, that nothing is certain. Should these conditions change, violence might well emerge. If, for instance, the already fragile economy were to deteriorate abruptly and popular unrest were to increase, the elites might be tempted to use force rather than compromise. The potential instrument of that force has been emerging in recent years. Technically, Costa Rica abolished its military in the 1940s. However, the Reagan administration, intent on pressuring the Sandinistas, persuaded the Costa Rican government to modernize and strengthen its Civil Guard. To date, U.S. military aid has trained small border units and increased the Civil Guard's firepower and equipment. The security forces remain small by Central American standards, and Costa Rican observers report little apprehension about an impending militarization.[2] However, if the absence of a military establishment in the past has been a factor favorable to democracy in Costa Rica, any military resurgence should be viewed with concern.

Conceivably, the domestic tranquility of Costa Rica might also be threatened by events taking place beyond its borders. In the now unlikely event that the Sandinistas are overthrown, hundreds of thousands of former government personnel and grass-roots organization members would likely flee, weapons in hand, into neighboring countries to avoid the inevitable bloody demobilization that a post-

Sandinista regime would have to carry out in order to govern. The implications for Costa Rica need not be spelled out. Indeed, this specter is probably one important reason why the Costa Rican government, which is certainly no friend of the Sandinistas, has long played a central role in the search for peace.

Honduras

The future of Honduras is less clear. It has only one of the two characteristics that seem to be most essential for domestic tranquility. That characteristic, the relative flexibility of its elite class, has contributed significantly to its largely nonviolent past. The other ingredient, social justice, is missing. Honduras is the poorest of the five countries we have studied. It has the worst social conditions. That those conditions have not generated the levels of unrest that would lead to widespread violence is due largely to the willingness of the elite to allow, rather than repress, grass-roots organizations and to pay lip service to, rather than openly resist, programs of reform. If the already bad economic situation were to deteriorate even more and the elites (backed by their burgeoning U.S.-supplied military) were to opt for force rather than accommodation, the spiral of violence might well begin. However, if past patterns of elite flexibility continue, the levels of violence exhibited in neighboring countries may be avoided for some time. Honduras has developed a disturbing pattern of death squad killings and security force human rights abuses since the early 1980s. These suggest at least some potential for the emergence of a terrorist demobilization campaign like those witnessed in Guatemala and El Salvador. In the long run, the best guarantee for peace in Honduras, as elsewhere, is social justice. For the poorest of Central America's countries, the possibility of genuine improvement in that realm seems remote.

Nicaragua

Ironically, Nicaragua in the first several years after the Sandinista revolution had embarked on precisely the type of change needed to bring true stability. As we noted earlier, the new government had encouraged and supported grass-roots organizations, had responded positively to their demands, and had institutionalized input from such organizations into decisionmaking at all levels. With the volunteer labor of members of the grass-roots organizations, the government had also embarked on a variety of programs in education, health, food distribution, social security, agrarian reform, and housing that had begun to narrow the social gulf between rich and poor. Finally, opposition was generally tolerated, within fairly broad limits, and state-sponsored terror—a fact of life in Guatemala and El Salvador—had become a thing of the past in Nicaragua. Accordingly, on their various visits to Nicaragua during that period, the authors observed an open and peaceful society in which the possibility of civil conflict seemed much reduced.

The end to that brief period of tranquility was externally imposed. Though a handful of right-wing guerrilla bandits had harassed the country prior to 1981, smuggling cattle and killing literacy crusaders, they were a trivial nuisance. After Ronald Reagan was inaugurated in Washington, however, the situation changed radically. A U.S.-organized, U.S.-trained, U.S.-equipped, and U.S.-advised contra army was disgorged into Nicaragua from across both of its borders, and millions of dollars of CIA and National Endowment for Democracy funding were pumped into non-Sandinista media, party, and interest groups in order to maximize domestic internal polarization. The result was considerable death and destruction, a rapid reversal of previously improving economic conditions, and the imposition of various state-of-emergency restrictions on civil and political rights.

As this was being written, it appeared that the contra war was winding down. An agreement signed in El Salvador at the February 1989 Central American presidential summit provided for the dismantling of contra bases in Honduras. Even so, the damage the war had already inflicted on the economy, daily life, social programs, institutions, intraelite trust, and the human rights situation in that troubled country would, at best, take years to mend. Accordingly, the possibility of returning to the type of domestic peace that obtained in the period prior to the contra war was by no means certain.

Guatemala and El Salvador

The prospects for the emergence of long-term peace in El Salvador and Guatemala are very dim. Both of the conditions that, in any society, seem to be important for domestic tranquility—a relatively egalitarian social structure (or public policy that at least attenuates the worst effects of poverty) and a flexible elite willing to allow and accommodate grass-roots participation—are starkly absent in those two countries. It is doubtful that the formal holding of elections during, or in the wake of, bloody programs of demobilization will contribute in the long run to lasting domestic tranquility, even if those elections are technically clean, as they were in Guatemala in 1985. Regardless of the formal nature of government, the old and violent cycles of protest-mobilization-repression, protest-mobilization-repression, are likely to continue in both countries unless a firmer foundation for social peace is established.

Having discussed the long-term prospects for peace, let us now turn to policies or procedures that might end the current situation of violent civil strife in several countries, at least in the short run. One tactic for short-term peace that has been employed in various parts of the world, including Guatemala and El Salvador, is to try by the use of state terror to demobilize the opposition completely. It is true that if they are willing to be sufficiently brutal, governments can sometimes so terrorize a dissatisfied civilian population as to achieve temporary peace. The Salvadoran *Matanza* of 1932 provides a grisly Central American example: it politically demobilized a whole generation of Salvadorans. However, we would argue that such a tactic is not only morally reprehensible but also extremely short-sighted; peace achieved in this way is seldom permanent.

We believe that the best means for the reduction of tensions and the achievement of peace is negotiation leading to compromise and accommodation. We are not alone in this belief. Almost immediately after the Reagan administration came to power and began issuing bellicose statements about Central America, certain European and Latin American countries started calling for negotiated settlements of the conflicts there, rather than military confrontation. The response of the Reagan administration was a secret, but subsequently leaked, National Security Council planning document for Central America, which, among other things, observed, "We continue to have serious difficulties with U.S. public and congressional opinion, which jeopardize our ability to stay the course. International opinion, particularly in Europe and Mexico, continues to work against our policies." Later, under the category of "policy implications," the document declared that the administration should "step up efforts to co-opt [the] negotiations issue to avoid congressionally mandated negotiations, which would work against our interests."[3]

From then on, the United States took care to appear interested in negotiations (even to the extent of holding formal bilateral talks with Nicaragua in Manzanillo, Mexico, during the election year of 1984). It did so, however, while actually seeking to prevent negotiations between Nicaragua and other parties to the conflict and, where that failed, working to block the implementation of emerging settlements. Accordingly, the only genuine impetus for a peaceful settlement came from within Latin America.[4] In early 1983, representatives of Colombia, Mexico, Panama, and Venezuela met on the Panamanian island of Contadora to begin work on the drafting of a comprehensive peace plan for Central America. By early fall of 1984, the Contadora Group in consultation with the governments of Central America had produced an "Act for Peace and Cooperation in Central America." It provided for democratic and representative government, honest elections, national reconciliation, a prohibition of foreign military bases and support for irregular armed forces in other countries, a reduction in armaments, and a withdrawal of foreign military advisers. It was reported that "officials from Honduras, Guatemala, El Salvador and Costa Rica [had] indicated their Governments would be willing to sign the treaty."[5] And while expressing doubt that the Sandinistas would sign, U.S. Secretary of State George Shultz called it "an important step forward."[6] However, when Nicaragua then announced that it had decided to sign the act "in its totality, immediately and without modifications,"[7] the United States and its four Central American allies did a quick about-face, denouncing the treaty as inadequate and offering voluminous new suggestions for revision.

Henceforth, the United States would continued to endorse publicly the Contadora and other peace efforts, while at the same time working assiduously behind the scenes to present obstacles to the actual implementation of an accord. Though the outcome of the September 1984 initiative and the U.S. opposition to it were disappointing, the Contadora Group did not give up. By 1986, the group produced a second draft treaty, one that included many of the amendments proposed by U.S. allies in Central America when they had rejected the 1984 act. In addition, the Contadora Group enlisted the backing of a second quartet of Latin American countries, which became known as the Contadora Support Group—Argentina, Brazil, Peru, and Uruguay. The eight countries involved represented over 80 percent of Latin America's population. After much arduous negotiation, Nicaragua agreed to accept the 1986 document, provided that the United States, the major promotor of the contras, would also sign. Washington refused, arguing, in essence, that it was not a party to the conflicts.

In late 1986 the Iran-Contra scandal broke, plunging U.S. Central American policy into disarray and seeding grave doubts among Central American leaders about the future of U.S. actions, especially the administration's ability to keep funding the contra war. In the resultant vacuum of U.S. initiative, the peace process sputtered on into 1987. Early that year, president Oscar Arias Sánchez of Costa Rica began drafting a peace proposal. Late that summer Ronald Reagan, anxious to renew military aid to the contras and to lift U.S. policy out of its doldrums, enlisted Speaker of the House Jim Wright as a cosponsor of a "peace plan" for Central America. The provisions of this bipartisan proposal were so clearly unacceptable to the Sandinistas that many informed observers recognized it for what it apparently was, a deliberately foredoomed proposal that, upon inevitable rejection by Managua, could be used as a pretext to finally unite a bipartisan majority in Congress behind support for lethal contra aid.

The Wright-Reagan plan was announced just days before the presidents of Central America were scheduled to meet in Esquipulas, Guatemala, to discuss the Arias plan. Proposed by the United States virtually without prior consultation with the Central American countries or the contras, the Wright-Reagan plan apparently so alarmed and offended the Central Americans that it gave them the final incentive they needed to sign their own agreement. On August 7, 1987, all five presidents of Central America initialed a revised version of the Arias proposal, the Procedure for the Establishment of a Strong and Lasting Peace in Central America (also known variously as the Central American Peace Accord, the Esquipulas accord, or the Arias Peace Plan). With provisions designed to promote national reconciliation, cessation of hostilities, democratization, free elections, cessation of assistance to irregular forces, the nonuse of national territory for irregular forces attacking other states, international and internal verification, the 1987 peace accord caught the Reagan administration temporarily off balance, won worldwide acclaim, and earned Oscar Arias a Nobel Peace Prize. Speaker Wright quickly broke ranks with the White House and enthusiastically endorsed the Central American accord, thus undercutting the White House ploy for contra aid.

As it turned out, the peace accord was much easier to sign than to implement. None of the countries was willing or able to carry out fully all of its provisions. And the major outside actor, the U.S. government, took a variety of steps—seeking Congressional support for more contra aid, increasing daily aerial supply drops to the contras inside Nicaragua, pressuring Honduras to continue to allow the contras to operate from inside its territory—that appeared deliberately designed to sabotage the peace process.

The peace plan itself included provisions for the international monitoring of its own implementation. An International Verification and Follow-up Commission composed of representatives of the United Nations, the Organization of American States, all eight countries of the Contadora and Contadora Support groups, as well as the five Central American countries, were to monitor the process and meet and report their findings in January 1988. Unfortunately, there was one fatal flaw: the five Central American countries (all of them parties to the conflict and four of them allies of the major foreign actor in the regional drama) had reserved to themselves the right to veto any objectionable aspect of the report. Just prior to the plenary meeting of the commission, the representatives of the UN, the OAS, and the eight Contadora and Contadora Support countries to the International Verification and Follow-up Commission met and unanimously approved an initial report that tended to be far more critical of the U.S. government and its four Central American allies than it was of Nicaragua. Among other things, the draft prepared by the Verification Commission included the statement (Paragraph 21):

> Despite the appeals made by the Central American Presidents, it remains the policy and practice of the United States Government to provide assistance, particularly military assistance, to irregular forces operating against the Government of Nicaragua. The definitive termination of such assistance is still an indispensable prerequisite for the success of peace efforts and the success of the Procedure as a whole.[8]

There were also statements that Nicaragua's compliance with key provisions of the Esquipulas accord had been greater than the compliance of other isthmian nations, especially Guatemala, El Salvador, and Honduras.

Such conclusions, of course, embarrassed the other Central American regimes and angered the Reagan administration, which was trying to discredit and remove the Sandinista government. Therefore, smarting under the commission's criticism and under heavy U.S. pressure, El Salvador and Honduras demanded, as a condition for continuation of the accord at the January 1988 Central American presidential summit, elimination of the International Verification and Follow-Up Commission. For over a year each nation would verify its own compliance—tantamount to no supervision. The draft of the commission's offending report was quashed and a version much more acceptable to the United States and its Central American allies (i.e., less favorable to Nicaragua) was ultimately published.[9]

Though partly emasculated by its own authors, the Central American peace effort continued into 1989. One interesting development connected with it was eventual direct negotiations between the Sandinistas and the contras. Technically, the government of Nicaragua was not obliged to negotiate directly with the contras. The accord stipulated only that efforts would be made to work out cease-fires, and that "the corresponding governments will initiate a dialogue with all unarmed internal political opposition groups and with those who have availed themselves of the amnesty."[10] Nevertheless, from the start, the Reagan administration loudly trumpeted the false notion that the peace accord required Nicaragua to negotiate directly with the contras, something that the Sandinistas had consistently refused to do. The U.S. media never contradicted that distortion. Heavy political and diplomatic pressure, both in the United States and abroad, was mustered behind the demand for contra-Sandinista talks.

Thus the Sandinistas found themselves in the curious position of having to take a major step beyond the accord in order not to appear to the U.S. public and Congress (then being pressed for more aid to the contras) to be in fundamental violation of that agreement. Accordingly, the Sandinistas agreed first to indirect negotiations and finally, in 1988, to direct talks. One of these, which took place in Sapoá, Nicaragua, actually resulted in a temporary cease-fire agreement. Again the Reagan administration was caught off balance, this time by the surprisingly independent behavior of its own surrogates. Moderate contra leaders who were inclined towards peace were berated by their CIA handlers, and the precipitous slide towards peace was stopped only after several hundred contras, including the leaders who had promoted the peace effort, were removed from leadership and staff positions worldwide.[11] The contra negotiating team was also reconstituted to include the head of the most hard-line faction.

As of early 1989, presidents or representatives of the five Central American countries were still meeting periodically in an effort to keep the peace process alive. At foreign ministers' and presidential meetings in January and February, new international verification procedures (mobile third-party observer teams with free access throughout the region) were agreed upon, as was a decision to close Honduran contra bases. Nicaragua agreed to further domestic political reforms, including electoral law changes and to an earlier date for the 1990 elections.[12]

As this was being written, the most unpredictable variable was the role that would be played by the new Bush administration. Prior to the election of the new U.S. president in November 1988, both authors had been told by well-placed, informed sources that the new team in Washington would likely pursue diplomatic rather than military solutions in Central America. However, the fact that, in February 1989, Bush succumbed to conservative pressure and nominated procontra activist, Bernard Aronson, to be assistant secretary of state for Inter-American affairs did not seem to bode well. Not propitious either were the administration's skeptical reaction to the agreements reached by the Central American presidents the same month and its defiance of that accord when, in March, it persuaded Congress to extend "humanitarian" aid for the contras in their Honduran base camps. One thing, however, was clear: The peace process was not likely to succeed without U.S. support, or at least U.S. acquiescence.

PROSPECTS FOR ECONOMIC, SOCIAL, AND POLITICAL DEVELOPMENT

In the late 1980s, the possibilities of economic growth, human development, and meaningful democracy in Central America were being held hostage by the continuing turmoil in that region. Over the previous decade, the devastation and other expenses of the war had caused a significant decline in per capita income and a diversion of public resources away from social programs in those countries most affected. What is more, civil and political liberties had been restricted in the name of wartime national emergency. Logically, then, a continuation of the armed conflicts appeared likely to cause further decay and deterioration in these conditions.

But even if peace were achieved in the short run, the problems facing Central American development were likely to continue to be immense. Progress toward their solution would depend on an understanding on the part of important internal and external actors that social, economic, and political factors are interrelated. For instance, our examination of the economic evolution of Central America would indicate that economic growth per se is not always a good thing. Poorly distributed growth, such as occurred in the region in the 1960s and early 1970s, can be socially and politically disruptive and ultimately destabilizing. In grossly unequal societies such as those of northern Central America, income tends to be highly concentrated—especially during bursts of growth. It is essential, therefore, that governing elites have both the will and the power to manage the process of growth in such a way as to prevent its impact from being socially regressive and politically destabilizing.

In Central America, socially distributive programs in health, education, food distribution, agrarian reform, and so forth could reduce the worst effects of poverty. However they can be implemented only through a reduction of military spending and the termination of the wasteful destruction of public and private infrastructure occasioned by armed conflict. Priority in the allocation of scarce public and international credit should be placed much more heavily than in the past on assistance to small producers, peasant cooperatives, and worker-owned enterprises and on labor-intensive activities geared toward production for local or regional markets. Though the extension of credit to large-scale agro- or urban-industrial activities oriented largely toward export production is financially safer and easier to manage, it is socially regressive and politically destabilizing if allowed to predominate, as it has in the past.

There are also important political reforms that must be undertaken. Historically, the most basic political problem in Central America has been the lack of concern on the part of local elites for the plight of the poor and the problem of reducing the region's most debilitating inequities. This indifference is probably related to the essential powerlessness of the poor majority. As we noted in Chapter 9, benefits in any political system tend to flow to groups and individuals in rough proportion to the power they can bring to bear on that system. Balanced economic growth capable of propelling true social development is not likely to take place without a more equitable distribution of political power. As it is now, the elites that control countries such as Guatemala and El Salvador are the same groups that benefit from the social and economic system as it is. Authentic democracy, involving effective citizen participation—that is, real input by the poor majority—is essential to meaningful economic and social development. The holding of technically clean and periodic elections, although useful and important as one tool in building such participation, is simply not sufficient to represent the needs of the majority to entrenched power holders.

In making predictions about the intertwined phenomena of economic, social, and political development, we conclude with observations that are analogous to those we made about the prospects for peace. The future of balanced development is somewhat brighter in Costa Rica, with its relatively more egalitarian society and more participatory political system, than it is in El Salvador and Guatemala, with their highly unequal societies, intransigent elites, and strikingly nonparticipatory political systems. Prospects for Honduras and Nicaragua, though for different reasons, lie somewhere between those of the Costa Rican and Guatemalan/Salvadoran cases.

Though the most backward in economic and social development, Honduras has the advantage of having an elite that, because of its relative weakness, has traditionally allowed some grass-roots participation. Whether such participation will grow and become institutionalized to the point of effecting social and economic development is an open question.

Nicaragua, prior to about 1984, when the contra war and the U.S. program of economic destabilization began taking their toll, was making significant strides in all three areas of development. Agrarian reform, loans to small and cooperative producers, and other economic measures in line with what the Sandinistas called "the logic of the majority" had contributed to Nicaragua's modest economic growth in the four years from 1980 through 1983, a period in which the economies of all the other Central American countries had declined markedly.[13] Social development in the form of significant strides in health, education, agrarian reform, and food distribution programs and advances in political participation and empowerment brought about through the new emphasis on adult literacy and the encouragement of grass-roots organizations were also changing the previously elite-dominated society. But by 1989, the damage and exigencies of war had significantly reversed virtually all of these advances and the future of Nicaraguan social, economic, and political development had become clouded.

THE FUTURE OF U.S. FOREIGN POLICY TOWARD THE REGION

It is clear that the United States has tremendous capacity to affect the future of Central America. The United States has almost ten times the population of

Central America, and orders of magnitude of greater natural and technical resources and economic and military power. Washington can bestow or withhold economic and military aid; block or expedite badly needed loans from the International Monetary Fund, the World Bank, and the Inter-American Development Bank; and increase, decrease, or totally cut off access to U.S. markets and products. It can and does use the U.S. Central Intelligence Agency, the National Endowment for Democracy, and other institutions and resources to manipulate local media and create or amplify opposition for its enemies or support for its friends. The United States can recruit, train, and deploy surrogate armies of so-called freedom fighters to undermine and possibly overthrow its chosen enemies. And in extreme cases, it can invade and conquer. In recent years, the most significant constraints on U.S. government behavior in Central America have been domestic opinion, resistance to administration policy in the U.S. Congress, and world opinion. However, the U.S. public tends to be ill informed about world affairs[14] and members of Congress are subject to manipulation through red-baiting. Hence, both are susceptible to unexamined "patriotic" appeals or political maneuvering.

If we were to project from the past, we would logically have to predict that although specific tactics may change from time to time, the essentially conservative, status quo–reinforcing thrust of U.S. policy toward the isthmus is not likely to be altered, at least not in the foreseeable future. In all likelihood, U.S. policy vis-à-vis Central America will continue to respond more to politically manipulated domestic perceptions in the United States than to the actual reality of that region. However, we see some glimmers of hope for a happier future. And since pessimism is rarely productive, we will examine those glimmerings and then offer a series of constructive suggestions.

One cause for hope, though in reality it has little to do with Central America, may ultimately affect U.S. policy toward it. Here we speak of the process of reforms taking place in the Soviet Union under Mikhail S. Gorbachev in the late 1980s. We continue to maintain that the threat of pro-Soviet Communist expansion in Latin America in general and Central America in particular has been modest, at least until recent U.S. intervention in Nicaragua drove the Sandinistas into ever-greater dependence upon the Soviet Union. Nevertheless, in matters of this sort, perception is what counts. As long as a cold, repressive, and apparently warlike regime existed in Moscow, it was possible for many people in the United States to argue with at least some superficial plausibility that the Soviets were intent on gobbling up the world. Therefore, legitimate pressure for change in Central America could be described as a Communist-inspired threat to U.S. national security, and independent, reform-minded governments such as those of Guatemala in the early 1950s and Nicaragua since 1979 could be depicted as Communist extensions of Soviet power. However, if the Gorbachev reforms take root and prosper, we might reasonably expect that policy arguments based on the threat of a demonic world Communist conspiracy would lose some, if not all, of their power. This might free Washington to deal with Central American reality rather than cold war myths about the region. One ray of hope that a more commonsense approach might soon emerge was the fact, mentioned earlier, that informed sources close to candidate (and later president) George Bush had suggested to both authors that the incoming administration might let the contra war lapse and turn instead to serious diplomatic negotiation. Such a change in policy, though insufficient by itself, would certainly be a step in the direction of pragmatism.

There are several changes in policy that we believe the United States should make within the overall objective of harmonizing its legitimate interests with those of the peoples of Central America. The first and most important would be to begin to support and promote the Central American peace process. Although negotiation is not likely to bring an end to conflicts in Guatemala and El Salvador (where civil war is rooted in social, economic, and political injustice), it would almost certainly bear fruit in Nicaragua, if allowed by the United States to prosper. The contras were created by, and are dependent on, the United States. The Sandinistas have long expressed willingness to negotiate a settlement that would address the legitimate security concerns of the United States, including the reduction of military strength, the expulsion of foreign military advisors, the signing of agreements guaranteeing the territorial integrity of neighboring states and prohibiting the use of Nicaraguan territory for foreign military bases and Nicaraguan support for insurgents in other countries. The United States should, therefore, actively engage Nicaragua in meaningful negotiations that would test Sandinista sincerity.

The Sandinistas, who have also been willing to engage in dialogue with their internal opposition, have made civil and political concessions that are virtually unheard of in Marxist-led governments or in countries in a serious state of internal conflict. Thus it would appear that an end to the war and a normalization of civil and political rights could take place very rapidly if the United States would lend its support to a negotiated solution.

We also believe that the United States should actively promote a reversal of the current arms race in Central America. Nicaragua has built up its armed forces significantly, first as a deterrent to possible attack by its neighbors and by the United States, and later to combat the contras and their campaign of rural terror. The reduction of Nicaraguan armed strength could be pursued through the termination of the contra war, improved relations with the United States, and U.S. negotiations with Nicaragua and with its major arms supplier, the Soviet Union. Of course there would have to be guarantees of Nicaragua's security as well and significant arms reductions throughout the rest of Central America, especially in the three countries to the north. It would be incumbent on the United States to reduce arms shipments to Guatemala, El Salvador, and Honduras and to persuade its close ally, Israel, to do the same. Such a reversal in policy should present very little security threat to the regimes in northern Central America, especially if it were negotiated in the context of a regional peace agreement. History shows that armed insurgencies rarely succeed and certainly do not when ruling elites behave in a humane and flexible, rather than brutal and rigid, manner. By helping to remove part of the military crutch and by reducing intraregional tensions, the United States would be creating both an incentive for flexibility and the resources for reform that might actually improve some regimes' chances for survival. Though adaptation, reform, and survival would be the most likely outcome of such a process, it is at least remotely possible that under this scenario, a rebel insurgency might defeat a traditional elite-dominated regime. But that should not cause alarm. Given its great resources and power advantage, the United States should have confidence in itself and in the basic pragmatism of Central Americans. The simple truth is that the United States has far more to offer any government in Central America—even a revolutionary one—than does any other power in the world.

We also believe that the United States should assist the Central American governments—revolutionary and nonrevolutionary alike—to pursue programs that promote genuine social, economic, and political development based on grass-roots majority participation. In the economic realm this would mean eschewing the customary expedient of simply endloading money onto pro-U.S. regimes regardless of their social behavior and honesty or underwriting large export-oriented domestic and multinational "development" projects. Rather, as we indicated earlier, a much larger portion of scarce foreign aid funds should be set aside for assistance to small producers, peasant cooperatives, worker-owned enterprises, and labor-intensive activities geared toward local and regional markets. Preferably, these funds would be channeled through private and international organizations with experience in grass-roots economic development. And, in order to strengthen the economies of the region and help to decrease their socially destabilizing dependence on foreign markets, the United States should actively promote and encourage the resurrection and development of the Central American Common Market.

In addition, if only as a pragmatic strategy for relieving politically destabilizing pressures, the United States should support, encourage, and where possible, help fund social programs aimed at bringing greater equality and social justice to the region. Genuine agrarian reform involving free and unintimidated grass-roots participation in community decisionmaking is absolutely crucial in this poor agricultural region. Programs in health, literacy, housing, and nutrition, facilitated by massive and uninhibited grass-roots participation, should also be encouraged and supported.

The United States should begin to support participatory democracy. It should cease abusing the concept of democracy, in contrast to what it has recently done in Guatemala and El Salvador and to a lesser extent Honduras when the United States promoted and praised the election of essentially powerless governments by violently intimidated and demobilized electorates. Instead, Washington should stand for the same right in Central America that is considered essential to the functioning of democracy in the United States: the right of all citizens—not just a privileged minority—to form and participate in interest groups and parties to protect collective interests and to pressure and shape government policy. Especially critical here would be uniform and even-handed pressure on all governments of the isthmus to respect human rights and to permit meaningful citizen participation.

Finally, the United States should, as far as is possible, pursue each of the above objectives in multilateral arenas and with multilateral means. Despite its immense resource and power advantages, the Reagan administration proved unable to remove the FSLN from power in Managua or to end the Salvadoran insurgency, and Soviet influence in Central America became greater than ever. This is partly because of domestic limits on administration actions, but it is also due to widespread international disapproval of U.S. means over the last decade. The United States became isolated in Central America in the 1980s and lacked the approval and cooperation of other actors. Multilateral programs under the auspices of the United Nations, Organization of American States, European Community, Contadora Group, Contadora Support Group, and the Central American states themselves can muster resources and political will to reduce Soviet military influence, increase political stability, and manage destabilizing economic and social problems in the region.

In conclusion, though we may shock many self-styled foreign policy "realists" in the United States, we would argue that a U.S. policy toward Central America that is genuinely "kinder and gentler" would almost certainly prove to be wiser and more pragmatic. As long as the U.S. government remains a de facto ally of the privileged minorities of the region, acquiescing or aiding in programs of bloody demobilization, it will simply be underwriting continuing instability. Only a very different policy—one that actively supports and promotes free and open grass-roots economic, social, and political participation—will provide for long-term stability in Central America.

APPENDIX

Table 1 Percent Growth in Per Capita Gross Domestic Products, Central American Countries, 1950-1987

	Costa Rica	El Salvador	Guatemala	Honduras	Nicaragua
1950	-1.0	-	-3.0	0.5	13.6
1951	-2.4	-0.9	-1.9	2.7	3.8
1952	7.0	4.6	-1.2	1.1	13.9
1953	10.6	4.3	0.4	5.2	-0.6
1954	-4.3	-1.8	-1.4	-8.4	6.3
1955	6.5	2.2	-0.8	-0.1	3.7
1956	-8.0	5.0	5.8	5.4	-3.1
1957	3.4	2.4	2.3	1.9	5.4
1958	7.3	-0.7	1.4	0.5	-2.6
1959	0.2	1.6	1.6	-0.2	-1.5
1960	5.2	1.2	-0.9	3.0	-1.3
1961	0.7	-0.2	1.8	-0.6	4.8
1962	2.6	8.3	1.0	2.6	8.2
1963	5.1	0.6	7.0	0.5	8.2
1964	1.4	5.6	2.1	2.0	9.0
1965	5.6	1.7	1.9	5.4	6.8
1966	4.3	3.4	3.0	2.6	0.6
1967	2.6	1.7	1.6	2.4	4.3
1968	4.2	-0.5	6.3	2.7	-1.4
1969	3.2	-0.2	2.2	-2.4	4.0
1970	4.1	-0.7	2.7	-1.1	-2.5
1971	4.1	1.5	2.6	0.1	1.4
1972	-1.7	2.6	4.3	0.2	0.3
1973	5.5	2.1	3.5	1.0	1.7
1974	3.0	3.5	3.1	-3.2	9.0
1975	-0.3	2.5	-1.2	-5.2	-1.1
1976	0.3	1.0	4.2	2.6	1.6
1977	6.3	2.8	4.6	2.0	2.8
1978	3.3	1.4	2.4	4.1	-10.2
1979	1.8	-5.9	1.9	1.4	-27.2
1980	-1.8	-11.7	0.8	-0.4	7.4
1981	-5.0	-9.6	-1.8	-2.4	2.0
1982	-9.7	-6.5	-6.1	-4.9	-4.4
1983	0.0	-0.2	-5.4	-3.9	1.3
1984	5.1	0.5	-2.8	-0.3	-4.8
1985	-1.7	0.1	-3.7	-1.8	-5.9
1986	-8.6	-0.6	-2.5	2.4	-4.0
1987	0.7	0.9	-0.4	0.9	-1.7

Sources: Wilkie and Haber (1981: Table 22-3); CEPAL (1985: Table 2); CEPAL (1986: Table 3); Inter-American Development Bank (1988: Tables A-1, B-1).

Table 2 Selected Data by Country, 1960-1987

	Costa Rica	El Salvador	Guatemala	Honduras	Nicaragua
Population[a]					
1960	1,236	2,570	3,964	1,935	1,493
1980	2,284	4,525	6,917	3,662	2,771
1987	2,791	4,943	8,434	4,679	3,501
Mean annual population growth (%)					
1961-70	3.4	3.4	2.8	3.1	3.2
1971-80	2.8	2.3	2.8	3.4	3.0
1981-87	2.9	1.2	2.9	3.6	3.4
Percent urban population					
1960	33.2	36.4	34.0	22.5	41.7
1987	49.6	47.7	38.2	41.4	58.7
Percent literate					
1960	86.2	41.6	40.0	29.7	31.8[b]
1980	89.8	69.8	47.3	59.5	50.6[b]
University enrollment[a]					
1950	1.5	-	2.1	0.7	0.5
1980	51.0	27.1	37.8	20.4	19.8
GDP[c]					
1960	1,646	1,985	4,045	1,112	1,461
1970	2,932	3,437	6,911	1,905	2,849
1980	5,075	4,723	11,987	3,243	2,950
1987	5,611	4,440	11,604	3,657	3,079
GDP per capita[d]					
1960	1,332	772	1,020	575	879
1970	1,694	958	1,373	725	1,388
1980	2,222	1,044	1,732	886	1,065
1987	2,011	900	1,376	782	879
Percent[e] employed in					
Agriculture 1960	51.0	62.0	67.0	70.0	62.0
Agriculture 1980	29.0	50.0	55.0	63.0	39.0
Manufacturing c. 1950	11.0	11.0	12.0	6.0	11.0
Manufacturing 1983	16.0	14.0	15.0	13.0	15.0
Percent GDP from manufacturing					
1960	14.0	15.0	13.0	12.0	16.0
1980	22.0	18.0	17.0	16.0	25.0
1987	23.0	18.0	16.0	13.0	26.0

[a]Thousands.
[b]From Ministerio de Educación (1979: 140-141, 147).
[c]In millions of 1986 U.S. dollars.
[d]In 1986 U.S. dollars.
[e]Of economically active population.

<u>Sources</u>: Inter-American Development Bank (1988: Tables A-1, A-2, B-1, B-9); Torres Rivas (1982: Cuadro 4); Pérez Brignoli and Baíres Martínez (1983: Table 9); Castillo Rivas (1983b: Cuadro 1).

Table 3 Percent Change in Consumer Prices, 1963-1985

	Costa Rica	El Salvador	Guatemala	Honduras	Nicaragua
1963	3.0	0.9	0.1	2.9	0.8
1964	3.3	1.8	-0.2	4.6	9.6
1965	-0.7	1.4[a]	-0.7	3.2	3.9
1966	0.2	-0.9	0.6	0.2	3.9
1967	1.1	1.8	0.5	1.2	1.6
1968	4.0	1.8	1.8	2.6	3.1
1969	2.8	3.2[a]	2.2	1.8	2.0[b]
1970	4.6	2.6	2.4	2.9	5.9
1971	3.1	0.3	-0.5	3.1	5.6
1972	4.6	1.7	0.5	3.4	3.3[b]
1973	15.2	6.4	14.4	4.7	16.8[b]
1974	30.1	16.9	15.9	12.9	20.5[b]
1975	17.4	19.1	13.1	8.1	1.8
1976	3.5	7.0	10.7	5.0	2.9
1977	4.2	11.9	12.6	8.6	11.4
1978	6.0	13.3	7.9	5.7	4.6
1979	9.2	15.0	11.5	8.8	48.5
1980	18.1	17.3	10.7	18.1	35.9
1981	37.1	14.7	11.4	9.4	23.9
1982	90.1	11.7	5.0	9.4	24.8
1983	32.6	13.1	6.4	8.9	39.9
1984	12.0	13.0	5.0	4.8	48.1
1985	14.6	27.4	28.2	3.7	250.9

[a]Assigned mean value of other four nations as estimate.
[b]Estimates based on Nicaraguan Central Bank and other data; see Booth (1982: Table 5).

Sources: Data through 1979 from Wilkie and Haber, eds. (1981: Tables 2505, 2508, 2511, 2513); 1980-1985 data from Inter-American Development Bank (1983: country profile tables); U.S. Department of State (1985); CEPAL (1985: Table 5).

Table 4 Real Working Class Wage Indices, 1963-1984 (1973=100)

	Costa Rica	El Salvador[a]	Guatemala[b]	Honduras[c]	Nicaragua[d]
1963	80	90	-	-	92
1965	-	92	109	-	125[e]
1967	94[e]	93	115	-	137
1970	96	92	109	-	121
1971	107	93	109	-	119
1972	103	94	107	96	114
1973	100	100	100	100	100
1974	108	98	96	94	100
1975	91	90	95	91	106
1976	103	95	97	102	106
1977	113	85	81	95	97
1978	123[e]	87	84	101	88
1979	128	84	84[e]	103	77[e]
1980	129[e]	82	84[e]	97	64[e]
1981	114[e]	76[f]	86[e]	93[f]	64[e]
1982	92[e]	68[f]	92[e]	101[f]	56[e]
1983	102[e]	60[f]	85[f]	92[f]	49[e]
1984	110[e]	57[f]	84[e]	89[f]	46[e]

[a]Excludes construction (after 1974); data drawn from Wilkie and Perkal (1984: Table 1405).
[b]Unweighted average of all sectors reported in Wilkie and Perkal (1984: Table 1405).
[c]Unweighted average wages in manufacturing, construction, and agriculture (agricultural wages not included in 1972 and 1973 figures).
[d]Includes wages in manufacturing, transportation (only), and construction.
[e]Data drawn from Wilkie and Lorey (1987: Table 1413).
[f]Data drawn from Gallardo and López (1986: 168).

Sources: Based on Wilkie and Haber (1981: Tables 1400, 1401, 1402, 1403); Wilkie and Perkal (1984: Table 1405) and consumer price data in Table 3 above. The 1978 and 1979 data for Nicaragua are from Mayorga (1985: 65). Value of the indices represent an unweighted average of wages in manufacturing, construction, transport, storage, and communication, and in agriculture, corrected for consumer price changes except for items under note [e] above, which are wages only for persons included in national social security systems.

Table 5 Compensation of Employees as Percent of National Income (1962 = 100)

	Costa Rica		Honduras		Nicaragua	
	%	Index	%	Index	%	Index
1962	45.0	100	46.2	100	57.5	100
1965	51.0	113	42.4	92	65.0	113
1967	52.2	116	41.8	90	65.3	114
1968	51.6	115	42.5	92	65.3	114
1969	51.3	114	42.0	91	65.6	114
1970	50.8	113	42.1	91	65.3	114
1971	52.0	116	43.7	95	65.5	114
1972	52.5	117	44.6	97	65.6	114
1973	49.4	110	45.0	97	69.7	121
1974	48.6	108	42.8	93	58.9	102
1975	49.8	111	-	-	59.1	103

Source: Wilkie and Haber (1981: Table 1404).

Table 6 Unemployment Trends, 1970-1984 (percentages)

	Costa Rica	El Salvador[a]	Guatemala[b]		Honduras[c]	Nicaragua
1970	3.5[d]	16.0	4.8	-	-	3.7
1971	-	-	-	-	8.8	3.6
1972	-	17.0	4.9	24.5	7.7	6.0
1973	7.6[e]	-	-	-	7.4	9.1
1974	-	-	-	-	6.9	7.3
1975	-	18.0	5.1	26.5	9.7	-
1976	4.9[e]	-	-	-	9.4	-
1977	4.4[e]	-	-	-	8.9	13.1[f]
1978	4.6	21.0	5.3	28.6	9.2	14.5
1979	4.7	-	-	-	-	22.9
1980	5.9	24.0	5.5	31.2	15.2	17.8
1981	8.1	25.0	6.0	32.6	18.3	16.6
1982	15.0	30.0	7.0	36.7	21.1	19.9[g]
1983	8.6[g]	33.0	8.0	40.1	22.9	15.2[g]
1984	6.6[g]	30.0	10.0	43.4	23.9	16.3[g]

[a]Salvadoran figures for 1970, 1972, 1975, and 1978 are estimates based on Central American mean unemployment trends (IICA 1982: 256) and data for 1981 on from U.S. Department of State (1985).
[b]First column of Guatemalan data refers to unemployment; second column refers to combined unemployment and underemployment. These figures are data reported by the Guatemalan Ministry of Labor, cited in *La Nación Internacional* (1982: 12), and by the Guatemalan Secretariat of Economic Planning, reported in *Inforpress Centroamericana* (1985a: 18). Also used were data for 1981 on from the U.S. Department of State (1985). Figures for 1972, 1975, and 1978 are estimates based on earlier and later reported data.
[c]Figures for 1971-1978 are estimates based upon projections of economically active population from base years of 1974 and 1977 (Wilkie and Haber, 1981: Table 1301). Values represent number of unemployed as percent of economically active population. Figures for 1980-1984 are from Gallardo and López (1986: 198); computational method unknown.
[d]Gallardo and López (1986: 189).
[e]DGEC-Costa Rica (1980: Cuadro 196).
[f]From Booth (1982: Table 5.1). Data for 1978 on drawn from CIERA (1983: Cuadro 18).
[g]CEPAL (1985: Table 4).

Sources: Unless otherwise noted, data are drawn from Wilkie and Haber (1981: Table 1308).

Table 7 International Assistance (Approximate) to Nicaragua by Major Origins, 1979-1987 (millions of U.S. $)

	Multilateral	Western Countries	Socialist Countries	Total Assistance
1979	220	140	10	370
1980	190	500	160	850
1981	90	520	180	790
1982	110	320	280	710
1983	80	270	330	680
1984	20	180	600	800
1985	20	160	1,030	1,210
1986	40	120	390	550
1987	30	110	280	420

Source: Figures are estimates based on Conroy (1988: Figure 5).

Table 8 Central American Rebel Groups, 1959-1989

	Costa Rica	El Salvador	Guatemala	Honduras	Nicaragua
1959					various groups[b] (1959-61)
1960				FMLH[a]	
1961					FSLN
1962			MR-13, FAR, FGEI[c]		
1963					
1964					
1965					
1966					
1967					
1968					
1969					
1970		FPL			
1971			ORPA		
1972		ERP	EGP		
1973					
1974					
1975		FARN			
1976		PRTCS			
1977				PRTCH	FSLN splits[d]
1978			PGT-DN	MPL	
1979	La Familia	FAL			reunfication of FSLN, MPU/FPN[e]
1980	PRTC	FMLN[f] FMLN-FDR[g]	MRP-Ixim		
1981			URNG[h]	FPR	
1982					
1983				DNU[i]	
1984					
1985					
1986					
1987					
1988					
1989					

[a]Only sporadically active through late 1979s, when it resumed armed struggle.
[b]Of some 20 groups formed, only the FSLN survived beyond 1963.
[c]MR-13 disappeared after late 1960s counterinsurgency campaign; core of FAR survived to renew guerrilla activity in 1978; core of FGEI survived counterinsurgency and helped form EGP.
[d]Under heavy counterinsurgency pressure, FSLN split into three factions with tactical differences.
[e]MPU/FPN coalitions linked broad-front political opposition to FSLN.
[f]FMLN included all five Salvadoran guerrilla organizations.
[g]FMLN-FDR linked FMLN guerrillas to broad-front political opposition coalition.
[h]URNG linked the guerrilla groups EGP, FAR, ORPA, and the PGT-DN; MRP-Ixim not a member.
[i]DNU linked the MPL, FPR, and FMLH guerrilla organizations.

Sources: Booth (1982: Ch. 7), Ropp (1984: 241-245), Montgomery (1982b: 124), Black et al. (1984: 66-77, 103-108).

Table 8 (Continued)

<u>Key to groups</u>

DNU	National Directorate of Unity
EGP	Guerrilla Army of the Poor
ERP	Revolutionary Army of the People (Ejército Revolucionario del Pueblo)
FAL	Armed Forces of Liberation (Fuerzas Armadas de Liberación)
FAR	Revolutionary Armed Forces
FARN	Armed Forces of National Resistence (Fuerzas Armadas de Resistencia Nacional)
FDR	Revolutionary Democratic Front
FGEI	Edgar Ibarra Guerrilla Front
FMLH	Morazan Front for the Liberation of Honduras
FMLN	Farabundo Marti National Liberation Front
FPL	Popular Forces of Liberation (Fuerzas Populares de Liberación)
FPN	National Patriotic Front
FPR	Lorenzo Zelaya Popular Revolutionary Forces
FSLN	Sandinista National Liberation Front
La Familia	The Family
MPL	Popular Movement for Liberation
MPU	United People's Movement
MR-13	13th of November Revolutionary Movement
MRP-Ixim	People's Revolutionary Movement-Ixim (Movimiento Revolucionario del Pueblo-Ixim)
ORPA	Organization of the People in Arms
PGT-DN	Guatemalan Labor Party-National Directorate (Partido Guatemalteco del Trabajo-Dirección Nacional)
PRTC	Revolutionary Party of Central American Workers (Partido Revolucionario de Trabajadores Centroamericanos-Costa Rica)
PRTCS	Revolutionary Party of Central American Workers (Partido Revolucionario de Trabajadores Centroamericanos-El Salvador)
PRTCH	Revolutionary Party of Central American Workers (Partido Revolucionario de Trabajadores Centroamericanos-Honduras)
URNG	Guatemalan National Revolutionary Union

Table 9 Selected Data on Deaths, Disappearances, and Refugees, El Salvador, 1980-1984

Annual Number of Deaths and Disappearances

	1980	1981	1982	1983	1984	1980-84
Deaths	13,194	16,376	12,617	5,826	2,206	50,219
Detained/ disappeared	979	927	1,177	526	196	3,805
TOTAL	14,173	17,303	13,794	6,352	2,402	54,024

Deaths and Disappearances, by Occupation (%)

Occupation	Deaths	Disappearances
Workers	14.6	15.3
Students	7.2	17.3
Peasants	67.9	10.6
Merchants	2.6	3.2
Employees	4.5	6.6
Teachers	1.2	1.6
Professionals	1.3	1.0
Housewives	0.3	2.2

Salvadoran Refugees Abroad, by Country (est.)

Country	Number	Country	Number
United States	500,000	Costa Rica	10,000
Mexico	250,000	Panama	1,500
Guatemala	70,000	Nicaragua	20,000
Belize	7,000	Honduras	32,000

TOTAL 890,500

Source: CDHES (1984: 87-89).

Table 10 Comparative Data on Central Government Expenditures (percent of budget)

	Costa Rica		El Salvador	Guatemala		Honduras	Nicaragua
	1978	1983	1984	1978	1984[a]	1976	1976
1. Defense	2.7	3.0	24.6	11.0	13.7	10.5	12.8
2. Education	24.5	19.4	15.5	13.0	12.7	20.7	16.9
3. Health	3.6	22.5	8.1	7.1	7.5	14.7	4.1
4. Social security/welfare	28.3	14.5	3.7	4.1	3.9	4.7	19.9
5. Total percent on education, health and social security/welfare (2+3+4)	56.3	56.3	27.3	24.2	24.1	40.1	40.9
6. Ratio of human services to defense (5:1)	21:1	19:1	1:1	2:1	2:1	4:1	3:1

[a]Slightly different budget breakdowns are used between Wilkie and Perkal and Wilkie and Lorey on the one hand and _Inforpress Centroamericana_ on the other. The 1984 Guatemala data for the social security and welfare category on this measure are assumed be the same as _Inforpress_'s "labor" and "government" lines combined.

Sources: Wilkie and Haber (1981: Table 2323); Wilkie and Lorey (1987: Table 3010); _Inforpress Centroamericana_ (1985a: 5).

ACRONYMS

AID	Agency for International Development
AMNLAE	Luisa Amanda Espinosa Nicaraguan Women's Association (Asociación de Mujeres Nicaragüenses Luisa Amanda Espinosa)
AMPRONAC	Association of Women Confronting the National Problem (Asociación de Mujeres Frente a la Problemática Nacional) (N)
ANEP	National Association of Private Enterprises (Asociación Nacional de Empresas Privadas) (ES)
ARDE	Revolutionary Democratic Alliance (Alianza Revolucionaria Democrática) (CR-based contra forces)
ARENA	Nationalist Republican Alliance party (Alianza Republicana Nacionalista) (ES)
ATC	Rural Workers' Association (Asociación de Trabajadores del Campo) (N)
BPR	Revolutionary Popular Bloc (Bloque Popular Revolucionario) (ES)
CACM	Central American Common Market
CDC	Civil Defense Committee (Comité de Defensa Civil) (N & H)
CDS	Sandinista Defense Committee (Comité de Defensa Sandinista) (N)
CEB	Christian base communities (*comunidades eclesiales de base*)
CGUP	Guatemalan Committee of Patriotic Unity (Comité Guatemalteco de Unidad Patriótica)
CIA	Central Intelligence Agency
COSEP	Superior Council of Private Enterprise (Consejo Superior de la Empresa Privada) (N)

Abbreviations of countries: CR = Costa Rica; ES = El Salvador; G = Guatemala; H = Honduras; N = Nicaragua

COSIP	Superior Council of Private Initiative (Consejo Superior de la Iniciativa Privada) (N)
CPI	consumer price index
CRM	Revolutionary Coordinator of the Masses (Coordinadora Revolucionaria de Masas) (ES)
CST	Sandinista Workers' Federation (Central Sandinista de Trabajadores) (N)
CUC	Peasant Unity Committee (Comité de Unidad Campesina) (G)
DC	Christian Democratic party (Partido Demócrata Cristiano) (G)
DINADECO	National Community Development Directorate (Dirección Nacional de Desarrollo de la Comunidad) (CR)
DNC	Joint National Directorate (Dirección Nacional Conjunta) (N)
DNU	National Directorate of Unity (Dirección Nacional de Unidad) (H)
EGP	Guerrilla Army of the Poor (Ejército Guerrillero de los Pobres) (G)
FAO	Broad Opposition Front (Frente Amplio Opositor) (N)
FAPU	United Popular Action Front (Frente de Acción Popular Unida) (ES)
FAR	Revolutionary Armed Forces (Fuerzas Armadas Revolucionarias) (G)
FDCR	Democratic Front Against Repression (Frente Democrático Contra la Represión) (G)
FDN	Nicaraguan Democratic Force (Fuerzas Democráticas Nicaragüenses)
FDR	Revolutionary Democratic Front (Frente Democrático Revolucionario) (ES)
FGEI	Edgar Ibarra Guerrilla Front (Frente Guerrillera Edgar Ibarra) (G)
FMLH	Morazán Front for the Liberation of Honduras (Frente Morazanista para la Liberación de Honduras)
FMLN	Farabundo Martí National Liberation Front (Frente Farabundo Martí para la Liberación Nacional) (ES)
FP-13	January 13th Popular Front (Frente Popular 13 de Enero) (G)
FPN	National Patriotic Front (Frente Patriótico Nacional) (N)
FPR	Lorenzo Zelaya Popular Revolutionary Forces (Fuerzas Populares Revolucionarias "Lorenzo Zelaya") (H)
FSLN	Sandinista National Liberation Front (Frente Sandinista de Liberación Nacional) (N)
FUR	United Front of the Revolution (Frente Unido de la Revolución) (G)
GDP	gross national product

LP-28	28th of February Popular Leagues (Ligas Populares 28 de Febrero) (ES)
MLN	National Liberation Movement (Movimiento de Liberación Nacional) (G)
MLP	Popular Liberation Movement (Movimiento de Liberación Popular) (ES)
MNR	National Revolutionary Movement (Movimiento Nacional Revolucionario) (ES)
MPL	Popular Movement for Liberation (Movimiento Popular de Liberación) (H)
MPU	United People's Movement (Movimiento Pueblo Unido) (N)
MR-13	13th of November Revolutionary Movement (Movimiento Revolucionario del 13 de Noviembre) (G)
OAS	Organization of American States
OPEC	Organization of Petroleum Exporting Countries
ORDEN	Nationalist Democratic Organization (Organización Democrática Nacionalista) (ES)
ORPA	Organization of the People in Arms (Organización del Pueblo en Armas) (G)
PCH	Honduran Communist party (Partido Comunista de Honduras)
PCN	National Conciliation party (Partido de Conciliación Nacional) (ES)
PCS	Communist Party of El Salvador (Partido Comunista de El Salvador)
PDC	Christian Democratic party (Partido Demócrata Cristiano) (ES)
PDCH	Christian Democratic Party of Honduras (Partido Demócrata Cristiano de Honduras) (H)
PGT	Guatemalan Labor party (Partido Guatemalteco del Trabajo)
PID	Institutional Democratic party (Partido Institucional Democrático) (G)
PINU	Innovation and Unity party (Partido de Inovación y Unidad) (H)
PLH	Honduran Liberal party (Partido Liberal de Honduras)
PLN	Liberal Nationalist Party (Partido Liberal Nacionalista) (N)
PLN	National Liberation party (Partido de Liberación Nacional) (CR)
PR	Revolutionary party (Partido Revolucionario) (G)
PRTCH	Revolutionary Party of Central American Workers of Honduras (Partido Revolucionario de Trabajadores Centroamericanos de Honduras)
PRUD	Revolutionary Party of Democratic Unification (Partido Revolucionario de Unificación Democrática) (ES)
PSD	Democratic Socialist party (Partido Socialista Demócrata) (G)

PUSC	Social Christian Unity party (Partido de Unidad Social Cristiano)(CR)
RN	Nicaraguan Resistance (Resistencia Nicaragüense)
UDEL	Democratic Liberation Union (Unión Democrática de Liberación) (N)
UDN	Democratic National Union (Unión Democrática Nacionalista) (ES)
UFCO	United Fruit Company
UN	United Nations
UNAG	National Union of Farmers and Ranchers (Unión Nacional de Agricultores y Ganaderos) (N)
UNO	National Opposition Union (Unión Nacional Opositora) (N & ES)
URNG	Guatemalan National Revolutionary Union (Unión Revolucionaria Nacional Guatemalteca)

NOTES

NOTES TO CHAPTER 1

1. National Bipartisan Commission on Central America, *Report of the National Bipartisan Commission on Central America* (Washington, D.C., January 1984), p. 15.

2. Coauthor John Booth informally surveyed Central America scholars, reviewed lists of the commission's consultants, and discussed at length the commission's operation with one of its members.

3. See, for instance, Policy Alternatives for the Caribbean and Central America, *Changing Course: Blueprint for Peace in Central America and the Caribbean* (Washington, D.C.: Institute for Policy Studies, 1984); Inter-American Dialogue, *The Americas in 1984: A Year for Decisions, Report of the Inter-American Dialogue* (Washington, D.C.: Aspen Institute for Humanistic Studies, 1984); William M. LeoGrande, "Through the Looking Glass: The Kissinger Report on Central America," *World Policy Journal* (Winter 1984) pp. 251–284.

4. Here, and in certain other parts of this volume, much of the wording is from Thomas W. Walker's unsigned contribution to: Presbyterian Church (USA), *Adventure and Hope: Christians and the Crisis in Central America: Report to the 195th General Assembly of the Presbyterian Church* (Atlanta, 1983), pp. 57–91, 97–101. The authors wish to thank the Presbyterian church for its kind permission to publish this material (which Walker wrote in 1982 while he was part of the UPCUSA [United Presbyterian Church (USA)] Task Force on Central America) here in this form.

5. Population estimates for Central American countries based on Maria Eugenia Gallardo and José Roberto López, *Centroamérica: La crisis en cifras* (San José, Costa Rica: Instituto Interamericano de Cooperación para la Agricultura [IICA]–Facultad Latinoamericano de Ciencias Sociales [FLACSO], 1986), p. 35.

6. National Bipartisan Commission, pp. 88–91.

NOTES TO CHAPTER 2

1. Inter-American Development Bank (IADB), *Economic and Social Progress in Latin America: Labor Force and Employment: 1987 Report* (Washington, D.C., 1987), Table I-1, p. 2.

2. Ibid., country statistical profiles.

3. Ibid.

4. Ibid.

5. Population Reference Bureau, *1981 World Population Data Sheet* (Washington, D.C., 1981).

6. Ibid.

7. Wallace W. Atwood and Helen Goss Thomas, *The Americas* (Boston: Ginn and Co., 1929), p. 45.

8. For an overview, see, for instance, Ronald H. Chilcote and Joel C. Edelstein, *Latin America: Capitalist and Socialist Perspectives of Development and Underdevelopment* (Boulder, Colo.: Westview Press, 1986).

NOTES TO CHAPTER 3

1. Good histories are Ralph Lee Woodward, Jr., *Central America: A Nation Divided*, 2nd ed. (New York: Oxford University Press, 1985), and Mario Rodríguez, *Central America* (Englewood Cliffs, N.J.: Prentice Hall, 1965).

2. See David Richard Radell, "An Historical Geography of Western Nicaragua: The Spheres of Leon, Granada, and Managua, 1519–1965," Ph.D. dissertation, University of California, Berkeley, 1969, pp. 66–80.

3. For excellent coverage of the Walker period and its aftermath, see Karl Bermann, *Under the Big Stick: Nicaragua and the United States since 1848* (Boston: South End Press, 1986).

4. Honduras never really developed a landowning aristocracy; economic and political power remained in the hands of regional *hacendados* and newer urban industrial-commercial-financial entrepreneurs.

5. Enrique A. Baloyra, "Reactionary Despotism in Central America," *Journal of Latin American Studies* 15 (November 1983), pp. 295–319.

6. Ibid., pp. 309–310.

7. In Honduras, agrarian colonization and expanding employment in the modern capitalist sector of agriculture continued to absorb much of the growth of the rural labor force.

8. Victor Bulmer-Thomas, *The Political Economy of Central America Since 1920* (Cambridge: Cambridge University Press, 1987), pp. 177–180.

9. John Weeks, "The Industrial Sector," in Thomas W. Walker, ed., *Nicaragua: The First Five Years* (New York: Praeger, 1985), pp. 281–296; and John Weeks, *The Economies of Central America* (New York: Holmes and Meier, 1985), pp. 101–151.

10. Weeks, *The Economies of Central America*, p. 284.

NOTES TO CHAPTER 4

1. John A. Booth, "Representative Constitutional Democracy in Costa Rica: Adaptation to Crisis in the Turbulent 1980s," in Steve Ropp and James Morris, eds., *Central America: Crisis and Adaptation* (Albuquerque: University of New Mexico Press, 1984), Table 5.1. Other material on the evolution of Costa Rica drawn from Mitchell A. Seligson and Miguel Gómez, "Ordinary Elections in Extraordinary Times: The Political Economy of Voting in Costa Rica," in John A. Booth and Mitchell A. Seligson, eds., *Elections and Democracy in Central America* (Chapel Hill: University of North Carolina Press, 1989);

and from interviews by Booth with Costa Rican scholars and political experts during author's visits there in August 1987 and January 1988.

2. From Robert J. Shafter, *A History of Latin America* (Lexington, Mass.: D. C. Heath, 1978), p. 474.

3. Ibid.

4. Paul Levy, as quoted in Jaime Wheelock Román, *Imperialismo y dictadura: Crisis de una formación social* (México: Siglo Veintiuno Editores, 1975), p. 29.

5. See Tommie Sue Montgomery, *Revolution in El Salvador: Origins and Evolution* (Boulder, Colo.: Westview Press, 1982); and Enrique Baloyra, *El Salvador in Transition* (Chapel Hill: University of North Carolina Press, 1982).

6. As quoted in Montgomery, *Revolution in El Salvador*, p. 46.

7. Enrique A. Baloyra, *El Salvador in Transition* (Chapel Hill: University of North Carolina Press, 1982), p. 35.

8. Tommie Sue Montgomery, "El Salvador: The Roots of Revolution," in Steve C. Ropp and James A. Morris, eds., *Central America: Crisis and Adaptation* (Albuquerque: University of New Mexico Press, 1984), p. 78.

9. See Stephen Webre, *José Napoleón Duarte and the Christian Democratic Party in Salvadorean Politics: 1960–1972* (Baton Rouge: Louisiana State University Press, 1979).

10. See Montgomery, *Revolution in El Salvador*, pp. 97–117.

11. George Black et al., *Garrison Guatemala* (New York: Monthly Review Press, 1984), p. 13.

12. Jerry L. Weaver, "Guatemala: The Politics of a Frustrated Revolution," in Howard J. Wiarda and Harvey F. Kline, eds., *Latin American Politics and Development* (Boston: Houghton Mifflin, 1979), p. 337.

13. Richard H. Immerman, *The CIA in Guatemala: The Foreign Policy of Intervention* (Austin: University of Texas Press, 1982), Chapters 2–7.

14. Richard Newbold Adams, *Crucifixion by Power: Essays on Guatemalan National Social Structure, 1944–1966* (Austin: University of Texas Press, 1970), p. 195.

15. See John Sloan, "The Electoral Game in Guatemala," Ph.D. dissertation, University of Texas at Austin, 1968.

16. Black, *Garrison Guatemala*, p. 43.

17. Ibid.

18. Lars Schoultz, "Guatemala: Social Change and Political Conflict," in Martin Diskin, ed., *Trouble in Our Backyard: Central America and the United States in the Eighties* (New York: Pantheon, 1983), pp. 188–189.

19. Americas Watch, *Little Hope: Human Rights in Guatemala, January 1984–1985* (New York, February 1985); British Parliamentary Human Rights Group, *"Bitter and Cruel . . .": Report of a Mission to Guatemala by the British Parliamentary Human Rights Group* (London: House of Commons, 1985).

20. See John A. Booth et al., *The 1985 Guatemalan National Elections: Will the Military Relinquish Power?* (Washington, D.C.: International Human Rights Law Group–Washington Office on Latin America, 1985); David Carliner et al., *Political Transition and the Rule of Law in Guatemala* (Washington, D.C.: International Human Rights Law Group–Washington Office on Latin America, January 1988).

21. Interviews by Booth in Guatemala during visits in April 1987, January 1988, and September 1988. See also the Latin American Studies Association, *Extraordinary*

Opportunities . . . and New Risks: Final Report of the LASA Commission on Compliance with the Central American Peace Accord (Pittsburgh: LASA, March 15, 1988), pp. 15–20.

22. Thanks to José García of New Mexico State University for his insight on these matters. See James A. Morris, "Honduras: The Burden of Survival in Central America," in Ropp and Morris, *Central America*, pp. 189–223.

23. James A. Morris, "Honduras: A Unique Case," in Wiarda and Kline, eds. *Latin American Politics and Development*, p. 349.

24. As quoted in "Commentary: The Region," *Mesoamérica*, September 1982, p. 1.

25. See Eva Gold, "Military Encirclement," in Thomas W. Walker, ed., *Reagan Versus the Sandinistas: The Undeclared War on Nicaragua* (Boulder, Colo.: Westview Press, 1987), pp. 39–56.

26. The 1985 election followed the Uruguayan model, which combined a primary and general election. Several candidates ran for president under each major party banner. The Liberals gained the most votes; therefore, their leading vote-winner (Azcona) won the presidency, even though one National party candidate had more votes than he.

27. Mark Rosenberg, "Honduras: The Reluctant Democracy," *Current History* 85 (December 1986), pp. 417–420, 438, 448; and "Can Democracy Survive the Democrats? From Transition to Consolidation in Honduras," in Booth and Seligson, eds., *Elections and Democracy in Central America*, pp. 40–57.

NOTES TO CHAPTER 5

1. For example, see Thomas O. Enders, "The Central American Challenge,"*AEI Foreign Policy and Defense Review* 4, No. 2 (1982), p. 9.

2. Ronald Reagan, "U.S. Responsibility in Central America," address to Congress, April 28, 1983; and Jeane Kirkpatrick, "This Time We Know What's Happening," both in M. Falcoff and R. Royal, eds., *Crisis and Opportunity: U.S. Policy in Central America and the Caribbean* (Washington, D.C.: Ethics and Public Policy Center, 1984).

3. National Bipartisan Commission on Central America, *Report of the National Bipartisan Commission on Central America* (Washington, D.C., 1984), p. 87.

4. Many are summarized in Donald E. Schulz, "Ten Theories in Search of Central American Reality," in D. Schulz and D. Graham, eds., *Revolution and Counterrevolution in Central America and the Caribbean* (Boulder, Colo.: Westview Press, 1984), pp. 3–64.

5. Schulz, in "Ten Theories," examined "ten theories in search of Central American reality"; most prove to be merely approaches to data, analytical themes, or myths, rather than theories.

6. E.g., Donaldo Castillo Rivas, "Modelos de acumulación, agricultura, y agroindustria en Centroamérica," in D. Castillo Rivas, ed., *Centroamérica: Más allá de la crisis* (México: Ediciones SIAP, 1983); see also Douglas H. Graham, "The Economic Dimensions of Instability and Decline in Central America and the Caribbean," in Schulz and Graham, eds., *Revolution and Counterrevolution*, pp. 157–189.

7. Héctor Pérez Brignoli with Yolanda Baíres Martínez, "Growth and Crisis in the Central American Economies, 1950–1980," *Journal of Latin American Studies* 15 (November 1983), p. 365.

8. Victor Bulmer-Thomas, "Economic Development Over the Long Run—Central America Since 1920," *Journal of Latin American Studies* 15 (November 1983), p. 291. See also Bulmer-Thomas, *The Political Economy of Central America since 1920* (Cambridge: Cambridge University Press, 1987).

9. See, for example, Gabriel Aguilera Peralta, "Guatemala: Estado, militarismo, y lucha política," in Castillo Rivas, ed., *Centroamérica*, pp. 61–90; Enrique Baloyra, "Reactionary Despotism in Central America," *Journal of Latin American Studies* 15 (November 1983), pp. 295–319.

10. E.g., Michael McClintock, *The American Connection*, Vol. 1: *State Terror and Popular Resistance in El Salvador* (London: Zed Books, 1985); Howard J. Wiarda, "The Central American Crisis: A Framework for Understanding," *AEI Foreign Policy and Defense Review* 4, No. 2 (1982), pp. 2–7.

11. E.g., Phillip Berryman, *The Religious Roots of Rebellion: Christians in Central American Revolutions* (Maryknoll, N.Y.: Orbis, 1984); Michael Dodson and Tommie Sue Montgomery, "The Churches in the Nicaraguan Revolution," in Thomas W. Walker, ed., *Nicaragua in Revolution* (New York: Praeger, 1982).

12. For example, Thomas P. Anderson, *Politics in Central America: Guatemala, El Salvador, Honduras, and Nicaragua* (New York: Praeger, 1982); Phillip Berryman, *Inside Central America* (New York: Pantheon Books, 1985).

13. E.g., Stephen C. Gorman, "Social Change and Political Revolution: The Case of Nicaragua," in S. Ropp and J. Morris, eds., *Central America: Crisis and Adaptation* (Albuquerque: University of New Mexico Press, 1984); see also Heinrich-W. Krumweide, "Regimes and Revolution in Central America," in W. Grabendorff et al., eds., *Political Change in Central America: Internal and External Dimensions* (Boulder, Colo.: Westview Press, 1984).

14. For example, see Castillo Rivas, "Modelos"; Walter LaFeber, *Inevitable Revolutions: The United States in Central America* (New York: W. W. Norton, 1983); see also Francisco Villagrán Kramer, "The Background to the Current Political Crisis in Central America," in R. Feinberg, ed., *Central America: International Dimensions of the Crisis* (New York: Holmes and Meier, 1982).

15. Edelberto Torres Rivas, *Crisis del poder en Centroamérica* (San José, Costa Rica: Editorial Universitaria Centroamericana, 1981), p. 86, authors' translation.

16. Ibid., pp. 100–101.

17. A. S. Cohan, *Theories of Revolution: An Introduction* (New York: Wiley-Halsted Press, 1975); Barbara Salert, *Revolutions and Revolutionaries: Four Theories* (New York: Elsevier, 1976); Stan Taylor, *Social Science and Revolutions* (New York: St. Martin's Press, 1984).

18. E.g., James C. Davies, "Towards a Theory of Revolution," *American Sociological Review* 27 (1962), pp. 5–18; and Ted R. Gurr, *Why Men Rebel* (Princeton: Princeton University Press, 1971).

19. Taylor, *Social Science*, p. 84.

20. E.g., ibid.; Rod Aya, "Theories of Revolution Reconsidered: Contrasting Models of Collective Violence," *Theory and Society* 8 (June-December 1979), pp. 39–100; Cohan, *Theories of Revolution*; Salert, *Revolutions and Revolutionaries*.

21. Theda Skocpol, *States and Social Revolutions* (Cambridge: Cambridge University Press, 1979); John Walton, *Reluctant Rebels: Comparative Studies in Revolution and*

Underdevelopment (New York: Columbia University Press, 1984); and Aya, "Theories of Revolution Reconsidered."

22. Charles Tilly, *From Mobilization to Revolution* (Reading, Mass.: Addison-Wesley, 1978).

23. Louis Kriesberg, *Social Conflicts*, 2nd ed. (Englewood Cliffs, N.J.: Prentice-Hall, 1982), p. 29.

24. Skocpol, *States and Social Revolutions*, p. 13.

25. Walton, *Reluctant Rebels*, p. 13.

26. Jeffrey M. Paige, *Agrarian Revolution: Social Movements and Export Agriculture in the Underdeveloped World* (New York: The Free Press, 1975); Eric Wolf, *Peasant Revolts of the Twentieth Century* (New York: Harper and Row, 1969).

27. Walton, *Reluctant Rebels*, pp. 161–162.

28. Kriesberg, *Social Conflicts*, pp. 66–106.

29. Aya, "Theories of Revolution Reconsidered," pp. 41–44; Tilly, "Introduction," in L. A. Tilly and C. Tilly, eds., *Class Conflict and Collective Action* (Beverly Hills: Sage, 1981), pp. 21–23.

30. Walton, *Reluctant Rebels*; Skocpol, *States and Social Revolutions*.

NOTES TO CHAPTER 6

1. The values are an index indicating relative change for each country, set arbitrarily to equal 100 in 1973. Particular values for Nicaragua should be compared only to other values for Nicaragua, not to other nations' values.

2. Centro de Investigaciones y Estudios de la Reforma Agraria (CIERA), *Informe de Nicaragua a la FAO* (Managua: Ministerio de Desarrollo Agropecuario y Reforma Agraria, 1983), pp. 40–41.

3. Mario A. DeFranco and Carlos F. Chamorro, "Nicaragua: Crecimiento industrial y empleo," in Daniel Camacho et al., *El fracaso social de la integración centroamericana* (San José, Costa Rica: Editorial Universitaria Centroamericana, 1979), Cuadro 2.

4. John A. Booth, *The End and the Beginning: The Nicaraguan Revolution*, 2nd ed. (Boulder, Colo.: Westview Press, 1985), Chapter 5.

5. Note that computational methods vary from nation to nation, so that cross-national comparisons of raw data should not be made. Trends within nations, however, are usefully disclosed.

6. Jaime Wheelock Román, *Imperialismo y dictadura: Crisis de una formación social* (México: Siglo Veintiuno Editores, 1979), pp. 141–198; Amaru Barahona Portocarrero, *Estudio sobre la historia contemporánea de Nicaragua* (San José, Costa Rica: Instituto de Investigaciones Sociales, Universidad de Costa Rica, 1977), pp. 33–44.

7. Donaldo Castillo Rivas, "Modelos de acumulación, agricultura, y agroindustria en Centroamérica," in D. Castillo Rivas, ed., *Centroamérica: Más allá de la crisis* (México: Ediciones SIAP, 1983), pp. 202–205; Consejo Superior Universitaria Centroamericana (CSUCA), *Estructura Agraria, dinámica de población, y desarrollo capitalista en Centroamérica* (San José, Costa Rica: Editorial Universitaria Centroamericana, 1978), pp. 204–254.

8. CIERA, *Informe de Nicaragua*, p. 41.

9. One hectare equals roughly 2.5 acres.

10. Castillo Rivas, "Modelos," p. 203.

11. Material from Ricardo E. Chavarría, "The Nicaraguan Insurrection," in Thomas W. Walker, ed., *Nicaragua in Revolution* (New York: Praeger, 1982), pp. 28–29; Booth, *The End and the Beginning*, Chapter 6.

12. George Black, *Triumph of the People: The Sandinista Revolution in Nicaragua* (London: Zed Press, 1981), pp. 70–72; Centro de Información, Documentación y Análisis del Movimiento Obrero Latinoamericano (CIDAMO), "El movimiento obrero," in G. García Márquez et al., *Los Sandinistas* (Bogotá: Editorial Oveja Negra, 1979), pp. 171–176.

13. Michael Dodson and Tommie Sue Montgomery, "The Churches in the Nicaraguan Revolution," in Walker, ed., *Nicaragua in Revolution*, pp. 163–174; Laura Nuzzi O'Shaughnessy and Luis H. Serra, *The Church and Revolution in Nicaragua* (Athens: Monographs in International Studies, Latin American Series No. 11, Ohio University, 1986).

14. See also T. Walker, "Introduction," in Walker, ed., *Nicaragua: The First Five Years* (New York: Praeger Publishers, 1985), p. 20; Julio López C. et al., *La caída del somocismo y la lucha sandinista en Nicaragua* (San José, Costa Rica: Editorial Universitaria Centroamericano, 1979), pp. 98–112.

15. Thomas W. Walker, *The Christian Democratic Movement in Nicaragua* (Tucson: University of Arizona Press, 1970).

16. Omar Cabezas, *Fire From the Mountain*, trans. Kathleen Weaver (New York: New American Library, 1986).

17. Booth, *The End and the Beginning*, Chapter 8.

18. See ibid., pp. 97–104; López C. et al., *La caída del somocismo*, pp. 71–98.

19. Peter Kornbluh, "The Covert War," in Thomas W. Walker, ed., *Reagan Versus the Sandinistas: The Undeclared War on Nicaragua* (Boulder, Colo.: Westview Press, 1987), p. 21.

20. "A Secret War for Nicaragua," *Newsweek*, November 8, 1982, p. 44.

21. Tayacán [the CIA], *Psychological Operations in Guerrilla Warfare: The CIA's Nicaragua Manual* (New York: Vintage Books, 1985).

22. COSEP is the successor to COSIP following a name change made around 1979.

23. E.g., a detailed report by Latin Americanists, *The Electoral Process in Nicaragua: Domestic and International Influences* (Austin, Tex.: Latin American Studies Association, November 19, 1984); or Booth, *The End and the Beginning*, pp. 215–223.

24. For details, see Walker, ed., *Nicaragua in Revolution*, and *Nicaragua: The First Five Years*.

25. Lawyers Committee for International Human Rights, *Nicaragua: Revolutionary Justice* (New York: April 1985), pp. 33–40.

26. John Spicer Nichols, "*La Prensa:* The CIA Connection," *Columbia Journalism Review* 28, No. 2 (July-August 1988), pp. 34, 35.

27. *Los Angeles Times*, June 27, 1986, p. 15.

28. Martin Diskin et al., "Peace and Autonomy on the Atlantic Coast of Nicaragua: A Report of the LASA Task Force on Human Rights and Academic Freedom," Part 2, LASA *Forum* 17 (Summer 1986), p. 15.

29. Americas Watch, *On Human Rights in Nicaragua* (New York, May 1982), pp. 58–80.

30. See Martin Diskin et al., "Peace and Autonomy on the Atlantic Coast of Nicaragua: A Report of the LASA Task Force on Human Rights and Academic Freedom," Part 1, LASA *Forum* 17 (Spring 1986), pp. 1–16; and Part 2, pp. 1–16.

31. Americas Watch, *On Human Rights in Nicaragua*, pp. 58–80.

32. See O'Shaughnessy and Serra, *The Church and Revolution in Nicaragua*.

33. *Los Angeles Times*, June 27, 1986, p. 15; June 30, 1986, p. 7; *New York Times*, July 5, 1986, p. 2.

34. "Latin Presidents Announce Accord on Contra Bases," *New York Times*, February 15, 1989, pp. 1, 4; *New York Times*, February 16, pp. 1, 6; "Nicaragua Pins Hopes on Turning Bureaucrats into Farmers," *Dallas Morning News*, February 22, 1989, p. 12A; and Booth's conversations with Mauricio Díaz of the Popular Social Christian party and Pedro Joaquín Chamorro Barrios, former director of the Nicaraguan Resistance, Montezuma, New Mexico, February 1989.

35. Joseph R. Thome and David Kaimowitz, "Agrarian Reform," in Walker, ed., *Nicaragua: The First Five Years;* and Forrest D. Colburn, *Post-Revolutionary Nicaragua: State, Class, and the Dilemmas of Agrarian Policy* (Berkeley: University of California Press, 1986).

36. John Weeks, "The Industrial Sector," and Michael E. Conroy, "Economic Legacy and Policies: Performance and Critique," in Walker, ed., *Nicaragua: The First Five Years;* and interviews by Booth with COSEP members in León, August 1985.

37. Michael E. Conroy, "Nicaragua: Structure, Dynamics, and Conditions of the Economy in 1988: The Economic Dilemmas of Peace and Democracy," paper presented at the VII Congreso Centroamericano de Sociología, October 10–15, 1988, Guatemala City, passim; and John A. Booth, "Nicaragua," in James M. Malloy and Eduardo Gamarra, eds., *Latin American and Caribbean Contemporary Record*, Vol. 7 (New York: Holmes and Meier, forthcoming).

NOTES TO CHAPTER 7

1. Hugo Molina, "Las bases económicas del desarrollo industrial y la absorción de fuerza de trabajo en El Salvador," in Daniel Camacho et al., *El fracaso social de la integración centroamericana* (San José, Costa Rica: Editorial Universitaria Centroamericana, 1979), pp. 245–254; Phillip L. Russell, *El Salvador in Crisis* (Austin, Tex.: Colorado River Press, 1984), pp. 76–78; Victor Antonio Orellana, *El Salvador: Crisis and Structural Change* (Miami: Latin American and Caribbean Center Occasional Paper Series No. 13, Florida International University, 1985), pp. 5–9; Victor Bulmer-Thomas, *The Political Economy of Central America Since 1920* (Cambridge: Cambridge University Press, 1987), pp. 175–229.

2. See especially Tommie Sue Montgomery, *Revolution in El Salvador: Origins and Evolution* (Boulder, Colo.: Westview Press, 1982); Donaldo Castillo Rivas, "Modelos de acumulación, agricultura, y agroindustria en Centroamérica," in D. Castillo Rivas, ed., *Centroamérica: Más allá de la crisis* (México: Ediciones SIAP, 1983), pp. 204–207; James Dunkerley, *The Long War: Dictatorship and Revolution in El Salvador* (London: Junction Books, 1982), pp. 87–118.

3. Dirección General de Estadística y Censos (DGEC–El Salvador), *Anuario Estadístico, 1981*, Tomos III–V (San Salvador: Ministerio de Economía, 1983), Cuadros 311-01,311-02; Bulmer-Thomas, *Political Economy of Central America*, pp. 201–207.

4. Orellana, *El Salvador: Crisis*, pp. 5–10; Molina, "Las bases económicas," pp. 245–254.

5. Orellana, *El Salvador: Crisis*, pp. 5–7.

6. Montgomery, *Revolution in El Salvador*, pp. 94–95.

7. Orellana, *El Salvador: Crisis*, pp. 6–7.

8. Material based on Montgomery, *Revolution in El Salvador*; Dunkerley, *The Long War*, pp. 90–102; Jorge Cáceres Prendes, "Radicalización política y pastoral en El Salvador: 1969–1979," *Estudios Sociales Centroamericanos* 33 (September-December 1982), pp. 97–111.

9. Russell, *El Salvador in Crisis*, pp. 71–78; Tomás Guerra, *El Salvador en la hora de su liberación* (San José, Costa Rica: n.p., 1980), pp. 103–108; Enrique Baloyra, *El Salvador in Transition* (Chapel Hill: University of North Carolina Press, 1982), pp. 43–52.

10. DGEC–El Salvador, *Anuario Estadístico, 1981*, Tomos III–V.

11. Rafael Menjívar, *Formación y lucha del proletariado industrial salvadoreño* (San José, Costa Rica: Editorial Universitaria Centroamericano, 1982), pp. 115–162; Russell, *El Salvador in Crisis*, p. 71.

12. See Michael McClintock, *The American Connection*, Vol. 1: *State Terror and Popular Resistance in El Salvador* (London: Zed Books, 1985), pp. 156–209, for details on the rise of repression in El Salvador; see also Inforpress Centroamericano, *Central America Report*, January 20, 1984, p. 23.

13. McClintock, *The American Connection*, pp. 174–177.

14. Tommie Sue Montgomery, "El Salvador: The Roots of Revolution," in S. Ropp and J. Morris, eds., *Central America: Crisis and Adaptation* (Albuquerque: University of New Mexico Press, 1984), pp. 86–90.

15. Taken from DGEC–El Salvador, *Anuario Estadístico* for years 1965, 1966, 1968, 1969, 1971, 1977, 1980, and 1981; the figure reported in the table is the total number of "homicides" plus other, unexplained violent deaths.

16. Based on data reported in Baloyra, *El Salvador in Transition*, p. 190; and Richard Alan White, *The Morass: United States Intervention in Central America* (New York: Harper and Row, 1984), p. 44; and Inforpress Centroamericano, *Central America Report*, January 20, 1984, p. 23.

17. Comisión de Derechos Humanos de El Salvador (CDHES), *Primer Congreso de Derechos Humanos en El Salvador* (San Salvador, El Salvador: CDHES, November 1984), pp. 30–31, authors' translation.

18. Montgomery, *Revolution in El Salvador*, pp. 140–157.

19. Dunkerley, *The Long War*, p. 175.

20. Terry Karl, "Imposing Consent: Electoralism vs. Democratization in El Salvador," in P. Drake and E. Silva, eds., *Elections and Democratization in Latin America* (La Jolla: Center for Iberian and Latin American Studies–Center for U.S.-Mexican Studies, University of California, San Diego, 1986), p. 21. Data for 1989 from *Dallas Morning News*, March 19, 1989, pp. 1, 10–11, 12.

21. Baloyra, *El Salvador in Transition*; José Z. García, "El Salvador: Recent Elections in Historical Perspective," in John A. Booth and Mitchell A. Seligson, eds., *Elections and Democracy in Central America* (Chapel Hill, University of North Carolina Press, 1989), pp. 60–89.

22. Dunkerley, *The Long War*, p. 163.

23. For discussions of problems with the U.S.-backed elections in El Salvador in 1982, 1984, and 1985, see Terry Karl, "Imposing Consent"; Edward S. Herman and Frank Brodhead, *Demonstration Elections* (Boston: South End Press, 1984), pp. 93–152; and García, "El Salvador: Recent Elections," pp. 60–89.

24. See, for instance, Karl, "Imposing Consent," pp. 18–34; and Clifford Krauss, "El Salvador Army Gains on the Guerrillas," *Wall Street Journal*, July 30, 1986, p. 20.

25. Karl, "Imposing Consent."

26. Inter-American Development Bank (IABD), *Economic and Social Progress in Latin America: Science and Technology: 1988 Report* (Washington, D.C., 1988), Table B-1.

27. Krauss, "El Salvador Army Gains," p. 20.

28. Inforpress Centroamericana, *Guatemala: Elections 1985* (Guatemala City, 1985), p. 19.

29. Guatemala was judged to be one of the countries most affected by rising unemployment in the early 1980s. See Eugenio Rivera Urrutia, Ana Sojo, and José Roberto López, *Centroamérica: Política económica y crisis* (San José, Costa Rica: Editorial Departamento Ecuménico de Investigaciones—Universidad Nacional Autónoma, 1986), pp. 138–141.

30. Ibid.; Thomas P. Anderson, *Politics in Central America: Guatemala, El Salvador, Honduras, and Nicaragua* (New York: Praeger, 1982), pp. 19–62; "Guatemala," *Mesoamérica*, May 1982; Consejo Superior Universitaria Centroamericana (CSUCA), *Estructura agrária, dinámica de población, y desarrollo capitalista en Centroamérica* (San José, Costa Rica: Editorial Universitaria Centroamericana, 1978), pp. 77–132; Technical Commission of the Great National Dialogue, *Economic and Social Policy Recommendations to the Head of State* (Guatemala City, 1985); Lars Schoultz, "Guatemala: Social Change and Political Conflict," in Martin Diskin, ed., *Trouble in Our Backyard* (New York: Pantheon, 1983), pp. 178–183.

31. Julio Castellano Cambranes, "Origins of the Crisis of the Established Order in Guatemala," in Ropp and Morris, eds., *Central America: Crisis*, Table 4.2.

32. Mitchell A. Seligson et al., *Land and Labor in Guatemala: An Assessment* (Washington, D.C.: Agency for International Development–Development Associates, 1982), pp. 1–18.

33. George Black et al., *Garrison Guatemala* (New York: Monthly Review Press, 1984), pp. 34–37; Schoultz, "Guatemala," p. 181; Seligson et al., *Land and Labor.*

34. Gustavo A. Noyola, "Integración centroamericana y absorción de mano de obra: Guatemala," in Camacho et al., *El fracaso*.

35. Richard Newbold Adams, *Crucifixion by Power: Essays on Guatemalan National Social Structure, 1944–1966* (Austin: University of Texas Press, 1970); Black et al., *Garrison Guatemala*, pp. 48–51.

36. John A. Booth, "A Guatemalan Nightmare: Levels of Political Violence, 1966–1972," *Journal of Interamerican Studies and World Affairs* 22 (May 1980), pp. 195–225.

37. Material here drawn mainly from Oscar Rolando Sierra Pop, "Iglesia y conflicto social en Guatemala," *Estudios Sociales Centroamericanos* 33 (September-December 1982), pp. 66–86; Black et al., *Garrison Guatemala*, pp. 61–107; Anderson, *Politics*, pp. 19–60; Inforpress Centroamericana, *Guatemala: Elections 1985*, pp. 8–11; Jonathan Fried et al., *Guatemala in Rebellion: Unfinished History* (New York: Grove, 1983), pp. 151–316.

38. Héctor Rosado Granados, *Guatemala 1984: Elecciones para Asamblea Nacional Constituyente* (San José, Costa Rica: Instituto Centroamericano de Derechos Humanos–Centro de Asesoría y Promoción Electoral, 1985), p. 41; "Guatemala," *Mesoamérica*, March 1982, pp. 2–4; Margaret E. Roggensack and John A. Booth, *Report of the International Human Rights Law Group and the Washington Office on Latin America Advance Election Observer Mission to Guatemala* (Washington, D.C., 1985), Appendix B; Robert Trudeau, "Guatemalan Elections: The Illusion of Democracy," paper presented to the National Conference on Guatemala, Washington, D.C., June 15, 1984.

39. Gabriel Aguilera Peralta, Romero Imery, et al., *Dialéctica del terror en Guatemala* (San José, Costa Rica: Editorial Universitaria Centroamericana, 1981); Americas Watch, *Human Rights in Guatemala: No Neutrals Allowed* (New York, 1982), and *Little Hope: Human Rights in Guatemala, January 1984–1985* (New York, 1985); John A. Booth et al., *The 1985 Guatemalan Elections: Will the Military Relinquish Power?* (Washington, D.C.: International Human Rights Law Group–Washington Office on Latin America, 1985); see also Gordon L. Bowen, "The Origins and Development of State Terrorism," in Donald E. Schulz and Douglas H. Graham, eds., *Revolution and Counterrevolution in Central America and the Caribbean* (Boulder, Colo.: Westview Press, 1984); and "Guatemala," *Mesoamérica*, July-August 1982, pp. 2–4..

40. Data for selected periods drawn from U.S. Embassy—Guatemala reports from 1966 through 1984, reported in Booth, "A Guatemalan Nightmare," and U.S. Department of State, *Country Report on Human Rights Practices* (Washington, D.C.: U.S. Government Printing Office, February 2, 1981), p. 441; later data came from Inforpress Centroamericana, *Central America Report*, February 1, 1985, p. 31; November 22, 1985, p. 357; January 21, 1988, p. 12.

41. For 1982 and after see U.S. Embassy—Guatemala, "A Statistical Comparison of Violence (1982–1985)," Guatemala City, xerox, 1985.

42. Quoted by Allan Nairn in "Guatemala Can't Take 2 Roads," *New York Times*, July 20, 1982, p. 23A.

43. Booth's conversation with U.S. Embassy personnel, Guatemala City, September 1985; see also Roggensack and Booth, *Report*.

44. Material based on Booth's field observations in Guatemala in 1985, plus Americas Watch, *Human Rights in Guatemala* and *Little Hope*; Booth et al., *The 1985 Guatemalan Elections*; Inforpress Centroamericana, *Guatemala: Elections 1985*; British Parliamentary Human Rights Group, *"Bitter and Cruel . . .": Report of a Mission to Guatemala by the British Parliamentary Human Rights Group* (London: House of Commons, 1985); and Black et al., *Garrison Guatemala*, pp. 61–113.

45. Black et al., *Garrison Guatemala*, pp. 107–109.

46. Interviews with Guatemalan labor sources, September–October 1985 and April–May 1987, Guatemala City; see Booth et al., *The 1985 Guatemalan Elections*, pp. 39–40, and David Carliner et al., *Political Transition and the Rule of Law in Guatemala* (Washington, D.C.: International Human Rights Law Group—Washington Office on Latin America, January 1988), pp. 7–8.

47. Booth et al., *The 1985 Guatemalan Elections*.

48. Interviews with spokesmen for various parties, September–October 1985, Guatemala.

49. See Latin American Studies Association (LASA), *Extraordinary Opportunities . . . and New Risks: Final Report of the LASA Commission on Compliance with the*

Central America Peace Accord (Pittsburgh: LASA, 1988), pp. 15–20; Booth's interviews with various Guatemalan political figures and expert observers,. September 1988; "Año de tumulto en Guatemala," *Excelsior* (Mexico City), December 30, 1988, p. 4A; *Christian Science Monitor*, February 14, 1989, p. 3.

50. See, for instance, Washington Office on Latin America, *Who Pays the Price? The Cost of War in the Guatemalan Highlands* (Washington, D.C., April 1988).

51. Carliner et al., *Political Transition;* and LASA, *Extraordinary Opportunities . . . and New Risks*, pp. 15–20.

NOTES TO CHAPTER 8

1. See also Victor Bulmer-Thomas, *The Political Economy of Central America Since 1920* (New York: Cambridge University Press, 1987), Table 10.7, p. 219; Víctor Hugo Céspedes, Alberto di Mare, and Ronulfo Jiménez, *Costa Rica: La economía en 1985* (San José, Costa Rica: Academia de Centroamérica, 1986), Cuadro 19, p. 71.

2. Víctor Hugo Céspedes, *Evolución de la distribución del ingreso en Costa Rica* (San José, Costa Rica: Instituto de Investigación en Ciencias Económicas, Universidad de Costa Rica, 1979), Cuadro 6; and Céspedes et al., *Costa Rica: La economía en 1985*, Cuadro 20, p. 73.

3. See also David Felix, "Income Distribution and the Quality of Life in Latin America: Patterns, Trends, and Policy Implications," *Latin American Research Review* 18, No. 2 (1983), pp. 3–34.

4. For further data, see John A. Booth, "Representative Constitutional Democracy in Costa Rica: Adaptation to Crisis in the Turbulent 1980s," in S. Ropp and J. Morris, eds., *Central America: Crisis and Adaptation* (Albuquerque: University of New Mexico Press, 1984), p. 171.

5. Mitchell A. Seligson, *Peasants of Costa Rica and the Development of Agrarian Capitalism* (Madison, University of Wisconsin Press, 1980), pp. 122–170; see also Francisco Barahona Riera, *Reforma agraria y poder político* (San José: Editorial Universidad de Costa Rica, 1980), pp. 221–422; Donaldo Castillo Rivas, "Modelos de acumulación, agricultura, y agroindustria en Centroamérica," in D. Castillo Rivas, ed., *Centroamérica: Más allá de la crisis* (México: Ediciones SIAP, 1983), pp. 210–213.

6. Thomas P. Anderson, *Politics in Central America: Guatemala, El Salvador, Honduras, and Nicaragua* (New York: Praeger, 1982), pp. 109–147.

7. Víctor Meza, *Honduras: La evolución de la crisis* (Tegucigalpa: Editorial Universitaria, 1982), pp. 19–29; J. Mark Ruhl, "Agrarian Structure and Political Stability in Honduras," *Journal of Inter-American Studies and World Affairs* 26 (February 1984), pp. 33–68.

8. "Guatemala," *Mesosamérica*, July-August 1982: 7; Castillo Rivas, "Modelos," pp. 199–201; Mario Posas, *El movimiento campesino hondureño* (Tegucigalpa: Editorial Guaymuras, 1981), pp. 34–42.

9. Booth's conversation with Lucas Aguilera, member of the executive committee of the Union Nacional Campesina, Tegucigalpa, and members of the Unión Maraíta cooperative farm, Departamento Francisco Morazán, August 21, 1985.

10. This material from John A. Booth, "Costa Rican Democracy," a paper presented at the Conference on Democracy in Developing Nations, The Hoover Institution, Stanford,

California, December 19, 1985, pp. 29–34; and Booth, "Representative Constitutional Democracy."

11. E. Lederman et al., "Trabajo y empleo," in Chester Zelaya, ed., *Costa Rica contemporánea*, Tomo II (San José: Editorial Costa Rica, 1979; James Backer, *La Iglesia y el sindicalismo en Costa Rica*, (San José: Editorial Costa Rica, 1978), pp. 135–207; Gustavo Blanco and Orlando Navarro, *El solidarismo: Pensamiento y dinámica social de un movimiento obrero patronal* (San José: Editorial Costa Rica, 1984).

12. Rodrigo Fernández Vásquez, "Costa Rica: Interpretación histórica sobre reforma social y acción eclesiástica: 1940–1982," *Estudios Sociales Centroamericanos* 33 (September-December 1982), pp. 221–248.

13. Lowell Gudmundson, "Costa Rica," in Jack W. Hopkins, ed., *Latin American and Caribbean Contemporary Record*, Vol. 3: *1983–1984* (New York: Holmes and Meier, 1985), pp. 499–508.

14. Mitchell A. Seligson and Edward Muller, "Democracy, Stability, and Economic Crisis: Costa Rica, 1978–1983," *International Studies Quarterly* 31 (September 1987), pp. 301–326; and Booth "Costa Rican Democracy."

15. Discussion of Honduras based on Víctor Meza, *Historia del movimiento obrero hondureño* (Tegucigalpa: Editorial Guaymuras, 1980), pp. 123–167, and Meza, *Honduras: La evolución*, pp. 14–41; Anderson, *Politics*, pp. 109–121; Posas, *El movimiento campesino*.

16. James A. Morris, "Government and Politics," in James D. Rudolph, ed., *Honduras: A Country Study* (Washington, D.C.: American University Foreign Area Studies series, U.S. Government Printing Office, 1984), pp. 168–193; Rosa María Pochet Coronado, "El reformismo estatal y la Iglesia en Honduras 1949–1982," *Estudios Sociales Centroamericanos* 33 (September-December 1982), pp. 155–188.

17. Steve C. Ropp, "National Security," in Rudolph, ed., *Honduras: A Country Study*, pp. 391–396.

18. Booth, "Representative Constitutional Democracy," pp. 173–176; Booth, "Costa Rican Democracy," pp. 39–40; Seligson, *Peasants*, pp. 105–114; U.S. Department of State, *Country Reports on Human Rights Practices* (Washington, D.C.: U.S. Government Printing Office, February 2, 1981), pp. 241–244.

19. Richard L. Millett, "Historical Setting," in Rudolph, ed., *Honduras: A Country Study*, p. 47.

20. Ramón Custodio, "The Human Rights Crisis in Honduras," in Mark Rosenberg and Phillip Shepherd, eds., *Honduras Confronts its Future* (Boulder, Colo.: Lynne Reinner Publishers, 1986), pp. 69–71.

21. U.S. Department of State, *Country Reports on Human Rights*, pp. 46; Morris, "Government and Politics," pp. 192–193; and James A. Morris, "Honduras: The Burden of Survival in Central America," in Ropp and Morris, eds., *Central America*, pp. 217–219; Anderson, *Politics*, pp. 116–132.

22. Americas Watch, *Review of the Department of State's Country Reports on Human Rights Practices for 1982: An Assessment* (New York, February 1983), p. 55. The discrepancy between this figure and the number of 40 cited earlier probably stems from a combination of two factors: different reporting agencies are involved, and they are reporting on somewhat different phenomena. The two figures may not, in fact, be incongruent.

23. *Washington Report on the Hemisphere*, October 28, 1987, pp. 1, 60.

24. James A. Morris, "Honduras: The Burden of Survival in Central America" in Ropp and Morris, *Central America*, pp. 201–204.

25. Mark Rosenberg, "Can Democracy Survive the Democrats? From Transition to Consolidation in Honduras," in John A. Booth and Mitchell A. Seligson, eds., *Elections and Democracy in Central America* (Chapel Hill, University of North Carolina Press, 1989), Latin American Studies Association (LASA), *Extraordinary Opportunities . . . and New Risks: Final Report of the LASA Commission on Compliance with the Central American Peace Accord* (Pittsburgh: LASA, 1988), pp. 20–26.

NOTES TO CHAPTER 9

1. Paper presented by Thomas W. Walker to the U.S. Department of State conference on Central America: U.S. Policy Interests and Concerns, Washington, D.C., March 19, 1979. This paper was subsequently published as "The U.S. and Central America," *Caribbean Review* 8, No. 3 (Summer 1979), pp. 18–23.

2. The only modification we would now make to the 1979 statement is that surprisingly, even in the late 1980s, flawed U.S. policy still had not produced high levels of anti-Americanism. Even in Nicaragua, most citizens, including most Sandinistas, were able to distinguish between the American people, on the one hand, and the U.S. government, on the other. Rightly or wrongly, the former were not held responsible for the behavior of the latter.

3. Charles W. Anderson, "The Latin American Political System," in his *Politics and Economic Change in Latin America: The Governing of Restless Nations* (New York: Van Nostrand Reinhold Co., 1967), pp. 87–114.

4. For a sophisticated analysis of democratic theories, see Robert A. Dahl, *A Preface to Democratic Theory* (Chicago: University of Chicago Press, 1956). For a critical analysis of the significance of participation as a basis for democratic process, see E. E. Schattschneider, *The Semisovereign People: A Realist's View of Democracy in America* (New York: Holt, Rinehart, and Winston, 1960).

5 See, for instance, John A. Booth and Mitchell A. Seligson, eds., *Elections and Democracy in Central America* (Chapel Hill: University of North Carolina Press, 1989), passim.

6. National Bipartisan Commission on Central America, *Report of the National Bipartisan Commission on Central America* (Washington, D.C., 1984), p. 30.

7. Paulo Freire, *The Pedagogy of the Oppressed* (New York: Herder and Herder, 1968).

8. Coauthor Thomas W. Walker served as a U.S. Peace Corps volunteer in Mompós, Colombia, from 1963 to 1965.

9. Second General Conference of Latin American Bishops, *The Church and the Present-Day Transformation of Latin America in the Light of the Council* (Washington, D.C.: United States Catholic Conference, 1973).

10. For more information about the changing Catholic church in the past three decades, see Edward L. Cleary, O.P., *Crisis and Change: The Church in Latin America Today* (Maryknoll, N.Y.: Orbis Books, 1985).

11. After the victory, the women's organization changed its name to the Luisa Amanda Espinosa Nicaraguan Woman's Association (Asociación de Mujeres Nicaragüenses Luisa Amanda Espinosa–AMNLAE) and the CDCs became the Sandinista Defense

Committees (Comités de Defensa Sandinista—CDS), but other than that, all five movements remained essentially the same.

12. This information was revealed on June 25, 1985, by an official in the U.S. Embassy to a group of which coauthor Thomas Walker was part.

13. For more information about mobilization in Nicaragua, see Luis Serra, "The Grass-Roots Organizations," in Thomas W. Walker, ed., *Nicaragua: The First Five Years* (New York: Praeger, 1985), pp. 65–89, or Gary Ruchwarger, *People in Power: Forging a Grassroots Democracy in Nicaragua* (Granby, Mass.: Bergin and Garvey Publishers, 1987).

14. See Deborah Barndt, "Popular Education," in Walker, ed., *Nicaragua: The First Five Years*, pp. 317–345.

15. The only Central American country in which some popular mobilization and socioeconomic reform has succeeded with U.S. support is Costa Rica, where the social-democratic reformers of the National Liberation party were associated with a political movement that ousted Communists from power in 1948.

16. For an illuminating discussion of the nature of the U.S. policymaker's perception of a Communist threat in Latin America, see Lars Schoultz, "Communism," in his *National Security and United States Policy Toward Latin America* (Princeton: Princeton University Press, 1987), pp. 106–139.

17. Michael McClintock, *The American Connection, Volume 1: State Terror and Popular Resistance in El Salvador* (London: Zed Books, 1985), p. 47.

18. See Michael Klare, *War Without End* (New York: Alfred A. Knopf, 1972), Chapter 9.

19. Americas Watch, *Review of the Department of State's Country Reports on Human Rights Practices for 1982: An Assessment* (New York: February 1983), pp. 1–9, 37–46, 55–61, 63–70. The report stated, for instance, that "a special effort appears to have been made to exculpate current leaders considered friends of the United States—such as . . . President Ríos Montt of Guatemala" (p. 5).

20. Latin American Studies Association, *The Electoral Process in Nicaragua: Domestic and International Influences* (Austin, Tex.: LASA, 1984), p. 17.

21. Mary B. Vanderlaan, *Revolution and Foreign Policy in Nicaragua* (Boulder, Colo.: Westview Press, 1986), p. 322.

22. Excerpts from State Department and Pentagon, *Congressional Presentation Document*, Security Assistance Programs, FY 1981, as reproduced in Robert Matthews, "The Limits of Friendship: Nicaragua and the West," NACLA *Report on the Americas*, 19 (No. 3, May/June 1985), p. 24.

23. Michael McClintock, *The American Connection, Volume II: State Terror and Popular Resistance in Guatemala* (London: Zed Books, 1985), pp. 32–33. This volume is also a source of documentation for the general observations in the next two paragraphs. For additional information about demobilization in Guatemala see Tom Barry and Deb Preusch, *The Soft War: The Uses and Abuses of U.S. Economic Aid in Central America* (New York: Grove Press, 1988).

24. Lindsey Gruson, "Terror's Toll Builds Again in El Salvador," *New York Times*, December 20, 1988, p. 1.

25. Just prior to the Sandinista victory in Nicaragua, coauthor Thomas Walker and two other U.S. academicians were invited to speak at a dinner seminar for high-level U.S. government officials from various foreign policymaking departments. Though the seminar

was designed explicitly to "focus on the prospects for political and economic stability in . . . [Central America], paying particular attention to the impact of a radical, pro-Cuban regime in Managua," Walker accepted the invitation on the condition that he be allowed to deliver a sharply critical evaluation of U.S. policy. The condition was accepted in writing on July 18, and the event took place on August 2, 1988. After the short academic presentations, the government officials in attendance, including CIA Director Admiral Stansfield Turner, broke into a remarkably frank strategy discussion in which the ideas contained in the three sentences in the text preceding this endnote number emerged as part of an apparent consensus among the policymakers.

26. See McClintock, *The American Connection*, Vol. 1.

27. For a good description and documentation of the role of James Cheek, see Tommie Sue Montgomery, *Revolution in El Salvador: Origins and Evolution*, 2nd ed. (Boulder, Colo.: Westview Press, forthcoming), Chapter 7.

28. For material on U.S. officials' efforts to persuade El Salvador to improve its human rights performance, see "El Salvador," *Mesoamérica*, November 1982, p. 6; "El Salvador," *Mesoamérica*, October 1983, p. 6; "El Salvador," *Mesoamérica*, November 1983, p. 6; and "El Salvador," *Mesoamérica*, December 1983, pp. 5–6; and the *Miami Herald*, December 19, 1983, p. 1.

29. One can get a sense of this barbarity by reading, for instance, Organization of American States, *Report on the Situation of Human Rights in Nicaragua: Findings of the "On-site" Observation in the Republic of Nicaragua, October 3–12, 1978* (Washington, D.C.: General Secretariat of the OAS, 1978).

30. Richard L. Millett, *Guardians of the Dynasty: A History of the U.S.-Created Guardia Nacional de Nicaragua and the Somoza Family* (Maryknoll, N.Y.: Orbis Press, 1977), p. 252.

31. A 1985 U.S. Congressional investigation revealed that forty-six of the forty-eight officers in the main contra army were former Somoza officers (Arms Control and Foreign Policy Caucus, the U.S. House of Representatives, "Who Are the Contras?" *Congressional Record* 131, 48 [Daily Edition, April 23, 1985], H2335). Though this embarrassing revelation led the Reagan administration to expand and reshuffle the officers' corps, the real control of the contras in the field remained firmly in the hands of ex-guardsmen. Indeed, the head of the contras as this was being written was still a former guard officer, Enrique Bermúdez.

32. Tayacán [the CIA], *Operaciones sicológicas en guerra de guerrillas*, [1983]. This was later translated and published commercially as *Psychological Operations in Guerrilla Warfare: The CIA's Nicaragua Manual* (New York: Vintage Books, 1985).

33. The documentation of contra brutality is massive. The numerous reports of Americas Watch are good sources. Others are Reed Brody, *Contra Terror in Nicaragua, Report of a Fact-finding Mission: September 1984–January 1985* (Boston: South End Press, 1985); and Christopher Dickey, *With the Contras: A Reporter in the Wilds of Nicaragua* (New York: Simon and Schuster, 1985).

34. Interamerican Research Center, *Nicaraguan Public Opinion: Preliminary Report of a Random Sample Poll Conducted in Managua by the Newly-Formed Nicaraguan Institute of Public Opinion* (Los Angeles: Interamerican Research Center, June 30, 1988).

NOTES TO CHAPTER 10

1. Walker, for instance, remembers with some embarrassment how, in the manuscript of a chapter on Nicaragua that he wrote early in 1978 for a textbook being edited by two other scholars, he confidently observed that even in the event of Somoza's overthrow, "it is unlikely that a socially revolutionary or progressive democratic government will come to power." At the time, the validity of the prediction had seemed obvious: Surely, he had reasoned, the Nicaraguan National Guard would have a sufficient instinct for self-preservation to get rid of Somoza, declare a reformist, superficially "democratic" regime, and thus avert a real social revolution or even significant reform. To Walker's chagrin, the chapter containing this prediction went to press early in 1979, at least a half-year after its author had come to an opposite conclusion and just months before the FSLN rebel army entered Managua and accepted the unconditional surrender of what remained of Somoza's armed forces. Thomas W. Walker, "Nicaragua: The Somoza Family Regime," in Howard J. Wiarda and Harvey F. Kline, eds., *Latin American Politics and Development* (Boston: Houghton Mifflin Co., 1979), p. 331.

2. Conversations of Booth with various Costa Rican scholars and expert observers during the mid- and late 1980s.

3. "National Security Council Document on Policy in Central America," *New York Times*, April 7, 1983.

4. For more detail and analysis concerning the Central American peace effort, see William Goodfellow, "The Diplomatic Front," in Thomas W. Walker, ed., *Reagan Versus the Sandinistas: The Undeclared War on Nicaragua* (Boulder, Colo.: Westview Press, 1987), pp. 143–156.

5. Stephen Kinzer, "Nicaraguans Say They Would Sign Proposed Treaty," *New York Times*, September 23, 1984, p. 20.

6. George Shultz, in a letter to foreign ministers of the European Economic Community, September 7, 1984.

7. A letter from the Nicaraguan junta president, Daniel Ortega, to the Contadora foreign ministers on September 21, 1984, as quoted in Goodfellow, "The Diplomatic Front," p. 149.

8. From a leaked "Translation from Spanish," titled "Comments, observations and conclusions of the International Verification and Follow-up Commission," p. 3. (The full report appears in Sung Ho Kim and Thomas W. Walker, eds., *Perspectives on War and Peace in Central America* [Athens: Papers in International Studies, Ohio University Press, forthcoming].) Though the report was ignored by the U.S. media, other reputable observer teams had come to conclusions very similar to those of the "The Ten." See, for instance, Latin American Studies Association, *Extraordinary Opportunities . . . and New Risks: Final Report of the LASA Commission on Compliance with the Central American Peace Accord* (Pittsburgh: LASA, 1988). [For information about obtaining the LASA report, write to The Latin American Studies Association, William Pitt Union, 9th Floor, University of Pittsburgh, Pittsburgh, PA 15260, or call (412) 648-7929.]

9. This version of the internal workings of the verification commission comes from conversations between Thomas Walker and an informed source involved in the work of

the commission who, because of his sensitive diplomatic position, has asked to remain anonymous.

10. Title 1, sub-title a, second paragraph, the Central American Peace Accord.

11. "Contras Lay off Political Staff Workers," *New York Times*, June 22, 1988, pp. 1, 3–4.

12. "Latin Presidents Announce Accord on Contra Bases," *New York Times*, February 15, 1989, pp. 1, 4; *New York Times*, February 16, 1989, pp. 1, 6.

13. For an excellent discussion of the Nicaraguan economic model, its success during the first four years, and the damage done to it by the Reagan administration's "low-intensity war," see Michael E. Conroy, "Economic Aggression as an Instrument of Low-Intensity Warfare," in Walker, ed., *Reagan Versus the Sandinistas*, pp. 57–79. As a curious addendum, it is interesting to note that in the waning weeks of the Reagan administration, the United States Information Agency decided to include Conroy's chapter in an "Economic Portfolio" that the agency's chief of copyright services indicated was "being prepared for priority shipment to our posts overseas" in order "to bring to the attention of foreign audiences a cross-section of current and authoritative writings" on "The International Legacy of Reaganomics," as the portfolio was to be titled.

14. In 1988, the National Geographic Society (NGS) commissioned the Gallup Organization to do a survey of the geographical literacy of adults in Canada, France, Italy, Japan, Mexico, Sweden, the United Kingdom, the United States, and West Germany. The survey revealed that U.S. citizens ranked among the bottom third of those tested. Most ominous of the NGS findings was the fact that the youngest U.S. group of voting age, those eighteen to twenty-four years old, did worse than that age group in all other countries tested, including Mexico, where young adults have an average of only a few years of formal education. See Julie D. Edgeworth, "Americans Get Low Grades in Gallup Geography Test," *National Geographic Society Update*, Fall 1988.

BIBLIOGRAPHY

Adams, Richard Newbold. 1970. *Crucifixion by Power: Essays on Guatemalan National Social Structure, 1944–1966*. Austin: University of Texas Press.

Aguilera Peralta, Gabriel. 1983. "Guatemala: Estado, militarismo, y lucha política." In Castillo Rivas, ed. 1983a.

Aguilera Peralta, Gabriel, Romero Imery, et al. 1981. *Dialéctica del terror en Guatemala*. San José, Costa Rica: Editorial Universitaria Centroamericana.

Americas Watch. 1982a. *Human Rights in Guatemala: No Neutrals Allowed*. New York.

———. 1982b. *On Human Rights in Nicaragua*. New York. May.

———. 1983. *Review of the Department of State's Country Reports on Human Rights Practices for 1982: An Assessment*. New York. February.

———. 1985. *Little Hope: Human Rights in Guatemala, January 1984–1985*. New York. February.

Anderson, Charles W. 1967. "The Latin American Political System." In Charles W. Anderson, *Politics and Economic Change in Latin America: The Governing of Restless Nations*. New York: Van Nostrand Reinhold, 1967.

Anderson, Thomas P. 1982. *Politics in Central America: Guatemala, El Salvador, Honduras, and Nicaragua*. New York: Praeger.

"Año de tumulto en Guatemala." 1988. *Excelsior* (Mexico City). December 30: 4A.

Arms Control and Foreign Policy Caucus, U.S. House of Representatives. 1985. "Who Are the Contras?" *Congressional Record* 131, 48 (Daily Edition, April 23), H2335.

Atwood, Wallace W., and Helen Goss Thomas. 1929. *The Americas*. Boston: Ginn and Co.

Aya, Rod. 1979. "Theories of Revolution Reconsidered: Contrasting Models of Collective Violence." *Theory and Society* 8 (June-December): 39–100.

Backer, James. 1978. *La Iglesia y el sindicalismo en Costa Rica*. San José, Costa Rica: Editorial Costa Rica.

Baloyra, Enrique A. 1982. *El Salvador in Transition*. Chapel Hill: University of North Carolina Press.

———. 1983. "Reactionary Despotism in Central America." *Journal of Latin American Studies* 15 (November): 295–319.

Barahona Portocarrero, Amaru. 1977. *Estudio sobre la historia contemporánea de Nicaragua*, San José, Costa Rica: Instituto de Investigaciones Sociales, Universidad de Costa Rica.

Barahona Riera, Francisco. 1980. *Reforma agraria y poder político*. San José, Costa Rica: Editorial Universidad de Costa Rica.

Barndt, Deborah. 1985. "Popular Education." In Walker, ed. 1985b.

Barry, Tom, and Deb Preusch. 1988. *The Soft War: The Uses and Abuses of U.S. Economic Aid in Central America*. New York: Grove Press.

Bermann, Karl. 1986. *Under the Big Stick: Nicaragua and the United States since 1948*. Boston: South End Press.

Berryman, Phillip. 1984. *The Religious Roots of Rebellion: Christians in the Central American Revolutions*. Maryknoll, N.Y.: Orbis Books.

______. 1985. *Inside Central America*, New York: Pantheon Books.

Black, George. 1981. *Triumph of the People: The Sandinista Revolution in Nicaragua*. London: Zed Press.

Black, George, with Milton Jamail and Norma Stoltz Chinchilla. 1984. *Garrison Guatemala*. New York: Monthly Review Press.

Blanco, Gustavo, and Orlando Navarro. 1984. *El solidarismo: Pensamiento y dinámica social de un movimiento obrero patronal*. San José: Editorial Costa Rica.

Booth, John A. 1980. "A Guatemalan Nightmare: Levels of Political Violence, 1966–1972." *Journal of Interamerican Studies and World Affairs* 22 (May): 195–225.

______. 1982. *The End and the Beginning: The Nicaraguan Revolution*. Boulder, Colo.: Westview Press.

______. 1984. "Representative Constitutional Democracy in Costa Rica: Adaptation to Crisis in the Turbulent 1980s." In Ropp and Morris, eds. 1984.

______. 1985a, "Costa Rican Democracy." Paper presented at the Conference on Democracy in Developing Nations, Stanford, California: The Hoover Institution. December 19.

______. 1985b. *The End and the Beginning: The Nicaraguan Revolution*. 2nd ed. Boulder, Colo.: Westview Press.

______. 1989. "Nicaragua." In Malloy and Gamarra, eds. forthcoming.

Booth, John A., and Mitchell A. Seligson, eds. 1989. *Elections and Democracy in Central America*. Chapel Hill: University of North Carolina Press.

Booth, John A., et al. 1985. *The 1985 Guatemalan National Elections: Will the Military Relinquish Power?* Washington, D.C.: International Human Rights Law Group–Washington Office on Latin America. February.

Bowen, Gordon L. 1984. "The Origins and Development of State Terrorism." In Schulz and Graham, eds. 1984.

British Parliamentary Human Rights Group. 1985. *"Bitter and Cruel . . .": Report of a Mission to Guatemala by the British Parliamentary Human Rights Group*. London: House of Commons.

Brody, Reed. 1985. *Contra Terror in Nicaragua, Report of a Fact-finding Mission: September 1984–January 1985*. Boston: South End Press.

Bulmer-Thomas, Victor. 1983. "Economic Development Over the Long Run—Central America Since 1920." *Journal of Latin American Studies* 15 (November): 269–294.

______. 1987. *The Political Economy of Central America Since 1920*. Cambridge: Cambridge University Press.

Cabezas, Omar. 1986. *Fire From the Mountain*. Kathleen Weaver, trans. New York: New American Library.

Cáceres Prendes, Jorge. 1982. "Radicalización política y pastoral en El Salvador: 1969–1979." *Estudios Sociales Centroamericanos* 33 (September-December): 97–111.

Camacho, Daniel, et al. 1979. *El fracaso social de la integración centroamericana*, San José, Costa Rica: Editorial Universitaria Centroamericana.

Carliner, David, et al. 1988. *Political Transition and the Rule of Law in Guatemala*. Washington, D.C.: International Human Rights Law Group–Washington Office on Latin America. January.

Castellano Cambranes, Julio. 1984. "Origins of the Crisis of the Established Order in Guatemala." In Ropp and Morris, eds. 1984.

Castillo Rivas, Donaldo, ed. 1983a. *Centroamérica: Más allá de la crisis*. México: Ediciones SIAP.

———. 1983b. "Modelos de acumulación, agricultura, y agroindustria en Centroamérica." In Castillo Rivas, ed. 1983a.

CDHES (Comisión de Derechos Humanos de El Salvador). 1984. *Primer Congreso de Derechos Humanos en El Salvador.* San Salvador, El Salvador. November.

CEPAL (Comisión Económica para América Latina y el Caribe). 1985. *Preliminary Overview of the Latin American Economy: 1985*. Santiago, Chile: United Nations. December.

———. 1986. *Preliminary Overview of the Latin American Economy: 1986*. Santiago, Chile: United Nations. December.

Céspedes, Víctor Hugo. 1979. *Evolución de la distribución del ingreso en Costa Rica*. San José, Costa Rica: Instituto de Investigación en Ciencias Económicas, Universidad de Costa Rica.

Céspedes, Víctor Hugo, Alberto di Mare, and Ronulfo Jiménez. 1986. *Costa Rica: La economía en 1985*. San José, Costa Rica: Academia de Centroamérica.

CIERA (Centro de Investigaciones y Estudios de la Reforma Agraria). 1983. *Informe de Nicaragua a la FAO*. Managua: Ministerio de Desarrollo Agropecuario y Reforma Agraria.

Chavarría, Ricardo E. 1982. "The Nicaraguan Insurrection." In Walker, ed. 1982.

Chilcote, Ronald H., and Joel C. Edelstein. 1986. *Latin America: Capitalist and Socialist Perspectives of Development and Underdevelopment*. Boulder, Colo.: Westview Press.

CIDAMO (Centro de Información, Documentación y Análisis del Movimiento Obrero Latinoamericano). 1979. "El movimiento obrero," in García Márquez et al., 1979.

Cleary, Edward L., O.P. 1985. *Crisis and Change: The Church in Latin America Today.* Maryknoll, N.Y.: Orbis Books.

Cohan, A. S. 1975. *Theories of Revolution: An Introduction*. New York: Wiley-Halstead Press.

Colburn, Forrest D. 1986. *Post-Revolutionary Nicaragua: State, Class, and the Dilemmas of Agrarian Policy.* Berkeley: University of California Press.

"Commentary: The Region." 1982. *Mesoamérica* (San José, Costa Rica). September: 1.

Conroy, Michael E. 1985. "Economic Legacy and Policies: Performance and Critique." In Walker, ed. 1985b.

———. 1987. "Economic Aggression as an Instrument of Low-Intensity Warfare." In Walker, ed. 1987.

———. 1988. "Nicaragua: Structure, Dynamics, and Conditions of the Economy in 1988: The Economic Dilemmas of Peace and Democracy." Paper presented at the VII Congreso Centroamericano de Sociología. October 10–15, Guatemala City.

"Contras Lay off Political Staff Workers."1988. *New York Times*. June 22: 1, 3–4.

CSUCA (Consejo Superior Universitaria Centroamericana). 1978. *Estructura agrária, dinámica de población, desarrollo capitalista en Centroamérica*, San José, Costa Rica: Editorial Universitaria Centroamericana.

Custodio, Ramón. 1986. "The Human Rights Crisis in Honduras." In Rosenberg and Shepherd, eds., 1986.

Dahl, Robert A. 1956. *A Preface to Democratic Theory*. Chicago: University of Chicago Press.

Davies, James C. 1962. "Towards a Theory of Revolution." *American Sociological Review* 27: 5–18.

DeFranco, Mario A., and Carlos F. Chamorro. 1979. "Nicaragua: Crecimiento industrial y empleo." In Camacho et al. 1979.

DGEC–Costa Rica (Dirección General de Estadística y Censos). 1980. *Anuario estadístico de Costa Rica, 1977*. San José, Costa Rica.

DGEC–El Salvador (Dirección General de Estadística y Censos). 1967. *Anuario Estadístico, 1965*. San Salvador: Ministerio de Economía.

______. 1968. *Anuario Estadístico, 1966*. San Salvador: Ministerio de Economía.

______. 1970. *Anuario Estadístico, 1968*. San Salvador: Ministerio de Economía.

______. 1971. *Anuario Estadístico, 1969*. San Salvador: Ministerio de Economía.

______. 1973. *Anuario Estadístico, 1971*. San Salvador: Ministerio de Economía.

______. 1979. *Anuario Estadístico, 1977*. San Salvador: Ministerio de Economía.

______. 1982. *Anuario Estadístico, 1980*. San Salvador: Ministerio de Economía.

______. 1983. *Anuario Estadístico, 1981*, Tomos III–V. San Salvador: Ministerio de Economía.

Dickey, Christopher. 1985. *With the Contras: A Reporter in the Wilds of Nicaragua*. New York: Simon and Schuster.

Diskin, Martin, ed. 1983. *Trouble in Our Backyard: Central America and the United States in the Eighties*. New York: Pantheon Books.

Diskin, Martin, Thomas Bossert, Salomon Nahmad, and Stefano Varese. 1986a. "Peace and Autonomy on the Atlantic Coast of Nicaragua: A Report of the LASA Task Force on Human Rights and Academic Freedom," Part 1. *LASA* [Latin American Studies Association] *Forum* 17 (Spring): 1–16.

______. 1986b. "Peace and Autonomy on the Atlantic Coast of Nicaragua: A Report of the LASA Task Force on Human Rights and Academic Freedom," Part 2. *LASA* [Latin American Studies Association] *Forum* 17 (Summer): 1–16.

Dodson, Michael, and Tommie Sue Montgomery. 1982. "The Churches in the Nicaraguan Revolution." In Walker, ed. 1982.

Drake, Paul, and Eduardo Silva, eds. 1986. *Elections and Democratization in Latin America*. La Jolla: Center for Iberian and Latin American Studies–Center for U.S.-Mexican Studies, University of California, San Diego.

Dunkerley, James. 1982. *The Long War: Dictatorship and Revolution in El Salvador*. London: Junction Books.

Edgeworth, Julie D. 1988. "Americans Get Low Grades in Gallup Geography Test." *National Geographic Society Update*. Fall.

"El Salvador." 1982. *Mesoamérica*. November: 5–6.

"El Salvador." 1983a. *Mesoamérica*. October: 5–6.

"El Salvador." 1983b. *Mesoamérica*. November: 4–7.

"El Salvador." 1983c. *Mesoamérica*. December: 5–6.

Enders, Thomas O. 1982. "The Central American Challenge." *AEI Foreign Policy and Defense Review* 4 (No. 2): 8–12.

Falcoff, Mark, and Robert Royal, eds. 1984. *Crisis and Opportunity: U.S. Policy in Central America and the Caribbean*. Washington, D.C.: Ethics and Public Policy Center.

Feinberg, Richard, ed. 1982. *Central America: International Dimensions of the Crisis*. New York: Holmes and Meier.

Felix, David. 1983. "Income Distribution and the Quality of Life in Latin America: Patterns, Trends, and Policy Implications." *Latin American Research Review* 18 (No. 2): 3–34.

Fernández Vásquez, Rodrigo. 1982. "Costa Rica: Interpretación histórica sobre reforma social y acción eclesiástica: 1940–1982." *Estudios Sociales Centroamericanos* 33 (September-December): 221–248.

Freire, Paulo. 1968. *The Pedagogy of the Oppressed*. New York: Herder and Herder.

Fried, Jonathan, et al. 1983. *Guatemala in Rebellion: Unfinished History*. New York: Grove.

Gallardo, María Eugenia, and José Roberto López. 1986. *Centroamérica: La crisis en cifras*. San José, Costa Rica: Instituto Interamericano de Cooperación para la Agricultura (IICA)–Facultad Latinoamericano de Ciencias Sociales (FLACSO).

García, José Z. 1989. "El Salvador: Recent Elections in Historical Perspective." In Booth and Seligson, eds. 1989.

García Márquez, Gabriel, et al. 1979. *Los Sandinistas*. Bogotá: Editorial Oveja Negra.

"Guatemala." 1982a. *Mesoamérica*. March: 2–4.

"Guatemala." 1982b. *Mesoamérica*. May: 2–3.

"Guatemala." 1982c. *Mesoamérica*. July-August: 2–3.

Gold, Eva. 1987. "Military Encirclement." In Walker, ed. 1987.

Goodfellow, William. 1987. "The Diplomatic Front." In Walker, ed. 1987.

Gorman, Stephen C. 1984. "Social Change and Political Revolution: The Case of Nicaragua." In Ropp and Morris, eds. 1984.

Grabendorff, Wolf, et al., eds. 1984. *Political Change in Central America: Internal and External Dimensions*. Boulder, Colo.: Westview Press.

Graham, Douglas H. 1984. "The Economic Dimensions of Instability and Decline in Central America and the Caribbean." In Schulz and Graham, eds. 1984.

Gudmundson, Lowell. 1985. "Costa Rica." In Hopkins, ed., 1985.

Gruson, Lindsey. 1988. "Terror's Toll Builds Again in El Salvador." *New York Times*. December 20: 1.

Guerra, Tomás. 1980. *El Salvador en la hora de su liberación*. San José, Costa Rica: n.p.

Gurr, Ted R. 1971. *Why Men Rebel*. Princeton: Princeton University Press.

Herman, Edward S., and Frank Brodhead. 1984. *Demonstration Elections*. Boston: South End Press.

Hopkins, Jack W., ed. 1985. *Latin American and Caribbean Contemporary Record*, Vol. 3: *1983–1984*. New York: Holmes and Meier: 499–508.

Immerman, Richard H. 1982. *The CIA in Guatemala: The Foreign Policy of Intervention*. Austin: University of Texas Press.

Inforpress Centroamericana. 1984. *Central America Report* (Guatemala). January 20.

———. 1985a. *Central America Report*. January 11.

———. 1985b. *Central America Report*. February 1.

———. 1985c. *Central America Report*. November 22.

———. 1985d. *Guatemala: Elections 1985*. Guatemala City.

———. 1988. *Central America Report*. January 21.

IICA (Instituto Interamericano de Cooperación para la Agricultura). 1982. "América Central frente a la década de los años ochenta." In *América Central frente a la década de los años de los 80*. Heredia, Costa Rica: Escuela de Relaciones Internacionales, Universidad Nacional Autónoma.

Interamerican Research Center. 1988. *Nicaraguan Public Opinion: Preliminary Report of a Random Sample Poll Conducted in Managua by the Newly-Formed Nicaraguan Institute of Public Opinion*. Los Angeles. June 30.

IADB (Inter-American Development Bank). 1983. *Economic and Social Progress in Latin America: Natural Resources. 1983 Report*. Washington, D.C.: Inter-American Development Bank.

———. 1987. *Economic and Social Progress in Latin America: Labor Force and Employment. 1987 Report*. Washington, D.C.: Inter-American Development Bank.

———. 1988. *Economic and Social Progress in Latin America: Science and Technology: 1988 Report*. Washington, D.C.: Inter-American Development Bank.

Inter-American Dialogue. 1984. *The Americas in 1984: A Year for Decisions; Report of the Inter-American Dialogue*. Washington, D.C.: Aspen Institute for Humanistic Studies.

International Verification and Follow-up Commission. 1988. "Comments, Observations and Conclusions of the International Verification and Follow-up Commission." In Kim and Walker, eds., forthcoming.

Karl, Terry. 1986. "Imposing Consent: Electoralism vs. Democratization in El Salvador." In Drake and Silva, eds. 1986.

Kim, Sung Ho, and Thomas W. Walker, eds. n.d. *Perspectives on War and Peace in Central America*. Athens: Papers in International Studies, Ohio University Press. Forthcoming.

Kinzer, Stephen. 1984. "Nicaraguans Say they Would Sign Proposed Treaty." *New York Times*. September 23, p. 20.

Kirkpatrick, Jeane. 1984. "This Time We Know What's Happening." In Falcoff and Royal, eds. 1984.

Klare, Michael. 1972. *War Without End*. New York: Alfred A. Knopf.

Kornbluh, Peter. 1987. "The Covert War." In Walker, ed., 1987.

Krauss, Clifford. 1986. "El Salvador Army Gains on the Guerrillas." *Wall Street Journal*. July 30: 20.

Kriesberg, Louis. 1982. *Social Conflicts*. 2nd ed. Englewood Cliffs, N.J.: Prentice-Hall.

Krumweide, Heinrich-W. 1984. "Regimes and Revolution in Central America." In Grabendorff et al., eds. 1984.

LaFeber, Walter. 1983. *Inevitable Revolutions: The United States in Central America*. New York: W. W. Norton.

La Nación Internacional (San José, Costa Rica). 1982. 26 August-1 September: 12.

LASA (Latin American Studies Association). 1984. *The Electoral Process in Nicaragua: Domestic and International Influences*. Austin, Tex. November 19.

———. 1988. *Extraordinary Opportunities . . . and New Risks: Final Report of the LASA Commission on Compliance with the Central American Peace Accord*. Pittsburgh. March 15.

"Latin Presidents Announce Accord on Contra Bases." 1989. *New York Times*. February 15: 1, 4.

Lawyers Committee for International Human Rights. 1985. *Nicaragua: Revolutionary Justice*. New York. April.

Lederman, E., et al. 1979. "Trabajo y empleo." In Zelaya, ed. 1979.

LeoGrande, William M. 1984. "Through the Looking Glass: The Kissinger Report on Central America." *World Policy Journal*. Winter: 251–284.

López C., Julio, Orlando Núñez S., Carlos Fernando Chamorro Barrios, and Pascual Serres. 1979. *La caída del somocismo y la lucha sandinista en Nicaragua*. San José, Costa Rica: Editorial Universitaria Centroamericano.

Malloy, James M., and Eduardo Gamarra, eds. n.d. *Latin American and Caribbean Contemporary Record*, Vol. 7. New York: Holmes and Meier. forthcoming.

Matthews, Robert. 1985. "The Limits of Friendship: Nicaragua and the West." *NACLA Report on the Americas* 19 (No. 3, May/June): 22–23.

Mayorga, Francisco J. 1985. *The Economic Trajectory of Nicaragua, 1980–1984: An Overview*. Miami: Latin American and Caribbean Center, Occasional Paper Series No. 14, Florida International University.

McClintock, Michael. 1985a. *The American Connection*, Vol. 1: *State Terror and Popular Resistance in El Salvador*. London: Zed Books.

———. 1985b. *The American Connection*, Vol. 2: *State Terror and Popular Resistance in Guatemala*. London: Zed Books.

Menjívar, Rafael. 1982. *Formación y lucha del proletariado industrial salvadoreño*. San José, Costa Rica: Editorial Universitaria Centroamericano.

Meza, Víctor. 1980. *Historia del movimiento obrero hondureño*. Tegucigalpa: Editorial Guaymuras.

———. 1982. *Honduras: La evolución de la crisis*. Tegucigalpa: Editorial Universitaria.

Millett, Richard L. 1977. *Guardians of the Dynasty: A History of the U.S.-Created Guardia Nacional de Nicaragua and the Somoza Family*. Maryknoll, N.Y.: Orbis Books.

———. 1984. "Historical Setting." In Rudolph, ed. 1984.

Ministerio de Educación. 1979. *Situación del sistema educativo después de 45 años de dictadura militar Somocista y perspectivas que plantea la revolución Sandinista*. Managua, Nicaragua.

Molina, Hugo. 1979. "Las bases económicas del desarrollo industrial y la absorción de fuerza de trabajo en El Salvador." In Camacho et al. 1979.

Montgomery, Tommie Sue. 1982a. "The Churches in the Nicaraguan Revolution." In Walker, ed. 1982.

———. 1982b. *Revolution in El Salvador: Origins and Evolution*. Boulder, Colo.: Westview Press.

———. 1984. "El Salvador: The Roots of Revolution." in Ropp and Morris, eds. 1984.

———. n.d. *Revolution in El Salvador: Origins and Evolution*. 2nd ed. Boulder, Colo.: Westview Press. Forthcoming.

Morris, James A. 1979. "Honduras: A Unique Case." In Wiarda and Kline, eds. 1979.

———. 1984a. "Government and Politics." In Rudolph, ed. 1984.
———. 1984b. "Honduras: The Burden of Survival in Central America." In Ropp and Morris, eds. 1984.
Nairn, Allan. 1982. "Guatemala Can't Take 2 Roads." *New York Times*. July 20: 23A.
National Bipartisan Commission on Central America. 1984. *Report of the National Bipartisan Commission on Central America*. Washington, D.C.
"National Security Council Document on Policy in Central America." 1983. *New York Times*. April 7.
"Nicaragua Pins Hopes on Turning Bureaucrats into Farmers." 1989. *Dallas Morning News*. February 22: 12A.
Nichols, John Spicer. 1988. "*La Prensa:* The CIA Connection." *Columbia Journalism Review* 28 (No. 2, July-August): 34, 35.
Noyola, Gustavo A. 1979. "Integración centroamericana y absorción de mano de obra: Guatemala." In Camacho et al. 1979.
Orellana, Víctor Antonio. 1985. *El Salvador: Crisis and Structural Change*. Miami: Latin American and Caribbean Center Occasional Paper Series No. 13, Florida International University.
OAS (Organization of American States). 1978. *Report on the Situation of Human Rights in Nicaragua: Findings of the "On-site" Observation in the Republic of Nicaragua, October 3–12, 1978*. Washington, D.C.: General Secretariat of the Organization of American States.
Ortega Saavedra, Daniel. 1984. Letter to the Contadora Foreign Ministers. September 21. Quoted in Goodfellow 1987.
O'Shaughnessy, Laura Nuzzi, and Luis H. Serra. 1986. *The Church and Revolution in Nicaragua*. Athens: Monographs in International Studies, Latin American Series No. 11, Ohio University Press.
Paige, Jeffrey M. 1975. *Agrarian Revolution; Social Movements and Export Agriculture in the Underdeveloped World*. New York: The Free Press.
Pérez Brignoli, Héctor, with Yolanda Baíres Martínez. 1983. "Growth and Crisis in the Central American Economies, 1950–1980." *Journal of Latin American Studies* 15 (November): 365–398.
Pochet Coronado, Rosa María. 1982. "El reformismo estatal y la Iglesia en Honduras 1949–1982." *Estudios Sociales Centroamericanos* 33 (September-December): 155–188.
Policy Alternatives for the Caribbean and Central America. 1984. *Changing Course: Blueprint for Peace in Central American and the Caribbean*. Washington, D.C.: Institute for Policy Studies.
Population Reference Bureau. 1981. *1981 World Population Data Sheet*. Washington, D.C.
Posas, Mario. 1981. *El movimiento campesino hondureño*. Tegucigalpa: Editorial Guaymuras.
Presbyterian Church (USA). 1983. *Adventure and Hope: Christians and the Crisis in Central America: Report to the 195th General Assembly of the Presbyterian Church*. Atlanta.
"Procedure for the Establishment of a Strong and Lasting Peace in Central America" [Central American Peace Accord]. 1987. August 7.
Radell, David Richard. 1969. "An Historical Geography of Western Nicaragua: The Spheres of León, Granada, and Managua, 1519–1965." Ph.D. dissertation, University of California–Berkeley.

Reagan, Ronald. 1983. "U.S. Responsibility in Central America." Address to Congress (April 28). In Falcoff and Royal, eds. 1984.

Rivera Urrutia, Eugenio, Ana Sojo, and José Roberto López. 1986. *Centroamérica: Política económica y crisis*. San José, Costa Rica: Editorial Departamento Ecuménico de Investigaciones–Universidad Nacional Autónoma.

Rodrígues, Mario. 1965. *Central America*. Englewood Cliffs, N.J.: Prentice Hall.

Roggensack, Margaret E., and John A. Booth. 1985. *Report of the International Human Rights Law Group and the Washington Office on Latin America Advance Election Observer Mission to Guatemala*. Washington, D.C.: International Human Rights Law Group–Washington Office on Latin America.

Ropp, Steve C. 1984. "National Security." In Rudolph, ed. 1984.

Ropp, Steve C., and James A. Morris, eds. 1984. *Central America: Crisis and Adaptation*. Albuquerque: University of New Mexico Press.

Rosado Granados, Hector. 1985. *Guatemala 1984: Elecciones para Asamblea Nacional Constituyente*. San José, Costa Rica: Instituto Centroamericano de Derechos Humanos–Centro de Asesoría y Promoción Electoral.

Rosenberg, Mark. 1986. "Honduras: The Reluctant Democracy." *Current History* 85 (December): 417–420, 438, 448.

______. 1989. "Can Democracy Survive the Democrats? From Transition to Consolidation in Honduras." In Booth and Seligson, eds. 1989.

Rosenberg, Mark, and Phillip Shepherd, eds. 1986. *Honduras Confronts its Future*. Boulder, Colo.: Lynne Reinner Publishers.

Ruchwarger, Gary. 1987. *People in Power: Forging a Grassroots Democracy in Nicaragua*. Granby, Mass.: Bergin and Garvey Publishers.

Rudolph, James D., ed. 1984. *Honduras: A Country Study*. Washington D.C.: American University Foreign Area Studies Series, U.S. Government Printing Office.

Ruhl, J. Mark. 1984. "Agrarian Structure and Political Stability in Honduras." *Journal of Inter-American Studies and World Affairs* 26 (February): 33–68.

Russell, Phillip L. 1984. *El Salvador in Crisis*. Austin, Tex.: Colorado River Press.

Salert, Barbara. 1976. *Revolutions and Revolutionaries: Four Theories*. New York: Elsevier.

Schattschneider, E. E. 1960. *The Semisovereign People: A Realist's View of Democracy in America*. New York: Holt, Rinehart, and Winston.

Schoultz, Lars. 1983. "Guatemala: Social Change and Political Conflict." In Diskin, ed. 1983.

______. 1987. *National Security and United States Policy Toward Latin America*. Princeton: Princeton University Press.

Schulz, Donald E. 1984. "Ten Theories in Search of Central American Reality." In Schulz and Graham, eds. 1984.

Schulz, Donald E., and Douglas H. Graham, eds. 1984. *Revolution and Counterrevolution in Central America and the Caribbean*. Boulder, Colo.: Westview Press.

Second General Conference of Latin American Bishops. 1973. *The Church and the Present-Day Transformation of Latin America in the Light of the Council*. Washington, D.C.: United States Catholic Conference.

"A Secret War for Nicaragua." 1982. *Newsweek*. November 8.

Seligson, Mitchell A. 1980. *Peasants of Costa Rica and the Development of Agrarian Capitalism*. Madison: University of Wisconsin Press.

Seligson, Mitchell A., and Edward Muller. 1987. "Democracy, Stability, and Economic Crisis: Costa Rica, 1978–1983." *International Studies Quarterly* 31 (September): 301–326.

Seligson, Mitchell A., and Miguel Gómez. 1989. "Ordinary Elections in Extraordinary Times: The Political Economy of Voting in Costa Rica." In Booth and Seligson, eds. 1989.

Seligson, Mitchell A., et al. 1982. *Land and Labor in Guatemala: An Assessment*. Washington, D.C.: Agency for International Development–Development Associates.

Serra, Luis. 1985. "The Grass-Roots Organizations." In Walker, ed. 1985b.

Shafter, Robert J. 1978. *A History of Latin America*. Lexington, Mass.: D. C. Heath.

Sierra Pop, Oscar Rolando. 1982. "Iglesia y conflicto social en Guatemala." *Estudios Sociales Centroamericanos* 33 (September-December): 66–86.

Skocpol, Theda. 1979. *States and Social Revolutions*. Cambridge: Cambridge University Press.

Sloan, John. 1968. "The Electoral Game in Guatemala." Ph.D. dissertation, University of Texas at Austin.

Tayacán. 1985. *Psychological Operations in Guerrilla Warfare: The CIA's Nicaragua Manual*. Prepared by the Central Intelligence Agency. New York: Vintage Books.

Taylor, Stan. 1984. *Social Science and Revolutions*. New York: St. Martin's Press.

Technical Commission of the Great National Dialogue. 1985. *Economic and Social Policy Recommendations to the Head of State*. Guatemala City.

Thome, Joseph R., and David Kaimowitz. 1985. "Agrarian Reform." In Walker, ed. 1985b.

Tilly, Charles. 1978. *From Mobilization to Revolution*. Reading, Mass.: Addison-Wesley.

______. 1981. "Introduction." In Tilly and Tilly, eds. 1981.

Tilly, Louise A., and Charles Tilly, eds. 1981. *Class Conflict and Collective Action*. Beverly Hills: Sage Publications.

Torres Rivas, Edelberto. 1981. *Crisis del poder en Centroamérica*. San José, Costa Rica: Editorial Universitaria Centroamericana.

______. 1982. "Cambio social y crisis en la década de los años ochenta." In *América Central frente a la década de los años de los 80*. Heredia, Costa Rica: Escuela de Relaciones Internacionales, Universidad Nacional Autónoma.

Trudeau, Robert. 1984. "Guatemalan Elections: The Illusion of Democracy." Paper presented to the National Conference on Guatemala, Washington, D.C. June 15.

U.S. Department of State. 1981. *Country Reports on Human Rights Practices*. Washington, D.C.: U.S. Government Printing Office. February 2.

______. 1985. Data in xerox ms. Office of Regional Economic Policy, Bureau of Inter-American Affairs. Washington, D.C.

U.S. Embassy—Guatemala. 1985. "A Statistical Comparison of Violence (1982–1985)." Guatemala City. Xerox.

Vanderlaan, Mary B. 1986. *Revolution and Foreign Policy in Nicaragua*. Boulder, Colo.: Westview Press.

Villagrán Kramer, Francisco. 1982. "The Background to the Current Political Crisis in Central America." In Feinberg, ed. 1982.

Walker, Thomas W. 1970. *The Christian Democratic Movement in Nicaragua*, Tucson: University of Arizona Press.

______. 1979a. Paper presented to the U.S. Department of State conference on Central America: U.S. Policy Interests and Concerns. Washington, D.C. March 19.

______. 1979b. "Nicaragua: The Somoza Family Regime." In Wiarda and Kline, eds. 1979.

______. 1979c. "The U.S. and Central America." *Caribbean Review* 8 (No. 3, Summer): 18–23.

______, ed. 1982. *Nicaragua in Revolution*. New York: Praeger.

______. 1985a. "Introduction." in Walker, ed. 1985b.

______, ed. 1985b. *Nicaragua: The First Five Years*. New York: Praeger.

______, ed. 1987. *Reagan Versus the Sandinistas: The Undeclared War on Nicaragua*. Boulder, Colo.: Westview Press.

Walton, John. 1984. *Reluctant Rebels: Comparative Studies in Revolution and Underdevelopment*. New York: Columbia University Press.

Washington Office on Latin America. 1988. *Who Pays the Price? The Cost of War in the Guatemalan Highlands*. Washington, D.C. April.

Washington Report on the Hemisphere. 1987. October 28.

Weaver, Jerry L. 1979. "Guatemala: The Politics of a Frustrated Revolution." In Wiarda and Kline, eds. 1979.

Webre, Stephen. 1979. *José Napoleón Duarte and the Christian Democratic Party in Salvadorean Politics: 1960–1972*. Baton Rouge: Louisiana State University Press.

Weeks, John. 1985a. *The Economies of Central America*. New York: Holmes and Meier.

______. 1985b. "The Industrial Sector." In Walker, ed. 1985b.

Wheelock Román, Jaime. 1975. *Imperialismo y dictadura: Crisis de una formación social*. México: Siglo Veintiuno Editores.

White, Richard Alan. 1984. *The Morass: United States Intervention in Central America*. New York: Harper and Row.

Wiarda, Howard J. 1982. "The Central American Crisis: A Framework for Understanding." *AEI Foreign Policy and Defense Review* 4 (No. 2): 2–7.

Wiarda, Howard J., and Harvey F. Kline, eds. 1979. *Latin American Politics and Development*. Boston: Houghton Mifflin.

Wilkie, James W., and Steven Haber, eds. 1981. *Statistical Abstract of Latin America*, Vol. 21. Los Angeles: University of California Latin America Center Publications.

Wilkie, James W., and David Lorey, eds. 1987. *Statistical Abstract of Latin America*, Vol. 25. Los Angeles: University of California Latin America Center Publications.

Wilkie, James W., and Adam Perkal, eds. 1984. *Statistical Abstract of Latin America*, Vol. 23. Los Angeles: University of California Latin America Center Publications.

Wolf, Eric. 1969. *Peasant Revolts of the Twentieth Century*. New York: Harper and Row.

Woodward, Ralph Lee, Jr. 1985. *Central America: A Nation Divided*. 2nd ed. New York: Oxford University Press.

Zelaya, Chester, ed. 1979. *Costa Rica contemporánea*, Tomo II. San José: Editorial Costa Rica.

INDEX